Moira House, Usher's Island, was the home of the Mendicity Institution for 130 years, from 1824–1954. (Print by Wm. Brocas Jnr courtesy of the National Library of Ireland)

DUBLIN OUTSIDERS

A History of the Mendicity Institution 1818–1998

Audrey Woods

A. & A. Farmar

A. & A. Farmar
Beech House
78 Ranelagh Village
Dublin 6
Ireland

Text design and setting by A. & A. Farmar
Cover design by Liam Furlong
Index by Amanda Bell
Printing and binding by Betaprint

ISBN 1 899047 49 2

Contents

List of Tables

FOREWORD

In 1993 the president of the Mendicity Institution Trust, the late Richard Tennant, became interested in the idea of recording its history. He was also chairman of the Friends of the Royal Hospital Donnybrook, whose history had been written by Dr Helen Burke, director of the Social Science Research Centre at University College Dublin. The Institution's committee of management decided to approach the Social Science Research Centre to write this history.

My thanks must go first to the committee of management of the Mendicity Institution Trust for commissioning the book. Individual committee members have been most helpful. Dorothy Browne and John Smiley provided interesting information about the Institution in former times and supplied me with copies of recent annual reports. Ann Coffey kindly took me along on her monthly visit to the dining room where we talked with the clientele and met the kitchen supervisor. The secretary, George Sheppard, was a fount of information about the present day Institution and its organisation. I am glad I had the opportunity to meet his predecessor, the much mourned Charles Smith, secretary to the Institution for fifteen years, who died in 1997, when he visited UCD with the president of the Institution, Richard White, and met members of the Social Science Research Centre.

Having mislaid the books several times over the years, the Institution finally entrusted its rich archive, comprising an almost complete record of its work, to the care of the National Library in the 1980s. The archive was a delight to research if at times hard on the eyesight. Warmest thanks to the staff in the National Library of Ireland for their assistance in so many ways. Ireland is fortunate to have a National Library where the friendly and courteous staff makes researching a pleasure and is a model for staff in similar establishments elsewhere.

I am grateful to my colleagues in the Social Science Research Centre for their support, particularly to Dr Helen Burke, who despite her own heavy workload, patiently read every word of the manuscript and made many helpful suggestions. Helen has always been a source of inspiration to me and I value her friendship and encouragment. Anne Coogan, Administrator of the Social Science Research, as always, was generous with advice and practical help in preparing the manuscript for publication. I deeply appreciate the meticulous attention to detail given by my editor, Sarah Jackson and my publisher, Tony Farmar. Finally, my thanks to my family for their encouragement, above all to Frank for his unfailing support.

A rapid preliminary survey of the material hinted at the breadth, vision and innovative nature of the Institution's work. Further research revealed the extent of the work with orphaned children, the unique transmission service, the establishment of the first public baths in Dublin, and the remarkable way the Institution adapted its work to meet current needs as the requirements of the poor changed.

The 180-year life-span of the Institution, 1818–1998, has seen major social and political change in Ireland. As the social organisation of poverty altered, the Institution adapted its work to meet the needs of a changing clientele. Innovation, adaptability and accountability have been notable characteristics throughout its history. Successive managing committees were always conscious that they were using the public's money and must account for every penny spent. That accountability is still evident in the annual report of the amount of provisions used down to the last pound.

The title of this history, *Dublin Outsiders*, reflects the essence of the Institution's work: first extending a helping hand to street beggars whom no other organisation would touch, to orphans who could not find a home in the Foundling Hospital or the House of Industry, to people excluded by the poor law authorities, to those stranded in Dublin who wished but could not afford to return home or to start a new life elsewhere, and to people who wanted to avoid the workhouse. Today the Mendicity Institution caters for a lonely, marginalised sector of society, not financially destitute, it is true, but needy in other ways.

Grateful acknowledgement is made to the National Library and the Old Dublin Society for permission to reproduce the illustrations.

CHAPTER ONE

Eighteenth-Century Dublin—A Tale of Two Cities

THE EIGHTEENTH CENTURY was a period of growing prosperity in Ireland; and Dublin, the capital, was the centre of development.[1] Liddy describes it as a time of elegant expansion for the city, with the formation of generous boulevards and the building of gracious mansions.[2] Competitions were held for the design of new buildings and prominent English architects, Gandon among them, vied for the opportunity to set their mark on the developing city. The splendid building housing the Royal Exchange reflected the wealth, power and prestige of Dublin merchants at the time.[3] Streets of houses soon followed the building of Powerscourt House, Leinster House and Mercers' Hospital. The city spread westward with the erection of several important buildings, among them Dr Steeven's Hospital and the Earl of Moira's beautiful house at Ushers Island, later to become the home of the Mendicity Institution.[4]

To the north of the city, the pleasure gardens supporting the new Lying-in Hospital, later known as the Rotunda Hospital, attracted development; and Rutland Square [now Parnell Square] was soon surrounded by extravagantly appointed houses, as was Mountjoy Square some years later.[5] Peers, members of parliament and bishops were among the occupants of these elegant houses and generated a rich and convivial social milieu.[6] Maxwell says visitors to Dublin 'were impressed by the air of gaiety in the houses of the well-to-do which went with a peculiarly splendid way of living—a multiplicity of servants, great profusion of dishes on the table, abundant wine'.[7] Masked balls were an especially popular feature of Dublin's social scene.[8]

In the second half of the century the Wide Streets Commissioners improved and beautified the city by building fine bridges across the River Liffey and removing a number of squalid buildings from the quays and the area around Christ Church and St

Patrick's cathedrals.[9] Thanks to their work, Dublin emerged from 'its mediaeval legacy of narrow streets and cramped lanes' and became a much admired city where many of the graceful streets ended with a magnificent building as a focal point.[10] Maxwell again: 'Dublin could now boast of a Parliament House, the Royal Exchange, the Custom House and Four Courts—a collection of buildings which, as Macaulay observed, would have been thought magnificent even in Paris.'[11]

Several fine barracks housed the many soldiers needed to put down the rebellious Irish. The Royal Barracks [later Collins] was described as 'the most magnificent, largest and most commodious of its kind in Europe'.[12] McDowell describes Dublin at that time as 'a great dominating and inspiring national phenomenon'.[13] Like London, the city attracted thousands of people from the countryside in search of new jobs and excitement.[14]

Greater prosperity did not eliminate poverty, and Dublin was a city of striking social contrasts.[15] As the splendid city grew, the level of poverty and deprivation in the back streets grew alongside.[16] Beggars gravitated naturally towards the capital where their misery contrasted sharply with the 'ostentatious luxury of the rich'[17] Dublin's slums, some of the worst in Europe, were usually outside the commercial and civic centre but never far away from the most beautiful buildings.[18] Once relatively prosperous areas, such as the Liberties, quickly degenerated into slum conditions when penal trade restrictions plunged many inhabitants into destitution.[19] In 1729 the Surveyor General commented: '70 persons have been known to live in a house, there being a family in each room, oftentimes in each floor and in the cellars, in the trading part of the city.'[20] Fever thrived in these crowded conditions and epidemics were frequent. When people became ill, family members were often forced to pawn clothing or furniture and run up debts to pay for medicines and medical care.[21]

The situation in the slums did not improve as the city continued to prosper. By the end of the century Malton described Dublin as having reached 'a climax of beauty' which could 'rank with the very finest cities of Europe for extent, magnificence, and commerce'.[22] Yet the Rev James Whitelaw, vicar of St Catherine's, who surveyed slum conditions in his parish, discovered a building that had once housed 108 occupants.[23] All of the other houses were multi-tenanted; rooms and even parts of rooms were sub-let, and the occupants lived in indescribably filthy conditions. In the contrasting lifestyles of its inhabitants, Dublin reflected what James describes as the paradox of Ireland's economic history in the eighteenth century: the increase of national wealth, accompanied by the persistence of widespread destitution.[24]

A capital city usually has a high population of beggars, but the extent of the problem in Dublin during the eighteenth century was 'grievous beyond the experience of other great cities'.[25] Many visitors commented on the extent of begging in the streets.[26] Maxwell describes the scene vividly:

> how Dublin beggars crowded round the doors of shops assailing customers as they went in and out; how they blocked up narrow entrances insisting on alms; and how even at night they would place themselves on street corners or upon the bridges 'roaring with hunger'.[27]

It is no surprise to find that shopkeepers frequently paid beggars to stay away from their premises.[28]

Many explanations have been given for the extent of begging in Dublin. Fagan considers that the vagrants and vagabonds who thronged into the city seeking alms were to a large extent a by-product of the upheavals which resulted from centuries of war and confiscation; and that their number was compounded by recurrent periods of unemployment.[29] Fownes, a contemporary observer, laid the blame for much of the poverty on workers spending their pay in ale-houses, often owned by their employers, who gave extended credit to their own employees.[30] He also considered that parents were responsible for the increasing number of young beggars on the streets. He blamed Dublin parents for allowing their young people to run wild around the city, and rural parents for sending their children to Dublin to learn trades or take up apprenticeships instead of having them trained or employed locally. As a result the Dublin labour market was swamped, there were far too many applicants for the jobs available, and many turned to begging to support themselves.[31] Dobbs, the Surveyor General, calculated in 1729 that only one in ten beggars was in genuine need. He believed that many 'sturdy' beggars pretended to be dumb, blind or lame, and even injured their children to arouse the compassion of the public and encourage them to give generously. He described begging as an actual and profitable trade, for which many people gave up their jobs or did not even seek work before starting to beg.[32] Forty years later, Bishop Woodward of Cloyne, a tireless advocate of a regular provision for the poor, also referred to the 'trade of begging' and 'repeated instances of journeymen quitting their looms for begging'.[33]

There is no doubt that the lack of any effective legislation for the Irish poor contributed significantly to the extent of begging in Dublin. In England, the impotent or 'deserving' poor, the sick, aged, infirm and children, had been made the responsibility of their local parishes by a series of laws culminating in the Elizabethan Poor Law of 1601. The able-bodied or 'undeserving' poor were sent to houses of correction.[34] In Ireland, the deserving poor were left to the vagaries of private charity, while an act passed in the parliamentary session of 1634–5 provided for the establishment of houses of correction.[35] Few such houses were built in Ireland as their provision depended on the grand jury system which was uneven in its operation.[36] The first effective provision for the Irish poor was made in 1704 with the passing of an act that established the Dublin workhouse and a corporation for relieving the poor and setting vagabonds and beggars to work.[37] This corporation was empowered to arrest beggars who would not work and confine them in the workhouse: a very important power as the Association for the Prevention and Suppression of Mendicity in Dublin was to discover a century later. The legislation also provided for the impotent and lunatic poor of Dublin. The measure was financed by a tax on licenses for hackney cabs and sedan chairs and a levy of three pence in the pound on every house in the city and the Liberties.[38] Fagan says Dublin would have needed a score of workhouses to deal adequately with its poor.[39] Perhaps the intended functions of the workhouse were too numerous. It was soon in financial trouble and operated mainly as a foundling hospital to cope with the great numbers of abandoned children in Dublin at that time. Burke says the city workhouse changed its function to meet a newly recognised need, although she doubts, with good reason, whether the needs of all those for whom it was originally intended were met elsewhere.[40]

Vagrancy became a transportable offence in Ireland in 1707, but the legislation was ineffectual and was followed by further Acts in 1729 and 1735.[41] Transportation of some vagrants to America continued until the Declaration of Independence in 1776. By that time, attitudes in Ireland were changing towards punishment for beggars; although transportation to Australia continued for felons, their ranks included very few beggars.[42]

A number of interesting and potentially successful plans were proposed in the eighteenth century to deal with the problem of paupers and begging. In 1725 Sir William Fownes, a member of Parliament and an advocate of the workhouse concept, devised an elaborate plan for 'regulating the Poor, Supporting of Some and Employing others, according to their several Capacities', by which he hoped all wandering beggars would be encouraged to return to their native parishes for support, thereby reducing the number on the streets of Dublin by at least one quarter.[43] He believed that the number of genuine beggars could be established by a system of badging persons who were entitled to help from their own parishes by being resident there for at least eighteen months. Persons capable of work could be trained in a workhouse, and imposters could be dealt with in a house of correction.[44] Fownes regarded the function of the workhouse as very different from that of the house of correction. The workhouse would employ and give training to the able-bodied poor and youths whose parents could not support them. The house of correction would compel vagabonds, sturdy beggars, and other offenders to beat hemp or flax until they promised to give up begging.[45]

Surveyor General Dobbs also formulated a plan for building workhouses supported by local taxes where the poor would be employed and relieved. He had no faith in houses of correction:

> for vagabonds are no sooner sent in, but they are allow'd to run away again, in case they have any bribe to give, or if not, it is too much trouble to the master to oblige them to work, for he connives at their escape, and makes Interest enough not to be call'd to account at the next Quarter Session. Thus our Laws are at present evaded and their execution slubber'd over.[46]

Instead, Dobbs suggested that each workhouse should include a vault for lazy workers who would be allowed only the food they could earn by working. Persistent idlers should be confined in a pumphouse 'where being chained by the foot, they must either pump or be drowned'.[47] Dobbs envisaged a charity school attached to each workhouse where a taste for work and an inclination to be industrious would be instilled in young people. Girls would learn to sew, spin, knit and clean house; boys would be taught spinning, net-making, gardening and planting. The growth of a new generation of beggars would consequently be inhibited. Until such workhouses were built, Dobbs suggested that the poor resident in a parish should be badged and allowed to beg for a short time. People who did not qualify as residents should be 'whipt' towards their native parish or to the nearest port to be shipped off to their native country.[48] Dobbs suggested that all the poor could be maintained in this way without the imposition of an unreasonable poor tax.

Although these ideas were not taken up at the time, several decades later, mainly due to the urging of Richard Woodward, Bishop of Cloyne, legislation was passed that provided for the establishment of corporations for the poor and workhouses, or houses of industry, in every county and city in Ireland.[49] At the same time the first of a series of acts permitting certain of the poor to beg by a system of badging was also passed.[50] Very few of these houses of industry were in fact built, and Dublin was the only place where the implementation of this legislation was in any way effective. Three years after it was opened in 1774, Bishop Woodward rejoiced that 'the nuisance [begging] . . . is actually suppressed on the founding of the Dublin House of Industry'.[51] The corporation calculated that the system of badging unmasked well over a thousand impostors, and there were other benefits.[52] Many liquor stores, previously the source of trouble in their neighbourhoods, closed down through loss of custom once begging was suppressed.[53] Bishop Woodward hoped that the trade would die out since 'no children are permitted to be trained up to begging'.[54]

This state of affairs did not last for long. The voluntary contributors who had responded to the bishop's initial plea to establish the House of Industry soon fell away once the institution was given a parliamentary grant. The Dublin House of Industry attracted the poor from many parts of the country. So many aged, infirm and sick needed accommodation that the confinement of 'sturdy' beggars was relegated to second place, and the number admitted to the House of Industry decreased every year. A report on the institution published in 1809 said that it had only moderately succeeded in its original intention—the suppression of beggars.[55] In Nicholls' opinion the legislation had no hope of succeeding as it coupled stringent provisions against mendicancy with conditional permission to practise it.[56] Relief of the poor was to be achieved by an organised system of begging: 'By combining two objects neither could be achieved...Vagrancy will not be put down nor poverty relieved.'[57] In addition, Nicholls regarded the distinction between the deserving poor who were permitted to beg and the undeserving poor who merited punishment for begging was not made sufficiently clear.[58]

The most effective provision for the Irish poor in the eighteenth century was directed towards the sick. An act passed in 1765 enabled the establishment of county infirmaries throughout the country and gave grants to several voluntary hospitals established in Dublin earlier in the century.[59] Although this act was not compulsory and relied upon voluntary donations to make it effective, it had important consequences. The subsequent establishment of infirmary and dispensary systems throughout the country was referred to by a contemporary writer as Ireland's poor law.[60] But this was far from sufficient to relieve Ireland's desperate poverty.

Beggary was prevalent in almost all European countries in the eighteenth century.[61] The most successful attempts to deal with the problem were made in Germany, where concerned men in different cities came to the conclusion that the poor were often forced to beg because they lacked useful skills and had never learned the habit or discipline involved in working. These men believed that the perception of work by the poor could be changed if they were encouraged to see it as an opportunity for a better life and not a punishment. The amount of begging in Hamburg was so appalling that two hundred of the most respected citizens, led by

Baron Caspar von Voght, united in an attempt to 'manage' the poor. For seven years they provided support, training, equipment, work, and medical relief for the poor, and education and training for their children. Alms-giving ceased because citizens were fined for giving to beggars on the street or at house doors.[62] During the period 1788–94, hardly a beggar was seen in Hamburg as a result of this strategy and 'the din of industry was heard where sloth or riot had inhabited before'.[63] The Hamburg approach was interesting and prescient because it gave help, such as medical assistance, to people on the borderline of poverty to prevent them from falling into destitution.[64]

In Bavaria, the scientist, inventor and philosopher, Count Rumford, firmly believed that the care of the poor was 'one of the most sacred duties imposed upon men in a civil society; one of those duties imposed immediately by the hand of God himself; and of which the neglect never goes unpunished'.[65] Shocked by the 'quite intolerable' number of beggars in Bavaria, he was determined to devise and execute a plan to clear the region of 'beggars, thieves and other vagabonds'.[66] He began in Munich, the regional capital, where he considered the 'quite incredible' situation worse than in any other German city.[67] It was almost impossible to cross the streets there without being forced to satisfy the demands of beggars. They even begged in the churches and disturbed people at prayer. Beggars and begging had gradually become accepted elements of Munich society, and the more their demands were satisfied, the greater the demands became.[68] Rumford appealed to the citizens of Munich to stop giving alms to beggars and instead to support an institution where the poor would be fed and supported, and employment would be provided for those capable of work once they agreed to stop begging. Their children were promised food, clothes and, from the age of six, training in simple tasks from which they could graduate to more difficult occupations and so acquire both the habit of working and a useful skill.[69] Rumford reversed the usual procedure; he believed by making people happy first that virtue would follow later. When his 'spacious and elegant' institution opened on 1 January 1790, a date chosen because it was a time for generous alms-giving and many beggars would be drawn to the streets, it took less than an hour to clear the streets of beggars.[70] Being the Commander in Chief of the army of the Duke of Bavaria, Count Rumford had the help of soldiers to accomplish this feat.[71]

Rumford visited the House of Industry in Dublin in 1796 where he examined the occupants' diet. He conducted experiments in the kitchen and concluded that it was impossible to invent a more nourishing or palatable kind of food than colcannon as it was made in Ireland. However, he recommended that it would be more economical to cut down on the amount of butter and use salted herrings as a substitute.[72] Having noted that the badly constructed boiler and fireplace were wasting fuel, he designed a new fireplace and boiler for the institution. He also designed a boiler for the Linen Hall in Dublin and a kitchen, laundry, chimney, fireplaces and a model of a lime kiln for the Dublin Society.[73] Forty years later, many of the poor law workhouses in Ireland used Count Rumford's recipes for feeding the poor.

Rumford's work was happily supported by the people of Munich once they saw how well his plan succeeded. His care was also clearly appreciated by the poor: when he became ill they went to the cathedral in procession to offer prayers for his recovery. Four years later when word was received that he had once again fallen ill while visiting Naples, the poor of Munich prayed for an hour each evening until he recovered.[74] Eventually, his institution offered help and advice on dealing with the poor to other cities and towns in Germany.[75] Rumford also laid down 'Fundamental Principles on which General Establishments for the Relief of the Poor may be formed in all Countries.'[76] Nearly thirty years later, the Committee for the Suppression of Mendicity in Dublin used many of these principles when establishing their institution. Despite the existence of the Poor Laws, English cities were thronged with beggars; and associations to suppress mendicity began in many towns during the early years of the nineteenth century, many following the example of Rumford and von Voght.[77]

The constitutional union of Great Britain and Ireland in 1800 radically changed the status of Dublin. Although Dublin retained most of the functions of a capital city, it was, nevertheless, a 'city bereft of its parliament'.[78] Maxwell says: 'The closing of the Parliament caused an exodus of people of wealth and fashion and the gradual fading of Dublin's brilliance.'[79] Parliament House was sold to the Bank of Ireland and many wealthy families sold their town houses. A sale relevant to this story was that of Leinster House, the town house of the Earls of Kildare, to the Dublin Society. The value of house property fell and places such as Rutland Square and its surroundings declined rapidly, eventually to become overcrowded tenements.[80] Many Dublin-based industries suffered by the removal of Parliament and the decline of the social season, notably the carriage-making, cabinet-making and gun-making industries, all major sources of employment. It was a bad time for the building trade, another major employer. The silk and poplin industry suffered a serious setback in the early years of the century, mainly due to changes in fashion.[81] The flood of English products into the Irish market led to the failure of many indigenous industries.[82] In general, after the union, there was an economic downturn and 'an age of affluence was suddenly and brutally replaced by an age of frugality'.[83]

The number of beggars on the streets increased as soldiers returning from the wars in Europe swelled the numbers of the unemployed. The House of Industry was full and could no longer cope with the numbers referred to it. The prevalence of fever and its social consequences were of great concern to many people. In an address to the Lord Lieutenant in 1815 members of the medical profession warned

> health among the lower orders of a community is the source of industry, economy and order, . . . [whereas] disease among the labouring poor leads to despondency and despondency prompts intoxication; indigence, beggary and crime complete the process of ruin.[84]

A particularly severe winter in 1816 compounded the misery of the poor. A contemporary account paints a horrific picture:

> the city presented a spectacle, at once afflicting and disgusting to the feelings of its inhabitants; the doors of carriages and shops, to the interruption of business, were beset by crowds of unfortunate and clamorous beggars, exhibiting misery and decrepitude in a variety of forms, and frequently carrying about in their persons and garments, the seeds of contagious disease; themselves the victims of idleness, their children were taught to depend on Begging, as affording the only

> means of future subsistence; every artifice was resorted to by the practised beggar to extort alms, and refusal was frequently followed by imprecations and threats. Mendicity developed a violent character... The benevolent were imposed upon—the modest shocked—the reflecting grieved—the timid alarmed. In short, so distressing was the whole scene, and so intolerable was the nuisance, that its suppression became a matter of necessity.[85]

This was the background against which a number of concerned gentlemen in Dublin puzzled over the difficulty of finding a solution to the problem of begging. Eventually, they came together and pooled their ideas. A public meeting was arranged at the Mansion House on 23 May 1817. At this meeting a resolution to suppress mendicity was passed and a committee appointed to draw up a plan to achieve this aim.[86] A pamphlet, pointing out that 'a beggar is not now to be seen' in the streets of Edinburgh as a result of the work of the Mendicity Association there, was published to promote the establishment of a similar organisation in Dublin.[87] The public was told that supporting such an organisation could save half of the estimated amount of £100,000 spent annually in answering the demands of beggars on the streets. An example was given of a healthy, strong woman who did not send her two little children to school because they could earn eight shillings a day begging on Great Russell Street.[88] The pamphlet also stressed the abuse to which children of beggars were exposed, citing the case of a little blind girl whose parents had withdrawn her from the Molyneux Asylum, where she had become quite proficient at music, and put her in Cavendish Row to earn money for them by begging. It was 'a powerful comment on the comprehensive evil of giving alms in the street'.[89]

CHAPTER TWO

Establishing the Institution: 1818–1819

THE COMMITTEE APPOINTED TO draw up a plan for the prevention and suppression of mendicity in Dublin spent some months carefully researching the experience of associations established with the same objective in Belfast, Edinburgh, Hamburg and Munich and presented an outline of their plan at a further public meeting held at the Rotunda Rooms on 22 January 1818.[1] The plan, based on 'the result of actual practice, crowned, in more instances than one, with the most complete success', was accepted and the Association for the Prevention and Suppression of Mendicity in Dublin came into being.[2] The founders included medical doctors, barristers, merchants and police magistrates and belonged to a sector of society dedicated to the improvement of the poorest elements in the city. Some of their names appear on the managing committees of other voluntary organisations working in the city at the time. Samuel Bewley, Roderick Connor, Dr Thomas Orpen and Francis Lear all served on the committee of the Association for the Improvement of Prisons and of Prison Discipline in Ireland. Dr Orpen was also a member of the committee of the Incorporated Society for Promoting English Protestant Schools in Ireland and a trustee of the Charitable Society for the Relief of Sick and Indigent Roomkeepers, while Samuel Bewley, Roderick Connor, John D La Touche and William L Guinness served on the committees of the Dublin Weekly and Daily Schools and the Society for Promoting the Education of the Poor of Ireland.[3] A long connection with the de Vesci family began with the appointment of Viscount de Vesci as one of the vice-presidents of the new Association, whose number also included that most generous of men, Thomas Pleasants.

Following Count Rumford's advice that the support of prominent people gives an organisation credibility and is vital for its success, the Lord Lieutenant was asked to become patron of the new Association and the Lord Mayor to become president.[4] The twelve vice-presidents included a duke, three earls, an archbishop, a bishop, and two viscounts. Although all annual subscribers of £3 or upwards were eligible for election to the general managing committee of forty-two members, the Lord Mayor, the Archbishops of Dublin and most of the senior members of the administration were among those appointed as ex officio members. In the election for the first committee, by mistake forty-three members were elected. Fortunately, William Thom, one of the successful candidates and later to become honorary secretary, sent in his resignation to prevent the necessity for a new election.[5] The meeting directed the general managing committee, the ex officio members, and the vice-presidents to put into effect the various resolutions that had been proposed for the organisation of the new Association.[6] (See Appendix A.)

The founders firmly believed that, as well as providing for the necessities of life, 'labour civilises and moralises the human species'.[7] Their philosophy that only by employment could 'the unruly passions, the idle and immoral habits of adults be restrained' was evident in the campaign plan, which was to support beggars at a meagre subsistence level while training them for simple employment and encouraging good industrious habits and a desire to support themselves independently.[8] During the training period, their children would be supported, educated and also trained in good habits.[9] No one would receive help who did not earn it: 'the revealed law is that 'he who will not work, will not eat'.'[10] The Association held that parents should support their children and adult children should support their aged parents, so as not 'to break those social ties, which are never disregarded without a corresponding relaxation in morals'.[11] Another reason underlying this seemingly worthy principle was to prevent people abandoning their children and their aged parents to be supported by the parish, a situation which could lead to the introduction of poor rates.

The managing committee needed to proceed with delicacy.[12] Although the experience of other cities had shown that a plan to train beggars for simple employment was workable, the employment of such people was a sensitive issue in Dublin and many objections were raised against it. In that era, so influenced by Adam Smith and the classical economists, some feared that employing beggars would interfere with the 'normal channels of employment' and take employment 'from a better class of persons'.[13] Others argued that the plan would encourage dependency in beggars. Yet another objection was that the plan was a harsh and cruel method of treating the poor, while a number of people considered that the whole idea was unworkable and not worth pursuing further. To allay these fears and to gain support for the Association, one member generously bore the cost of printing 20,000 copies of the proposed plan and an explanatory statement which were circulated widely around the city.[14]

Funding and membership were the new Association's two priorities, as people's money and time were vital for its success. A subscription of £1 or over entitled a donor to membership of the Association. The managing committee divided the city into sixty 'walks of collection' and two members of the Association were appointed to supervise the donations from each 'walk'. Once the plan was circulated, these members were given collection sheets and urged to begin work immediately.

Again following Rumford's advice, the managing committee was divided into six sub-committees, to deal with finance and accounts, employment, investigation, supply, education and superintendence of children, and health. The sub-committee of investigation seems to have been the most influential as it was responsible, not only for determining the best method of carrying out the Association's plan, but also for supervising an elaborate bureaucratic structure for the operation of district committees.[15]

To carry out the Association's primary objective, the prevention and suppression of mendicity, the managing committee divided the city into ten districts: College, Stephen's Green, Castle, Francis Street, Cork Street, James' Street, Royal Barracks [later Collins Barracks], Rutland Square, and Mountjoy Square. A committee would supervise each district and be responsible for dealing with the beggars resident in its area. Any member of the Association was eligible for election to a district committee of forty-two members, with clergymen of each denomination and churchwardens of all parishes in the area as ex officio members. Each district committee was to have six sub-committees corresponding to those of the managing committee. Rules and regulations were laid down about the premises each district committee was to rent, the number of rooms required, the function of each room, and even the type of furniture to be purchased. The plan was that materials would be distributed to outworkers from each district office. It was also hoped to divide each district into 'medical walks' where a medical member of the district committee would take care of sick beggars.[16] The plan was therefore both extensive and demanding. Nothing was left to chance. The duties of district committee members would be onerous. They would include attendance at at least two committee meetings a week, as well as supervision and investigation of beggars in the part of the district where a member was appointed as a 'visitor', and attendance in turn at the district office every morning once the operation was under way. They would be required to pay strict attention to record keeping and to make weekly returns to the managing committee. One district committee member and the secretary would represent the district at the weekly meetings of the managing committee.[17] The attention given to detail may be seen in the following recommendation:

> Each member of this sub-committee [of investigation] is requested to carry with him at all times, a small note book, in which he may enter any casual information he may obtain respecting the cases that have passed through his hands and to which he can instantly refer as the occasion may require.[18]

and demonstrating the discipline that was required of members:

> unless the [district] committees will work unremittingly, judiciously and in perfect unison with each other and with the Managing Committee, it will be in vain to expect even partial success unless they fully co-operate in one uniform principle of action and plan of management.[19]

These preliminary arrangements soon ran into trouble. It was essential that the Association's clients were both able and willing to work if its policy was to succeed. The Governor of the House of Industry agreed to take in all the aged and infirm beggars and abandoned children referred by the Association for whom he could find room. In return, the Association agreed to provide work or training for an equal number of able-bodied people released into its care from the House of Industry.[20] However, the Governor adamantly refused to admit sturdy beggars, those with 'rooted habits of idleness, vagrancy and vice'.[21] Many beggars roaming the streets belonged to this class, and the Association considered they would also disrupt its operation, where 'order and decorum must be indispensable requisites', even if they agreed to participate.[22] A sub-committee of barristers was appointed to examine the problem and reported that the powers of the police were limited to arresting beggars at night and charging them under the Vagrants Act, a charge which could lead to deportation and was considered 'at variance with the humane and mild principles which appear to govern this Association'.[23] The only other legal restraint on beggars was vested in the Corporation for the Relief of the Poor of Dublin, represented by the Governor of the House of Industry, who was now denying responsibility for them. The sub-committee suggested that the Association could qualify itself to become the Corporation for the Relief of the Poor of Dublin and thus assume legal powers to restrain beggars. As objections were immediately raised to this idea, the managing committee decided not to pursue the matter further, for fear of losing support for the whole project whose success depended so much on the goodwill and cooperation of the public.[24] It was, however, a major setback for the Association's plan. The objective of clearing the Dublin streets of beggars would be difficult to achieve if beggars who were unwilling to work in the Institution could not be satisfactorily placed elsewhere. Some members of the managing committee resigned on the grounds that this obstacle was unsurmountable.

The managing committee's reluctance to begin operations until all their elaborate arrangements were complete had allowed time for the previous objections to be raised again and to gain credence. Worst of all, a suggestion was now made that the plan could lead to the introduction of the dreaded poor rates. Although the Association stressed the important role of voluntary intervention in obviating the need for compulsory support of the poor, these objections cooled the Dublin public's initial enthusiasm for the plan and severely affected the collection of funds. During the first few months only £1,600 was collected and, due to the lower than anticipated membership, it was impossible to form all the proposed district committees. An important decision was required: to start with low funds and membership or to abandon the entire project.[25] Eventually, the managing committee decided to follow Rumford's example: in similar circumstances, he had gone ahead, proved the idea was workable, and gained the support of the people of Munich. The managing committee hoped that the Dublin public would be as sensible and generous as the Munich people and subscribe liberally to the Association once they saw the benefits.[26]

The original plan depended on the commitment of a substantial membership. When the hoped-for numbers failed to materialise, the managing committee were forced to adjust the plan, but never wavered in their principles.[27] At the outset, the Association had proposed to help all the poor without means of support in the hope of preventing them becoming mendicants. It had, after all, been founded to *prevent* as well as *suppress* mendicity. In the face of the unexpected difficulties and following long discussion, the managing committee decided to confine their initial attention to those already begging on the streets and to put a modified version of the plan into effect.[28]

A notice was placed in the newspapers announcing the registration of beggars from 8 June 1818 onwards and warning beggars of the consequences of continuing their 'trade': an empty threat, it now appeared, although the beggars were unaware of this. The general public was urged to stop giving alms in the street.[29] The mendicant poor who thought they would qualify for relief were invited to apply at a building in Hawkins Street. This building was the property of the Dublin Society, founded in 1731 to promote agriculture, manufactures, and the useful arts; and which later in turn founded and developed many of Ireland's best known institutions—among them the National Museum, the National Library and the Botanic Gardens. On a site previously occupied by one of the city's meat markets, the Dublin Society had erected and occupied the premises in Hawkins

Street before moving to Leinster House in 1815. The Society generously lent the building to the new Association and it became known as the headquarters of the Mendicity Institution. There, applicants were given a ticket referring them to the Association's district office in the area where they lived, if such an office had been established.[30] Otherwise, cases were processed in Hawkins Street. A questionnaire, adapted from one lent by the Edinburgh Mendicity Society, was used to investigate the circumstances of applicants.[31] (See Appendix B.)

Investigation was an important feature of all Mendicity Societies and of many voluntary organisations at that time. The idea of providing help for someone already receiving support elsewhere was against their principles. Investigation required manpower. An applicant's answers to the questionnaire were checked and verified by the committee member who acted as a visitor in the area where the applicant lived. The district sub-committee of investigation then decided on the treatment the applicant should receive.[32] Those considered unfit for work were supported for one month and recommended to the managing committee as suitable candidates for referral to the House of Industry. 'Strangers', people not natives or residents of Dublin for at least six months, were supported until they could be returned, at the Institution's expense, to friends or family in other parts of Ireland or to their native parishes in England or Scotland. People discovered lying about their circumstances were sent away and warned not to beg again. The remainder were offered work or training.[33]

Associations for the relief of the poor in Edinburgh, Belfast, Munich, and Hamburg had recommended the spinning of coarse yarn, straw-plaiting, knitting, picking oakum, whitewashing the residences of the poor, and sweeping the 'lanes, bye streets and crossways of the city' as possible sources of employment for Dublin beggars.[34] The Dublin Association tried all the suggested occupations, some proving to be more successful than others. The first committees advanced by a system of trial and error. They constantly looked for new ways in which to employ the poor. They were not afraid to admit their mistakes and were often forced to review, modify and adjust their approach. If something did not work, a special committee was usually appointed to ascertain the reason and to recommend a remedy. Being an active committee member of the Mendicity Association in the early years required great commitment. Ad hoc committees were frequently instructed to meet every day until a solution to a particular problem was found. The Association tried to meet needs and situations as they arose, but its brief quickly became much wider than originally envisaged. As the House of Industry was unable to accommodate all those referred for admission, the Association found itself helping increasing numbers of the aged, the infirm, and abandoned children as well as those fit for work.

Spinning was the most successful and the most profitable form of employment for the Dublin Association's clientele. A woman who could learn to spin twelve cuts of two-hank yarn in a day cost the Association very little for her support. Some women could reach this level of ability in three weeks. Due to shortage of funds the Institution was limited in the number of spinning wheels it could provide, but it also redeemed some wheels from the pawnbroker and provided their owners with materials so they could resume work. It was hoped that, when prices improved, the spinners would cease to be a charge on the Institution and would look for work elsewhere. Initially four hundred women were employed as spinners, but there was such a demand for the yarn they spun, the Institution claimed that it could have employed one thousand spinners had funds allowed.[35] The Institution was unable to meet the requirements of the Dublin and Drogheda markets, not to speak of supplying many orders from England and Scotland. One loom was reserved for spinning yarn for coarse clothing; and several women were employed to make it up into clothes for the most deserving mendicants, those who worked and behaved well, or 'in cases of extreme necessity to cover nakedness'.[36] In the winter, the public was asked to donate old clothes and carpeting to the Institution to be made into clothing, which provided more work for female mendicants. Plaiting straw, when the straw was given free as usually happened, also gave a fair return, even when the market for the finished article was poor. When the Linen Hall, the regulatory board for the industry, sent a quantity of yarn to be reeled, fifty mendicants were employed for three months and over £71 was earned for the Institution's funds.[37]

Some mendicants were employed as knitters, although this occupation yielded a very poor return. Adhering to the principle that no one should be freely helped if they were able to do even the smallest amount of work, the managing committee employed some of the elderly and infirm mendicants at knitting and also placed a few picking oakum. Some of the stronger mendicants were trained to work part of the oakum into doormats, the remainder was sold. Others learned how to make hearth rugs, and a large number were employed sweeping the streets.[38] A number of mendicants known as 'label men' were sent out daily with placards giving details of the number of poor in the Institution to alert the public about its existence and work. For a short period, some of the older boys in the Institution were allowed to participate in this work.

The managing committee were in a quandary about the rate at which the mendicants should be paid. The rate for manual labour in the city at that time was barely enough to support life. The Mendicity Institution certainly could not do less; yet it wanted to encourage its mendicants to become independent and seek other employment. In the beginning, to attract beggars away from their lucrative 'trade', it was found necessary to pay more than the normal wage, thus running the risk of attracting labourers already in work to seek help from the Institution.[39] The managing committee were caught between being too lenient (which would encourage over-long stays in the Institution) and too strict (which could leave mendicants without enough to live on and perhaps force them back to begging). Eventually, taking into account the price of potatoes at the time, a sum of four and a half pence daily was fixed as the appropriate rate of payment at the end of the summer in 1818.[40] Those who could not earn this sum by their work received the shortfall in food.

The Association established two schools for the children of mendicants in the Institution: one at Hawkins Street, where 227 children attended; the other at Brunswick Street in the Four Courts district where many of the expert spinners were employed, had 55 pupils. Children received elementary education and instruction in simple and useful employment and were fed by the Institution.[41]

All these initiatives made heavy demands on the Association's meagre funds. The Institution also supported mendicants whose work was non-productive because it gave no return, those for whom it was unable to provide work, and many who were unfit for any work. Women were paid to look after orphan children, apparently now also in the Institution's remit.[42] The Institution employed superintendents and teachers for the spinners, the straw-plaiters, and the schools. Even though expenses were kept to a minimum and whenever possible mendicants were employed in menial jobs, operating the Institution at Hawkins Street and the district offices was costly. The initial subscriptions were soon exhausted and the managing committee forced to make numerous appeals to the public for help, but with little result. They had over-estimated the generosity of Dublin's citizens. Extra contributions from members of the Association kept the Institution open, but every penny that came in was spent on daily expenses. No developments could take place nor improvements be made. The project seemed doomed to closure when it was less than three months in operation. In desperation, the managing committee paraded all the beggars currently being helped by the Association in a 'quiet well-ordered procession 'through the city streets on 7 September 1818, in order to demonstrate the effectiveness of its intervention.[43] The procession caused a 'considerable sensation'; many promises of support and some donations were received which enabled the Institution to remain open.[44]

Following a recommendation from the sub-committee of health, the managing committee decided, as winter approached, that relief should be given to all mendicants partly in money and partly in food. This strategy would ensure a better and more regular diet and help the mendicants to build up resistance to the fever epidemic attacking the city that year. The daily wage became ten ounces of bread, three pints of soup and twopence for lodging and other necessities. The new plan was not only cheaper for the Institution but meant that the mendicants could not waste money on unnecessary purchases such as alcoholic drink. The managing committee hoped that ineligible applicants would be deterred, as food would be less attractive than money. The plan provided a new source of employment for some female mendicants who went around the city households at stated times daily, collecting bones and scraps of food for the soup in provision carts. The public were urged to give left-over food to the cart women rather than to beggars on the doorstep.[45] To encourage them to work hard, the cart women received three farthings per stone of meat collected, in addition to their normal wages.[46]

An extract from an 'eloquent' sermon given by Rev W A Evanson at the Bethesda Chapel on 11 October 1818 gives some idea of the achievements of the Institution:

> The Mendicity Institution has banished from the City those hordes of beggars who had flocked from the remotest parts of the Island, to join the depradators upon public bounty, and to disseminate with still greater rapidity of effect the moral virus of Mendicity. It has purified the highways of our Metropolis from a noisome crowd of importunate and vicious supplicants, and we can now pursue our accustomed occupations without disturbing assaults on our feelings or our purses. It has equalized the distribution of a necessary maintenance amongst those who were daily passing from the extremes of riot and intoxication to the very depth of famine. It has given warmth and activity to limbs which were benumbed with cold, drenched in rain, and paralysed with idleness. It has rescued from the artifices of unfeeling Parents and the destructive influence of ill examples, those groups of miserable little ones who were daily initiating into hypocrisy and fraud, in whom every evil passion was inflamed by brutal excitement, and the very lineaments of the immortal man defaced by besotting ignorance. It has attempted to raise the character of the Female Mendicant, to somewhat of that elevated purity of her sex which is their glory and their ornament, by giving her employment for the hours which were continued in idle and polluting intercourse, and has thus begun to sow the seed of virtuous habits in hearts so lately overrun with the rankest weeds of vice.[47]

The Institution continued to drag on 'a precarious existence' until the managing committee were forced to call a public meeting at the Mansion House on 29 October 1818.[48] As a result of the Lord Mayor's appeal for subscriptions at this meeting, together with 'the receipts from public concerts, a munificent subscription from the Gentlemen of the University and Donations from individuals of distinguished liberality', the Association was able to support the Institution 'with extreme difficulty' until the end of the year.[49] Thus the first annual report of the Association could claim to have kept the streets almost free of beggars for seven months 'without coercion' and to have

> also drawn attention to, and excited an interest in behalf of a class of wretched beings, hitherto unjustly condemned, because entirely neglected—it has made the rich more acquainted with the poor, and, by so doing, has fostered that mutual feeling of interest, which, whenever exertions are made in the cause of benevolence, is usually found to unite the individuals benefited to their benefactors.[50]

The Association had also determined to some extent the amount of beggary in Dublin: 7,500 mendicants had been registered; of these 2,251 were assisted to leave the city and return home and 2,800 qualified for relief in the Institution. The average number helped daily was 2,600, including 600 children. Table 1 shows the number and occupation of the mendicants in the Institution during the last week of 1818. Although fever was rampant throughout the city during the winter of 1818–19, the Institution remained remarkably free from disease, a situation attributed to the improved diet of the mendicants. Above all, the Association had

Table 1: Number and Occupation of the Clientele in the Institution during the last week of 1818

Occupation	Number
Spinners	488
Knitters (stockings)	186
(rug mats)	12
Sweepers	288
Oakum pickers	20
Cart women	24
Label men and boys	55
Needle workers	20
Straw-plaiters	127
Weaver	1
Waiting for spinning wheels	708
Elderly and infirm	319
Children in school	282
Younger children	400
TOTAL	2,930

Source: 1st *Annual Report* of the Association, App 4, p 39

demonstrated that its plan worked. Many former beggars had learned a trade and had the opportunity to become 'virtuous and useful members of society'.[51] The Association also claimed to have made a great improvement in the morals of the poor: a claim that was supported by the police magistrates' report of a decrease in the amount of juvenile delinquency and in the number of women appearing before them since the Institution opened.[52]

The Association made several recommendations in its first annual report, to be repeated constantly in future years:

> 1. Powers to deal effectively and appropriately with sturdy beggars should be vested in the police magistrates. If they had this power during the last year, the Association considered that 'not a beggar would dare to infest this City.'[53]
> 2. Alms should not be given in the streets nor at the doors of houses. As long as this practice continued, beggars would be attracted to the streets. Ministers of religion, heads of businesses, and householders were urged to promote the cause of the Association and to discourage their congregations and subordinates from giving alms in this way.[54]

The Association had a strict policy with regard to religious practice in the Institution, 'the principle being not to interfere in the slightest degree, with the religious opinions of the poor'.[55] The Anglican and Roman Catholic archbishops of Dublin were interested members. Religious services, according to the rites of the church to which the mendicants respectively belonged, were held in the Institution each Sunday, followed by religious instruction for both children and adults from 'benevolent individuals of their own persuasion' for 'which they show[ed] the greatest attention and gratitude to their teachers'.[56] Indeed, the managing committee considered

> several of these poor have been thereby led to become constant attendants in a sacred duty they had previously neglected, and have been often seen to shed tears at the serious mention of that name, which had scarcely ever before been sounded in their ears but, in the curse of impiety or the cant of imposture.[57]

An additional benefit was that some of the adults and children learned to read during these lessons.[58] In line with the policy of religious freedom, children who needed nursing or fostering were always given to women of the same religion as that of their parents, and young people placed in service with employers of their own religion. Religious books were never allowed in the schoolroom. One anonymous complaint of proselytism against the Association proved to have no foundation and led to an assurance from the representatives of Dr Troy, the Roman Catholic Archbishop of Dublin, that they had every confidence that the managing committee would be vigilant in this respect.[59]

The new year was one of mixed fortunes for the Association. On the credit side, the trustees of the Linen Hall granted fifty spinning wheels and five reels to the Institution. A sale-room was set aside in Hawkins Street and wheelwrights were asked to send in any wheels they had on hand, in order to encourage visitors to purchase and donate them to the Institution when they saw the great need for them and 'the air of cheerfulness and comfort, which so remarkably characterises the industrious spinners'.[60] Ladies residing in the College district formed a 'penny-a-week society' and raised nearly £68 in two months to buy wheels.[61] Although the female mendicants in the Institution outnumbered their male counterparts by nearly ten to one, there were no women on the managing committee of the Association nor on any of the subcommittees. During the first two years, female participation in the management of the Association was limited to fund raising. Then, having been invited to follow the example of the 'ladies of Edinburgh', they supervised the management of the schools, taught sewing and good manners to the girls, and were regarded as a valuable asset by the gentlemen on the managing committee.[62] As a consequence of these measures, the spinning department was enlarged considerably and 735 spinners were employed. When more work became available, the number of applications for admission fell: many 'fled when they found industry had become the only terms on which even that pittance could be procured'.[63] Except for the sick and infirm, all the mendicants in the Institution had work by April 1819. Eighteen superintendents were employed and the managing committee could report that the Institution was 'in a state of progressive Improvement'.[64] The appearance of many of the mendicants had also improved. Most of the 'deserving' adults and nearly all the children had received fresh clothing. Their old garments were taken away and thoroughly cleaned or destroyed, if necessary, to prevent the spread of infection.[65]

According to the regulations, one-third of the members of the managing committee retired each year. Following the Annual General Meeting in January 1819, the new managing committee immediately set about streamlining their organisation to make better use of scarce resources. The number of district committees was reduced to four to avoid the expense of separate establishments.[66] Occupations that had proved unprofitable were given up. The street-cleaning experiment failed. Returning to the places where they had begged was a source of temptation for the mendicants: 'not only would the broom be thrown aside, but the old trade of begging occasionally resorted to'.[67] The managing committee also concluded that it was not a suitable occupation for female mendicants: 'a life spent on the public streets is not calculated to effect any moral change'.[68] Street-cleaning also required constant supervision; after a short time only a few elderly men were employed in this way. Knitting was also given up as the return was so poor. Although it was a suitable occupation for the aged and infirm, the time spent unravelling bad work and the loss of material were so costly, it was decided to confine knitting to able-bodied women while they were waiting to be supplied with spinning wheels.[69]

A new form of simple employment, preferably within the Institution, was needed for those unable to learn to spin. Pulverising oyster shells for manure was recommended by St Martin's Parish in London as an inexpensive method of employment, needing little skill and capable of producing a profit. All the extern workers, except the home spinners, the label men and the cart women, were called in and set to work in this way. The introduction of this occupation encouraged lazy spinners and bad attenders to improve their ways. Demotion to oyster shell duty was not a welcome prospect and 'the wheel became an object of attraction'.[70]

The managing committee turned their attention to the kitchen, where costs were high. Paying wages in food and money had proved expensive and the amount of free rations (meals) given out was large. The managing committee now believed that the system of paying the same allowance to every mendicant gave no incentive to work and encouraged idleness. They decided that only the aged, the infirm, mothers with small children, and mendicants in training would receive free food daily; new entrants would be given free rations for two days. Other mendicants would be paid in money and could purchase food from the kitchen at a reasonable price. As the quality of the soup and fine wheaten bread previously provided for the mendicants was 'totally beyond the powers of the class immediately above them in society to enjoy', the managing committee decided that a simpler and cheaper diet was necessary and fairer.[71] Following various experiments the new diet was launched. Meat and bones collected from city households were separated as carefully as possible from 'everything improper' and boiled with potatoes and vegetables; 'the whole was then thoroughly mixed together and properly seasoned' to form a 'wholesome, comfortable and highly nutritious mess'.[72] Every mendicant received or could purchase two rations daily, each consisting of two pounds of stew or 'lobscouse', as the mendicants called it. The new diet cost the Institution just over one penny per ration to make, less than half the cost of the soup and bread previously provided, and was sold to the mendicants at a halfpenny per ration. Selling food cheaply finally allowed the managing committee to fix the rate of the spinners' wages at the market standard. Applications for admission decreased and many left the Institution following this reduction from the rate paid the previous year. In the College district alone, more than half the mendicants left.[73]

The managing committee recognised that the mendicants might need some help to pay for lodgings following the reduction in their wages. Dublin being the capital, rents were 'necessarily high'.[74] A new allowance of twopence and a free ration of food was given to all who attended the Institution on Sundays. The allowance removed any reason for begging on that day, always a very lucrative time for beggars, and the source of many complaints by the public.

Next came the schools. The two schools were amalgamated into one at Hawkins Street where the children were given religious and moral instruction and taught to read, but no more. It was decided that 'education should cease to be the leading feature of their system', and children over seven years of age should be employed at simple work during the day to contribute as far as possible to their own support.[75] The managing committee justified these actions by arguing that 'forcing poor children on, in advanced stages of English education, no matter what their capacities, would be a serious misdirection of funds'.[76] They were also careful never to train the children for trades already overstocked with workers, nor in any accomplishment or useful art that might place them 'beyond their natural station in society'.[77] Girls were taught straw-plaiting, spinning and a few learned to sew. Boys learned to make nets, a skill which probably would not be of much future use to them, but the managing committee believed that 'the principle of calling forth exertion, and enforcing habits of industry' was valuable in itself.[78]

A special committee was appointed to superintend the straw-plait school. Its first objective was to establish habits of cleanliness and order among the girls. The first school had 127 pupils. They were paid a fixed rate, rather than for the quantity of work done. As a result, the quality of the work was very fine and it sold easily. A savings bank was started in the school where 'the trifle' saved each week enabled the 'little workers' to purchase clothes with money they had earned themselves.[79] The managing committee believed this system had many advantages: it taught the girls the value of thrift, encouraged them to work hard, gave them a degree of independence, made their lives more comfortable, and 'raised them one degree in the scale of society'.[80] A great improvement followed in their appearance, manners and spirits; and visitors to the Institution found it hard to believe their family history, 'so completely were the traces of 'Beggar's Child' thereby obliterated from their appearance'.[81] Their appearance also impressed prospective employers, who had not liked the previous 'coarse unseemly habit' which was all the Association could afford. Many of the girls easily obtained jobs in shops and factories or went into 'comfortable' service, silencing those who objected to mendicants wearing such fine clothes.[82] The Institution received favourable reports about the continuing good conduct of these girls from their satisfied employers.[83]

Despite the economies, the Association was still in a grave financial situation. By the end of January 1819, weekly subscriptions amounted to £87 less than weekly expenditure and the Association owed £800.[84] Subscription lists were sent to all households in the city to make it easier for people to contribute to the Association, but many people complained that this was too like a tax. The managing committee publicised the fact that subscriptions would be received by the banks or by any member of the Association.[85] A weekly account of donations received was published in the newspapers to encourage non-subscribers. Once again, the managing committee were forced to appeal to the Lord Mayor who issued a proclamation asking for subscriptions, this time with little result.[86] By the end of March the Association's debts had risen to almost £1,000. The proceeds from a public concert saved the situation but the managing committee's patience was exhausted.[87] A public meeting which drew great support was held on 2 April 1819 in the Great Room of the Rotunda, at which the managing committee gave notice that if the Institution went into debt again they would no longer be responsible: 'The next failure of funds would also be the failure of the Institution.'[88] The committee's time was so completely occupied by fundraising that it was impossible to supervise the Institution properly. Committee members had become public collectors rather than managers of the Institution; they had been compelled to beg for support from door to door, to depend on charity sermons or public entertainments, and 'to descend to every device, to undergo every fatigue, and yet to be in hourly fear of dissolution'.[89] They concluded by saying,

> they must resign their trust with feelings of indeed the deepest regret, but with the honest consciousness that if to have strained every nerve, to have given every warning, to have put into practice every shift in order to uphold so valuable an Institution was the duty of the managers, that duty has been fully and faithfully performed.[90]

This report caused a sensation. The managing committee were authorised to close the Institution if it went into debt again and the meeting was adjourned for two weeks to see if a solution could be found.[91] When it was re-convened, the managing committee were directed to employ professional collectors to approach every householder in the city for support.[92]

This was a major turning point for the Association. Although the managing committee had to make a further appeal for funds in August, the public began to take a greater interest and to recognise the benefits of the Institution's work. Ladies formed societies for contributing small sums weekly, or volunteered to collect funds for the purchase of spinning wheels, while others made and sold toys to raise money for the Institution. Several gentlemen 'possessing considerable influence in this City' promoted the Institution among their friends, and factory workers and servants contributed 'with cheerfulness' to weekly collections on its behalf.[93] A public sermon given by Rev James Dunn raised £529 14s 1d; a gentleman, who had only silver in his pocket in the church, later sent a donation of £1 10s 'as a token of his high respect for the Preacher and the effects of his persuasive eloquence'.[94] Two new occupations were introduced. An experiment in lace-making was begun in a small way. Only a few girls were taught at first as the equipment was expensive. Later, a special committee was placed in charge of the lace school, which expanded and made a profit. The girls became skilled and produced beautiful work, and many easily found jobs outside the Institution.[95] The manufacture of coarse blanketing from cow's hair was introduced as an occupation for adult mendicants. The objective was to provide cheap warm articles of covering which could be bought by the mendicants themselves, by paying a small amount weekly from their wages.[96]

The managing committee were now free to concentrate on managing the Institution and regulating its affairs. When fraud was discovered in the flax department, a rigid system of checks was introduced. Weekly statements of accounts were demanded with the result that costs decreased rapidly and expenses for the entire year of 1819, including the payment of all the outstanding debts, amounted to less than the costs of the eight months of 1818.[97] The 'infant body struggling to maintain life' during the first difficult year was finally able to advance 'towards maturity'.[98] By the end of the year the Institution had assumed 'rather the appearance of a regular workshop than an almshouse', and the first managing committee's objective had been achieved: there was a sufficient supply of spinning wheels for all who required them.[99]

However, the managing committee had little time to enjoy the benefits of the 'amended and more settled plan'.[100] At the Annual General Meeting in 1820, charges of such a serious nature were made against the outgoing committee that the meeting was adjourned and a public inquiry established to investigate the matter.

CHAPTER THREE

Finding a Home 1820–1823

THE PURCHASE OF A SHOWER BATH for £5 in August 1819 was the start of an unpleasant series of events for the managing committee.[1] Earlier that year *An Act for the Prevention of Contagious Diseases in Ireland* had been passed to establish regulations for cleaning and disinfecting the persons and clothes of the poor.[2] The managing committee were asked to forward the aims of this act among the mendicants in the Institution. After some research, it was decided to have a shower erected under the supervision of a physician in a discreet part of the premises, where the mendicants would not be overlooked while undergoing the cleansing procedure. It was also decided that, where necessary, their hair would be cut very short.[3]

These decisions led to charges against the managing committee of extreme cruelty to six mendicants. It was alleged that all six had become ill and three of them had died. When the matter was raised at the Annual General Meeting in 1820, a special committee of members and friends of the Association was set up to investigate the allegations. It is not clear from the minutes whether Daniel O'Connell was a member or a friend of the Association at that time, however he was appointed to this committee, which immediately held a sworn public inquiry into the matter. The committee reported to the adjourned Annual General Meeting that, in their opinion, the managing committee had acted in accordance with the terms of the act. No deaths had occurred as a result of the cleansing procedure and no evidence of cruelty was found. Sick and infirm mendicants had been examined by a physician before undergoing the shower bath; the practice, which only lasted a few moments, had never been carried out in bad weather; and exercise was always allowed afterwards. Although the managing committee were cleared of all charges, the affair had created such bad feeling among the poor, it was thought expedient to discontinue the compulsory cleansing of the mendicants in the Institution. It was considered safe to take this step as the spread of disease in the city had been halted to a great extent. Under the terms of the act, officers of health had full authority to take precautions if it became necessary to re-adopt them.[4] Later that year, Dr Harty, one of the founders of the Association, proposed that the process should be resumed, but other members of the managing committee disagreed with his proposal.[5]

The bad publicity did not help with another difficulty now faced by the Association. It urgently needed to increase its membership in order to replace some of the overworked members of the managing committee.[6] People were not unwilling to serve, but many were unable to give the time demanded of members. The committee often met twice weekly, and each of the members belonged to at least one sub-committee, not to speak of the special committees set up to examine particular issues. Dr Robert Perceval, a vice-president of the Association, had warned of this eventuality in 1818. From his wide experience of working with the marginalised sectors of Irish society, he observed that all voluntary organisations had this problem: once the novelty wore off, the work was left to a few committed individuals who then exhausted themselves on behalf of the organisation. He had proposed that the Mendicity Association should join with several other organisations, the Society for the Relief of Sick and Indigent Roomkeepers, the Charitable Society, the Strangers' Friend Society, and the Charitable Sisterhood, to organise a general system of relief for the poor. Hawkins Street could become a central office from which people needing help would be directed to the appropriate place, and where records of those helped could be kept.[7] Subsequently described by Burke as 'well ahead of his time', Dr Perceval's proposals were not adopted.[8] When the problem occurred in the Mendicity Association, the managing committee's solution was to abolish the remaining district committees, to open the membership of the managing committee to every member of the Association, and to create a new category of associate membership for people with a limited amount of free time.[9] Associate members could attend meetings and carry out the regulations, but did not have a vote. Their duties included:

1. Reporting on the extent of mendicity in their own neighbourhoods, particularly with regard to any increase or decrease; informing the managing committee of any 'remarkable beggar that may infect their district'; and examining special cases referred to them by the managing committee;[10]
2. Overseeing the provision carts and the conduct of the cart women and suggesting improvements;
3. Assisting collectors by their local knowledge and influence and overseeing the collections and subscriptions in their own neighbourhoods;
4. Assisting in their neighbourhoods in any way their free time allowed; carrying out the orders of the managing committee; and 'forwarding the objects of the Institution in any way their benevolence and experience could help'.[11]

One of the important results of the introduction of this category of membership was that retired members of the managing committee could become associate members. This allowed those dedicated founder members who so wished, to maintain an active interest in the Institution and ensured continuity of management.

Disregarding the 'temporary odium' caused by their cost-cutting procedures in 1819, the managing committee continued to operate with severity.[12] Clothes were now lent rather than given to the children, the old and infirm, and cases of extreme hardship. As usual 'a preference, as to the best articles, [was] to be given to the most deserving'.[13] The word MENDICITY was stamped in paint on the inside of all loaned garments and a number was stamped on the outside. Notices were placed in the newspapers warning pawn-brokers and second-hand clothes dealers that they would be prosecuted if they bought or dealt with the property of the Institution. In keeping with the meticulous approach always adopted, a register of clothing was kept, where the names of the mendicants and the items lent to them were entered.[14] After three months, mendicants were examined to make sure they still had the clothes.[15] Other mendicants were allowed to buy clothing cheaply from the Institution, the cost deducted in weekly instalments from their wages.[16]

In the kitchen, £30 a year was saved by replacing black pepper with allspice, chili powder, and ginger as seasoning for the mendicants' food. Previously, the pepper had not been sufficiently ground and thus wasted by the kitchen clerk, so strict instructions were given for grounding the allspice and using the correct amount of ingredients 'which should be dredged into the stew by degrees, not thrown into it'.[17] The cook was not pleased with these instructions. He complained that the allspice discoloured the food. As the mendicants liked the flavour of leeks, cheap scallions and onions in the stew, a note was added to the weekly notice of subscribers in the newspapers, requesting donations of these vegetables from the owners of gardens near Dublin, and all Dublin householders were asked to donate more liberally to the provision carts.[18] Mendicants were no longer allowed to use the term 'lobscouse' to describe the food. It was to be called 'Irish stew' or the 'stew' in future.[19]

The allowance to the aged and infirm was reduced to one and a half pence a day, although their Sunday allowance remained at two pence. Apart from their food and this minimal allowance for lodging, they now had to work for any extras they might need.[20] As they were only capable of light work, a quantity of junk, [old rope] was purchased so they could pick oakum.

Pulverizing oyster shells was made the initial employment of every healthy mendicant. It was a very laborious and unpopular job and those who persevered with this 'revolting occupation' were soon promoted to more pleasant work. Those who failed were considered not sufficiently in need of help and expelled.[21] This 'work test' proved more effective than the strictest investigation in determining who deserved admittance. In many instances, investigation had proved impracticable when neighbours wanted to help people seeking admission to the Institution and did not tell the truth about their circumstances.[22] The new system was also less time-consuming for the managing committee. In 1822, as it became more difficult to obtain oyster shells and the demand for the powder dropped, breaking limestone was substituted as the work test for mendicants in the Institution.[23] There was a great demand for this product, which was used to pave the streets.

The Institution's aim was to return mendicants to society as workers. To this end, it gave them no more than was barely enough to sustain life. Anything else was considered to be 'ruinous in its effects.'[24] The rapid turnover of mendicants, described in Table 2, showed the system was working. Expert workers were sought by outside businesses. Having checked the availability of jobs outside the Institution, the managing committee sometimes reduced wages to encourage mendicants to leave. When they did this in the straw-plait department, one hundred girls immediately found work elsewhere, seventy in factories and thirty in service. Another group of sixty-five girls then underwent training. As the Mendicity Institution qualified people to leave, it could never expect to make a profit, nor to break even. Once workers became expert, they went elsewhere, unlike regular apprentices who remained with their employers for a certain time after learning a trade. As a result, only the unskilled and those who were unemployable elsewhere remained in the Institution. Nor could the Institution take on more profitable work which might interfere with 'the industrious poor' who were already employed.[25] The managing committee often devised employment from which there was no return, in order to keep the mendicants occupied. As one member of the managing committee remarked:

> Therefore if the employment were only digging a hole and filling it up again, piling stones and taking them down again; it should be an indispensable rule, that in no case should a healthy adult receive relief as a pauper, except through the means of employment.[26]

Table 2: Turnover of the Institution's Clientele 1818–1820

	1818	1819	1820
Attendance	2,930	1,106	961
Number remaining from previous year		355	396

Source: 2nd and 3rd *Annual Reports* of the Association, p 20

However, the Institution initiated ideas for new industries by demonstrating to the public the lowest rate at which labour could be obtained, so that individuals were encouraged to undertake projects 'perhaps highly advantageous to the Country' that would not have been undertaken otherwise.[27] For example two businessmen, encouraged by the pool of cheap, skilled labour available from the Institution, started a poplin factory spinning fine woollen yarns which had been imported up to that time. Initially, they employed two hundred of the Institution's expert spinners and more were taken on later.[28]

The Institution also started new industries with a view to having them taken over by businessmen once they proved successful. For instance, twenty mendicants were employed in the Institution making hair quilts for which there was a high demand. When Trim gaol placed a large order for the quilts and there was a possibility that other gaols would adopt this form of covering for prisoners, it created an opportunity for an outside manufacturer to take on the project and make a good living from it.[29] The managing committee considered that 'absorbing the unemployed into the industrious classes of the community' was an important part of the Association's duty and that these projects also helped in accelerating the country's return to wealth and prosperity.[30]

The reduction in numbers seeking help in the Institution and the stringent reorganisation plan eased the financial situation considerably and enabled the managing committee to turn their attention to the wider picture of mendicity in the city. They now tried to implement fully the original intentions of the Association's founders: the *prevention* as well as the *suppression* of mendicity. One of the original resolutions of the Association had stressed the need

> to impress on the lower orders the necessity of providing for the future by the practice of industry, frugality and sobriety; and as the promotion of those virtues, the best and surest preventives of Mendicity, would be essentially aided by the establishment of such [savings] Banks.[31]

Saving was regarded as one of the great virtues in the nineteenth century, and the managing committee had always promoted it among mendicants in the Institution. All who earned were encouraged to save even the smallest amount each week. To encourage thrift, they were allowed to purchase clothing, tools and other necessary items by paying small sums weekly from their wages. Some of the mendicants went without a fire or candlelight in the evenings to save a weekly pittance.[32] The managing committee now made a strong recommendation that savings banks should be established in every parish in the city.[33]

Their second policy recommendation concerned the adoption of measures for improving the health of the poor. In 1818, the Association's sub-committee for health had carried out a survey of 600 mendicants and reported to the managing committee that 'there does not exist in Dublin a more prolific source of wretchedness, pauperism and mendicity, than disease'.[34] They warned that 'an association aiming at the suppression of mendicity [must] take serious cognizance of the health of the lower orders'.[35] Legislative provision in 1805 had enabled the establishment of local dispensaries funded partly by voluntary contributions and partly by grand jury presentments. Usually, several doctors operated a rota system and provided free medical care for the poor of a district. Many dispensaries provided vital help during the fever epidemics of 1816–19, but provision was haphazard and uneven.[36] The Association called for the establishment of dispensaries on a wide scale, especially in the east end, which was a particularly deprived part of the city. Few of the poor there, even if employed, could afford medicine and none could afford medical help.[37]

The Association considered that if savings banks and dispensaries were established throughout the city, independently from the Association, they would be 'powerful auxiliaries in preventing mendicity'.[38] While the Association provided for those who had already begged, savings banks would target potential paupers by encouraging and enabling them to save. By helping the 'industrious poor' to cope with minor illness, or by catching potentially serious conditions in time, dispensaries could be most useful in ensuring that such patients returned to their employment as quickly as possible and were not forced to resort to begging. The Hamburg Institution had reported 'the extension of the Medical Institution to those *not yet entitled* to receive support has prevented many a family from ever being in want of it'.[39] The Dublin Association also suggested to the city's employers that changing the day for the payment of wages from Saturday to either Tuesday or Wednesday would 'have very beneficial effects on the morals and comforts of the poor', by preventing them spending all of their pay on drink on Saturday night.[40]

The managing committee were always anxious that the public should be aware of the results of the Institution's work. The public was frequently invited to visit the project to witness the transformation that could be accomplished in beggars. A popular feature of each Annual General Meeting was a demonstration by the children of their skills at lace-making and straw-plaiting. Those present were always impressed by the children's modest and neat demeanour. Two female mendicants were each paid half a crown to take charge of the children on these occasions.[41] The managing committee also continued to plead with the government to give some body the power to deal with beggars. As long as the population continued to give alms on the streets and there were no effective measures to deal with beggars, the Association's aim to keep the streets of Dublin completely free of beggars would be impossible to achieve.

The managing committee received another unpleasant shock that year when the Institution was given notice to quit Hawkins Street. The premises at Hawkins Street had been a success from the beginning, being eminently suitable for the Institution's purpose. They were spacious and there was ample room for the employment projects, the training schools, a kitchen, stores and other offices all under one roof. When the managing committee decided to amalgamate the Brunswick Street and Hawkins Street schools, the premises easily accommodated all the children. Hawkins Street was also a very desirable location, nearly in the centre of the city and easily accessible to the public. Potential contributors could inspect the Institution, and members of the managing committee could supervise it and attend meetings regularly; yet it was in a sufficiently quiet position to avoid objections from neighbours. Apart from the building in Brunswick Street where many expert spinners were employed, with the collapse of the proposed district committee structure most activity had centred on Hawkins Street.[42]

During the first year of the Association's life, the managing committee frequently expressed gratitude to the Dublin Society for the loan of such spacious premises. However, in April 1819, when the Institution was only ten months old, the Dublin Society notified the Association of its intention to dispose of the building. Having failed to find suitable alternative accommodation, the managing committee offered to rent the Hawkins Street premises until they could find another location; thus, on 4 June 1819 the Association became the tenant of the Dublin Society at the reasonable rent of £300 per annum.[43] However, relations deteriorated between the two bodies during the following year. A dispute arose when part of the roof of an old laboratory at Hawkins Street, which the Association had been allowed to use at no extra cost, was stripped of lead. The managing committee's reluctance to pay the bill of £8 19s 6d and their stated intention to deduct the sum from the next instalment of the rent may have led to the otherwise inexplicable action of the now Royal Dublin Society on 5 August 1820, when the Association was given notice to quit Hawkins Street, the Society having arranged to rent the premises to Henry Harris who wished to build a theatre there.[44]

The Association was now in serious trouble. Over one thousand beggars were dependent on it, and to find satisfactory premises for the Institution in 1820 was no easier than it had been the previous year. When the government agreed to remove the staff of the Dublin militia from the South Great George's Street barracks and to rent the premises to the Institution at a modified rate because of the charitable nature of the project, the managing committee reluctantly decided it wiser to refuse the offer, as residents in its vicinity objected to the proposal to place an institution for beggars in their parish.[45] A deputation visited the Dean of St Patrick's Cathedral to see if these objections could be overcome, but had no success.[46] The managing committee met at least three times weekly during August 1820 to discuss the problem, and at the end of the month decided to meet daily until the matter of premises was resolved.[47] They requested the help of the Chief Secretary at Dublin Castle in finding appropriate premises and notified the citizens of Dublin of the emergency situation.

An advertisement was placed in all the daily and weekly newspapers:

> Wanted immediately by the Association for the Suppression of Mendicity, A Spacious Concern, capable of accommodating some hundreds of the working poor. Any person having such to let will send a description of the same with terms forthwith, directed to the Secretary at Hawkins Street.[48]

A special committee was appointed to deal with the many replies received to this advertisement. They viewed properties in Bishop Street, Abbey Street, Beresford Street and George's Quay, but none was suitable for the Institution's purposes. One was not large enough; several were in a bad state of repair; in most cases the rent asked was too high; and Beresford Street, in particular, was not considered to be a good neighbourhood for distinguished visitors to the Institution. It was feared that public interest would cool if the building was not centrally located so that the 'constant and scrutinizing control which distinguishes the Institution' could be maintained.[49] On 4 September, the managing committee decided to offer to pay the Royal Dublin Society full rent for Hawkins Street, while expressing regret that they had not been offered the chance to rent it before an agreement was made with Harris. They also decided to offer 'reasonable compensation' to Harris for any loss he might incur if he would give up the premises 'to preserve this great charity from ruin'.[50] Finally, the managing committee agreed to ask the Government to mediate in the matter. On the following day, a further meeting of the managing committee resolved:

> on maturely reconsidering the nature and probable result of our resolution of yesterday respecting the proposed appeal to Mr Harris and the ulterior applications to Government to interpose between him and the Dublin Society and having reason to fear that no successful issue could reasonably be anticipated from such a proceedings, that said Resolution be rescinded.[51]

This action certainly caused friction among the committee members. At the next day's meeting, it was resolved:

> although the circumstances in which the Institution were placed may

> justify the extreme measures adopted yesterday of rescinding the Resolutions of the preceding day—yet that for the future, no resolution adopted at any meeting of this Society be rescinded under a week's notice of such intention.[52]

Later, however, the committee asked and received permission from Harris to use the kitchen in Hawkins Street for a short time until one could be built in the new premises.[53]

Harris' Theatre Royal, where generations of Dubliners were entertained, opened on the premises in January 1821 with a production of *The Comedy of Errors* and *The Sleep Walker*. The opening address, by George Colman the younger, commemorated the former use of the site:

> Here once a market reared its busy head,
> Where sheep, instead of tragic heroes, bled,
> Soon Science came; his steel the butcher drops,
> And Learning triumphed over mutton chops!
> Again the scene was changed by Wisdom's rule,
> Want's refuge then succeeded Learning's School,
> No more in streets the shivering beggar stood,
> Vice found correction here and Famine food,
> Morality rejoiced at Sloth's defeat
> And Pity smiled to see the hungry eat.[54]

Today, the site houses the headquarters of the Department of Health.

This was a chaotic period for the Association. Committees were appointed daily to enter into negotiations for different properties. Finally, on 12 September 1820, the managing committee settled very reluctantly for a building at the back of Stanhope Gresham's premises in Castle Street, with an entrance on Copper Alley, at a rent of £222 15s per annum. Once again, people in the neighbourhood objected; but this time the managing committee were prepared and produced medical evidence to support their claim that the premises were suitable for accommodating large numbers. The premises were very private and sufficiently secluded not to interfere with anyone.[55] However, to defuse the situation and to reduce the numbers in Copper Alley, the managing committee rented a second premises at 64 Fleet Street for the schools and the children's workrooms at a rent of £80 per annum. The advantages of the Fleet Street premises included a quiet back door entrance where there would be few onlookers to see the children of begging families coming and going. Nevertheless, the managing committee received a letter from the Governors of the Bank of Ireland protesting at the imminent arrival of the children.[56]

The inadequacy of the 'confined and ill-ventilated' premises at Copper Alley was soon evident.[57] They were too small for the business of the Institution and conditions were very cramped. On many occasions, there was no water in the building.[58] Although fever in the city had been brought largely under control, the managing committee feared if it broke out again it could spread very rapidly in the crowded conditions in Copper Alley. The Institution could then be held responsible for spreading fever throughout the city, as mendicity had been blamed for spreading fever throughout the entire country during the recent epidemics.[59] Nor was Copper Alley suitable for meetings of the management committee: attendances fell as many of the members detested going there.[60] Following several unsuccessful attempts to find a suitable venue, it was decided to hold committee meetings in the schoolroom in Fleet Street until new premises could be found for the Institution.[61]

Another problem arose in Copper Alley as the days grew shorter on the approach of winter. The mendicants were unable to work once the daylight failed, and they could not earn enough to support themselves. If they were sent home early, they would need extra money for fire and candles and might be tempted to return to the streets.[62] One alternative was to allow a free ration of food each day from November until the end of February. Another was to raise the rate paid for their work, although this would help only the good workers. Following a vote, the managing committee decided to place lamps in the workrooms so the spinners could work in the evenings until 8 pm. Then it was discovered that whereas the Brunswick Street workroom was insured for the use of lamp-light, the workroom in Copper Alley was not. The managing committee were forced to take the unsatisfactory option of increasing the rate of payment for work done in Copper Alley.[63] As long as the Institution remained there, this problem continued to bother successive managing committees in winter each year. They were never keen to give extra money or rations for fear of creating a precedent, so different approaches were tried. One popular solution was to send all the expert spinners to the Brunswick Street workroom where they could work until 8 pm each evening.[64]

As 'the character of the Institution was threatened by continuing in Copper Alley', the search recommenced immediately for a permanent and suitable home, 'let the remove cost what it may'.[65] A special committee was appointed to look for new premises, but none of the many buildings inspected met all the Association's requirements. In despair, the premises committee suggested that the George's Street barracks should be reconsidered; however the managing committee considered the difficulties with that premises were 'insuperable'.[66] In July 1821, a meeting of the entire managing committee, including the ex officio members, was called to discuss the problem. A special committee was appointed solely to raise funds for the purchase or erection of a suitable building in a 'convenient and airy location'.[67] This was the second time that Daniel O'Connell was appointed to act on a special committee of the Association. At the Annual General Meeting of 1822, he became a member of the managing committee and was appointed to the regulations sub-committee. He probably attended meetings of this sub-committee, but there is no record of his attendance at any management committee meeting during the next four years, and unfortunately the minutes for the following five years are missing. The 1820s would have been a particularly busy time for Daniel O'Connell. It was during this period that he established the Catholic Association, 'the first popular democratic organisation of the modern world', won a seat at Westminster, and as a barrister spent considerable time travelling around the circuit.[68] He remained a member of the managing committee until his death in 1847, becoming president of the Association in 1842 during his term of office as Lord Mayor of Dublin.

Despite its disadvantages, Copper Alley saw the establishment of the Mendicity Institution dispensary. Although forced to abandon the original plan for medical walks in the city, the managing committee continued to worry about the disastrous consequences of illness for poor families. In response to requests for medical advice and aid from those working with the mendicants, they had arranged for physicians and surgeons from the nearby Poolbeg dispensary to provide medical care in Hawkins Street at a charge of £5 per quarter.[69] Ten thousand copies of the Hawkins Street sick certificate were printed, a number which perhaps reflects the amount of illness among mendicants. This certificate was used to verify illness. Following examination of the patient, the doctor decided the class to which each sick mendicant belonged:

> Class 1: Mendicants totally unfit to work received one and a half pence a day and their rations;
>
> Class 2: Mendicants able to work a little but not enough to support themselves fully received one and a half pence a day but no rations.[70]

On moving to Copper Alley, the managing committee was determined that the Institution should have its own dispensary. A number of physicians and surgeons agreed to give their services freely. They attended on a daily rota and treated any sick mendicants referred to them by the apothecary, who also visited sick mendicants in their homes and dispensed medicines. Sick mendicants were entitled to extra rations of food during their illness. According to the standards of the time, the clients of the Mendicity Institution were very well off for medical care compared with the poor outside the Institution.

After some time, problems developed in the dispensary at Copper Alley.[71] The attendance of the 'medical Gentlemen' became irregular, and on occasion the dispensary was left for several days at a time without any medical help, except for Buckley who had not practised as an apothecary for thirty-six years prior to working in Copper Alley. The managing committee wrote to the doctors expressing regret at this situation and asking them to notify the Institution if they did not wish to continue, so that medical help could be obtained elsewhere. An agreement was finally reached with the physicians and surgeons who guaranteed that at least one of them would attend daily and promised they would all deal with urgent medical and surgical cases, rather than specialising as previously.[72]

Apart from its location, Moira House at Usher's Island was the most suitable premises inspected by the premises committee. The former residence of the Earl of Moira, afterwards Marquess of Hastings, was once one of the most beautiful houses in Dublin and a popular subject for artists. John Wesley described it in his journal as one of the most magnificent palaces in Europe. During the rebellion of 1798, when Lord Edward Fitzgerald was arrested in Thomas Street, his wife, Pamela, was a guest in Moira House.[73] Its main drawback for the Mendicity Institution was the distance from the centre of the city: it was feared that members might not wish to travel so far. However, the committee optimistically hoped they could turn the location into an advantage and gain new members from the neighbourhood. The premises committee entered into negotiations with the owner, and an architect and builder inspected the premises on behalf of the Association.[74] In June 1822, the deal was nearing completion when a deputation from St Audoen's parish visited the managing committee to express 'surprise and disapprobation' at the committee's choice of premises for the Institution.[75] The deputation expressed respect for the ideals of the Mendicity Association but stated that it did not want the Institution in the neighbourhood. Its main arguments were:

1. Usher's Island, as the principal entrance to the city from the west, should be as agreeable in appearance as possible;
2. The presence of the Institution would force respectable individuals to leave their town houses and would halt improvements now taking place in the area;
3. The school children of the area would be seriously affected if they came into contact with 'such a mass of pauperism and wretchedness'.[76]

The managing committee wrote to the church wardens explaining that only the gentlemen of the committee and visitors to the Institution would use the Usher's Island entrance to Moira House; the clientele would use the Island Street entrance and so could not be a nuisance to anyone. During the day, the Institution was always very quiet and neighbours would not be disturbed. They promised that it would not differ at all from a private house in appearance.

The Association then received a letter from a solicitor acting for tenants of the late Earl of Moira concerning a clause in leases he had granted 'not to erect or bring in anything to annoy his tenants', subject to a penalty of £600.[77] An abstract of the title to Moira House and counsel's opinion on the matter was referred to a sub-committee of barristers. By February 1823, members of the managing committee were getting restless. They decided to ascertain finally if terms could be agreed on Moira House, otherwise they would look elsewhere for a building or a site on which to build.[78] For the next two months, the committee visited many vacant sites and viewed a number of premises. Even the building in Brunswick Street was examined to see if it could house the entire Institution. When it proved too small for this purpose, the managing committee decided to vacate. As a last resort, the premises committee tried to re-open negotiations with the agent for Moira House.[79] This effort came to an abrupt halt when trustees for Moira House announced in June 1823 that they did not wish to treat with the Mendicity Association.[80] The managing committee's worries were increased when notice to quit 64 Fleet Street was received because of impending alterations to the rear of the Bank of Ireland. Fortunately, this difficulty was quickly resolved when a committee appointed to find accommodation for the schools and a committee room rented new premises at 13 Fleet Street for £130 per annum.[81]

Finding a replacement for Copper Alley was not so easy. Once again a number of premises was inspected without success. In October 1823, the managing committee received word that Moira House had been sold to Patrick Reid of Linen Hall Street, who was willing to negotiate with the Association.[82] Not all members of the managing committee were satisfied with Moira House. Early in November, Thomas Wright gave notice of a motion to declare the premises unsuitable for the Institution. This motion was carried, following a vote at the next meeting of the managing committee.[83] Two weeks later, when the managing committee received an architect's report that Moira House would require £800 expenditure on repairs (a grossly inaccurate estimate) and, in his opinion, was 'extremely eligible' for the purposes of the Association, Paulus Singer gave notice of a motion to take Moira House, only to withdrew it a week later.[84] One can only wonder at what went on outside committee meetings. Some committee members viewed another possible building in Abbey Street.[85] Finally, on 9 December 1823, one of the founder members, Dr Orpen, was authorized to treat with Reid.[86] On 23 December, the managing committee resolved that 'Moira House is a fit and proper place for the Association' and agreed to Reid's proposal that the Mendicity Association should lease the premises at Usher's Island for a period of 900 years, with an option to surrender at the end of every two years at six months notice subject to the following conditions:

1. The name 'Moira House' was to be abolished;
2. A wall with solid gates was to be built between the house and the quay;
3. Mendicants would use the Island Street entrance; only the committee and visitors could use the front door and enter from Usher's Island;
4. If surrendered, the building was to be left in at least as good a condition as it was when the Institution took it over; any additional buildings erected should be left on site.[87]

What a Christmas present for the Association—a permanent home at last. Orpen, Oliver, Hort, Singer, and Lanigan were authorized to 'close forthwith for the House and the two gardens at the front and rere of Moira House' at an annual ground rent not exceeding £160 per annum.[88] The lease was signed on 30 December 1823, when the Association was given immediate possession with the first half year's rent due at the end of September 1824. A committee was immediately appointed to deal with the repairs to the roof of Moira House which needed urgent attention.[89] A sum of £400 was vested in 3 per cent government stock in the names of Dr Thomas H Orpen, Richard Cane and Robert Lanigan in trust for the Association

> for the purpose of indemnifying therefrom these gentlemen, their heirs, executors, administrators and assignees against any loss which may at any time be incurred by them on any or either of them from the surrender of the premises on Usher's Island at any time short of the period of two years for which the Society has bound itself to become responsible.[90]

To comply with the terms of the lease the premises were known from that time as Mendicity House.

CHAPTER FOUR
Clientele and Staff

IRELAND WAS A STRICTLY STRATIFIED society in the nineteenth century and stratification applied in the Mendicity Institution also. During the first year the mendicants were classified into distinct grades according to the type and quantity of work they were capable of and their wages and allowances were scaled accordingly.[1]

Class 1: Mendicants engaged in productive labour, sufficient for their support, received their wages in money and were paid the full value of their work. This class, which largely consisted of spinners, could purchase rations cheaply from the Institution kitchen.

Class 2: Mendicants training for productive labour received free rations during the training period and a fixed sum to enable them to pay for their lodging and other necessities. As their expertise grew and they became capable of earning money, the fixed sum was decreased by the amount of their earnings. When the six week (later extended to eight weeks) training period was over, all relief was stopped. Class 2 also included mendicants who worked in non-productive jobs or in jobs producing very little return. They were paid the full value of their work in money at a lower rate than Class 1 workers and received free rations until 1820. Soup carriers, cleaners, kitchen workers, label men, street-sweepers, oakum pickers, clothes menders, cobblers, cart women, needle workers, and net-makers all belonged to this class.

Class 3: Mothers with young children, and those who for other reasons such as weakness, lack of skill, or other incapacity except illness, were unable to do even half the amount of work required to support themselves, received free rations but were still expected to contribute to their own maintenance. They were encouraged to work as much as they could and were paid 'at as low a rate as can sustain life'.[2]

Class 4: The elderly and completely infirm received no wages, but were given food, clothing if necessary, and money for lodging until they could be sent to an appropriate asylum. In practice, mainly because of the lack of suitable accommodation elsewhere, the Institution continued to support great numbers of this class. The House of Industry was unable to cope with the large numbers who applied for admission. It occasionally had vacancies for male mendicants but seldom for females.[3] Some mendicants were reluctant to apply for admission to the House of Industry and were allowed to stay in the Mendicity Institution.[4] Consequently, the number of elderly and infirm mendicants in the Institution continued to increase, and the managing committee found it necessary to reduce their allowance and put any who were capable of very light work picking oakum, to uphold their principle that all who could must work to support themselves. Mendicants on the 'oakum list' were regularly examined by the doctors who often passed a number fit for spinning or other duties.[5]

Class 5: Children over six years of age capable of learning a useful trade were paid some wages in money (or it was given to their parents), and received their food. They were required to attend the school in the Institution.

Class 6: Children under six were fed in the Institution or an allowance in rations or money was given to their parents for them. The managing committee eventually provided a 'nursery room' for these children, so that their mothers could work in the Institution and contribute to their support.

Class 7: Sick and injured mendicants were sent to hospital, if necessary, or given medical aid organised by the Institution's subcommittee for health.[6] Once established, the Mendicity Institution's own dispensary catered for this class.

Far more women than men entered the Institution. Many were widowed or deserted, and brought their children with them. For several years the policy was that only those found begging in the street were eligible for admission to the Institution. However, street-begging was not the sole requirement for admission: applicants must have resided for at least six months within the circular road around the city; they must have no other means of support;

and if they had families, they were required to bring them to the Institution with them.

In March 1822, the managing committee decided to allow people who fulfilled these three criteria to enter the Institution, even though they might not have actually resorted to begging.[7] Despite opposition from some members of the managing committee, who made several unsuccessful attempts to have this decision reversed, mendicity was dropped as one of the requirements for admission from that time.[8] The minutes of the managing committee meeting of 15 July 1823, recording a proposal that people should not be admitted or readmitted to the Institution until they had been at least one week unemployed, reflect both the changing social profile of those seeking admission and the growing unemployment problem in Dublin.[9] As the provisional committee of the Hibernian Philanthropic Society noted at this time:

> In the city of Dublin, in a population exceeding two hundred and twenty thousand souls, we see a large portion of the youth rising up under our view, who have no means of gaining a livelihood save by thieving and prostitution. In every labouring and handicraft occupation there is a large surplus of hands, the decay of business having had a double operation, to drive the adult out of employment and to prevent the youth from being taken as apprentices.[10]

By 1826 unemployed factory workers were 'the most common and alarming group of beggars' in Dublin, and the Institution contained journeymen from almost every trade in the city.[11] A list of the previous occupations of over 700 people admitted in that year gives an interesting and vivid picture of changing lifestyles in early nineteenth-century Dublin and of the many industries under threat in the capital during the 1820s. (See Appendix C.) By this time the Institution's admission policy was exercised with a much greater degree of flexibility and discretion: the annual report for 1827 conceded that the Institution was supporting many who did not really qualify as clients.[12]

Because of the Association's policy of keeping families together, people were only admitted without their spouses in exceptional circumstances. One such occasion was when, on the recommendation of a country clergyman that she was unable to support herself and her children, Margaret Lackey was admitted with her children for two months while waiting for a passage to Australia where her husband was a convict in Botany Bay.[13] A blind eye was also turned to the rules when the demand for Irish labourers in England in the early 1820s led to many of their wives and children seeking and gaining admission to the Institution. Some were sent for later by their husbands, but many were deserted and remained on the Institution's books.[14]

The Foundling Hospital had been responsible for orphaned and deserted children since early in the eighteenth century.[15] In 1776, having found itself unable to accommodate the huge numbers requiring admission, it restricted entry to children under one year.[16] By the time the Association was established in 1818, it was difficult for orphans even of this age to find a home in the Foundling Hospital. In 1820, the House of Industry, which had taken over the care of orphaned and deserted children between one and eight years of age, ceased admitting them.[17] The Association believed that to bring up an orphan child was a very serious responsibility. As it did not consider itself capable of the task, a resolution was adopted initially to exclude orphaned children from the Institution. When no other institution would take responsibility for these children, the resolution was repealed and it was agreed to admit them only where '*exposure in the streets and starvation* would seem the *certain* result of an opposite procedure'.[18] The rota sub-committee, which was responsible for monitoring all applications to the Institution, admitted children provisionally until the next managing committee meeting when each case was investigated thoroughly.[19] There was more fraud found among these cases than in any other class of applications.[20] Some of the most well-behaved female mendicants in the Institution were paid a small wage to nurse and care for the orphans. Contrary to the policy of the Foundling Hospital 'to bring up all children in the Protestant religion, irrespective of the religion of their parents', the Mendicity Institution made every effort to determine the religion of each orphan's parents and to place the child with a woman of that religion.[21] On admission, the religion of each child was carefully entered against his or her name on the 'orphan list'. The minutes of 26 March 1822 record the case of Mary Ann Seares, otherwise Kidney. The managing committee insisted she should be brought up in the Protestant faith, as her mother, before her death, had brought the child to the Protestant church.[22] In one exceptional instance, with her clergyman's permission, a Protestant orphan, Mary Hyland, was allowed to go to work for a Catholic woman, a straw bonnet maker of Werburgh Street, who had originally recommended the child to the Institution.[23]

A particularly sad case was that of the Power children, Edward, aged ten, and his two brothers and two sisters: 'Father, John, a plasterer, killed more than a year back off a scaffold in Manchester—Mother, Anne died lately in the Lying in Hospital whence they were recommended by Doctor Collins'.[24] Edward, his two sisters, and one of his brothers were admitted to the Institution, and the other brother to the Foundling Hospital.

Children were sometimes placed on the orphan list when their parents were still living. Thomas Phillips, a turnkey at Newgate prison, had looked after John Hort, aged six, for a year following the transportation of the child's parents. When the turnkey could no longer care for him, John was admitted to the Institution.[25] When the Bevan children, John, aged eight, Michael, aged six, and Henry, aged four, were abandoned by their parents, they were also admitted as orphans.[26]

Orphans were often brought to the Institution by family members who could not look after them. Richard Ryan was brought by Jane Ryan, the legitimate widow of his father, as the boy's mother was also dead.[27] John and Robert Good, aged ten and five years of age respectively, whose parents were both dead, were admitted as orphans when brought in by their widowed aunt, Catherine. Robert died just over two years later. John eventually became apprenticed to a brazier in Cuffe Street. When that man's business failed, John went to work elsewhere for a time, but was finally readmitted to the orphan list in 1836 at the age of sixteen.[28] Ann Clarke, an eight year old Roman Catholic, whose father and mother were both dead, was brought to Institution by the matron of the Lock Hospital Laundry and placed on the orphan list.[29]

Children who had been in the Institution with their parents

were often admitted to the orphan list at a later date. May Langan was admitted in 1825 with her mother. Her father, a silk weaver, was then in England. When her mother died eleven years later and her father was still in England, the girl, then aged twelve, applied successfully to go on the orphan list.[30] William Warren, a widower, was admitted in May 1829 with his daughter Biddy, aged seven. Subsequently, he went into Cork Street Hospital where he died in July 1830. Although both were off the books at the time of his death, it was decided to readmit Biddy to the orphan list.[31] Children who left to work elsewhere occasionally applied for readmission. Eliza Nolan, aged twelve, was first admitted to the orphan list on 18 February 1834. She left to work with a bonnet maker in North King Street, who, after three months, did not need her any longer. The girl was then readmitted to the Institution.[32]

Some children were not kept in the Institution. When the following report was received from Mr Gibbons, the schoolmaster: 'Orphan Thomas Magee ran away from Rose Bond on Sunday morning with his two shirts on him, but returned on Sunday night when she secured one of the shirts from him; he went away on yesterday morning again and has not as yet returned'; Thomas was struck off the orphan list.[33] Anne Sweeting, originally admitted with her mother who left to work elsewhere, was readmitted by mistake. Children were not supposed to remain in the Institution without at least one of their parents, and although the child's grandmother was also in the Institution, Anne was struck off the books when the mistake was discovered.[34] Sarah Willock, aged four, was refused admission. On her mother's death, she had been abandoned by her father who went to England. A woman named Judith Nugent brought Sarah to the Institution and said on oath that her own daughter had gone to England with Willock either as a prostitute or had married him.[35] Another child not admitted was James Mangan, aged eleven. His parents were dead, but he had been living in the country with an aunt who brought him to the Institution.[36]

Other children remained for only a short time in the Institution. Mrs Walters, who ran a dress making shop in Wicklow Street, died leaving a widower, Patrick, who was an out of work servant, and five girls, the eldest of whom was twelve years old. Patrick Walters left his daughters with a cousin of their mother, who brought them to the Institution. They were admitted until their father could be found. The inspector employed by the Institution was ordered to search for him. A week later, Patrick Walters was found and brought to the police station where he was severely admonished. His children were then returned to him.[37] Patrick James, aged five, whose father was dead, and his mother reported to be working as a servant in Co Antrim, was admitted until his mother was found.[38] Jane Fitzpatrick was admitted as an orphan. It later transpired that her father was alive and kept a public house in Moore Street but did not want to look after her. He had not been married to her mother. Inspector Rogers was ordered to tell Fitzpatrick that the Institution would no longer support the child.[39] Mary Wise, aged ten, and her sister, Ellen, aged three, whose mother eloped with a man named Campbell after the death of their father, were admitted to the orphan list but were both returned to their mother two months later, when she called on the woman who was looking after them and demanded one of the children back.[40]

The Chief Secretary was asked to help in the case of a four-year-old boy who had been left on the door step of a police station and brought to the Institution when the police could not trace his parents. Neither the authorities in Jervis Street Hospital, who declared him to be an 'idiot', nor the House of Industry would take him. The Mendicity Institution provided him with food and arranged for someone to take care of him until a place in an appropriate asylum could be found for him.[41] There is no further mention in the minutes of the fate of this unfortunate child. On the recommendation of the Mendicity Institution, the Richmond Institution for the Blind agreed to admit a blind boy, Jeremiah Daly, and allowed him to take precedence over the queue of those waiting for admission.[42]

Unlike other establishments, the Institution did not provide accommodation for its clients, but preferred that they attended the Institution during the day and returned to their homes at night:

> their mode of procuring lodging is the same as that adopted by the lowest class of labourers in the city; one person renting a room at one to two shillings per week, and re-letting a portion of it to five or six, often many more, individuals, who pay three pence to four pence each. They generally sleep on straw—and frequently without any other covering than the clothes worn during the day. The houses thus let out are mostly in a ruinous and very filthy condition.[43]

Mendicants entered the Institution between 7 am and 9 am and remained there until 6 pm or until dusk in winter. New applicants could also be admitted between 1 pm and 2 pm when the gates were opened for this purpose. The different classes were assigned to different rooms in the Institution where they were supposed to work and remain during the day, except for meal times. The children had breakfast at 8 am and dinner at 2 pm; the adults ate at 9 am and 3 pm.[44] In summer, when the hot weather spoiled much of the food collected in the carts, and there were not sufficient bones or meat to make broth, the children were given stirabout and milk or bread and milk three times a week.[45] Mendicants who paid for their food were allocated a separate small dining hall. Four of the most competent women were appointed to serve the food and keep the halls clean. Following the refusal by some mendicants to eat the food on Ash Wednesday, Roman Catholic mendicants were dispensed from the obligation of fasting during Lent by the Archbishop of Dublin, Dr Troy.[46]

Many spinners left the Institution temporarily for the summer months and found employment weeding gardens around the city, returning to the Institution in the autumn.[47] A Christmas dinner was provided each year for the children; adult mendicants who attended on Christmas Day received free rations and an allowance of five pence.[48] In later years, Christmas dinner became a major occasion each year when over one thousand poor people from all parts of the city were entertained in the Institution. Good Friday was treated as a Sunday with religious services in the Institution and an allowance for all who attended.[49] Mendicants who needed assistance in legal matters, such as Eliza Turner 'who appears to be entitled to property to an amount of £400', could avail of the expertise of the barristers on the managing committee who willingly helped in these cases.[50]

The mendicants could complain about their treatment and they occasionally went beyond the managing committee with complaints. Each complaint was taken seriously and thoroughly investigated. In October 1819, a sub-committee was appointed to investigate a long list of complaints sent by the mendicants to the Lord Mayor. These included the recent reduction in their wages; the very poor quality of the food which they charged was only 'potato mash' and contained no meat; and having to pay for food, lodging and clothing. Some alleged they had been 'most cruelly beaten and treated unmercifully', and that many had been expelled from the Institution even though they were willing to work.[51]

The managing committee explained to the Lord Mayor that the mendicants' wages had been above the usual rate, and the reduction was necessary for fear of causing an injustice to the working class in general. Mendicants in the Institution also had the advantage of the opportunity to buy good food cheaply, and received free rations and an allowance of twopence on Sundays. The managing committee insisted that the food certainly did contain meat and almost all the mendicants bought it eagerly. Those who could earn very little received an extra allowance for lodging, and clothes were often given to children and to some adult mendicants as a reward for good behaviour. However, the managing committee conceded that about twenty mendicants had been summarily dismissed for insubordination or other improper conduct. As a result of this complaint, the managing committee decided all cases of bad conduct would be referred directly to them, and officers would no longer be entitled to expel mendicants who offended.[52]

The conduct and appearance of the mendicants were on-going sources of concern to the managing committee and on one occasion a sub-committee was appointed to look into ways 'for the more decent eating of the mendicants'.[53] As a consequence, the dining hall was enlarged to promote cleanliness and order, and tin bowls and scallop shells were provided and kept in a special pantry.[54] Another time, sixty pounds of soap were distributed among the mendicants because of the 'increasing growth of decency and cleanliness manifested in the persons of the mendicants'.[55] Some time later, the managing committee ordered that the 'laudable and desirable system' of giving out small pieces of soap to the most deserving mendicants should be resumed, since cleanliness had deteriorated since it had been stopped.[56] Material was bought at least twice a year to be made into clothes for the mendicants and old army jackets were also purchased. Occasionally, gifts of clothing from the public were distributed among the mendicants—the elderly and infirm, the longest inmates, the 'quiet ones', and those with young children receiving preference. Clothing was always given or lent as a reward for good conduct and not to anyone who might sell it.[57]

The managing committee paid particular attention to the appearance and manners of the children. The uniform for boys was a jacket, shirt and trousers, while girls wore a frock, petticoat, shift and bib. When the sub-committee for education reported that the boys' jackets and trousers were in a ragged state, the managing committee ordered the immediate purchase of corduroy and materials for trousers.[58] In April 1821, Mrs Dawson, one of the ladies interested in the Institution, presented enough clothing for seventy girls, but asked that they should not be allowed to take the clothing home but should wear it in the Institution 'to be decent and clean for the ladies who so kindly bestow their time for the benefit and instruction of those poor children'.[59] One of the chief benefits of clothing the children was the improvement it caused in their manners. The effect was so striking that sometimes new clothes were deliberately given to very badly behaved children to improve their behaviour. In the opinion of the managing committee, the new clothing also made the children 'indistinguishable from the better orders of the lower class' when they returned to society, some to find work, others to return to family or friends, which they had not wanted to do because of 'their raggedness and a sense of their degradation'.[60] The children were examined monthly to see if they still had all their new clothes, as their mothers often sold those garments least likely to be noticed. When this occurred, the loss was deducted from the mother's wages.[61]

After several years, the managing committee became aware that, whereas the boys' occupational training was minimal, their general education was far superior to that received by the girls who spent most of their time learning to straw-plait, make lace or sew. Girls spent only one and a half hours a day in the schoolroom at awkward hours: the lace makers very early in the morning before breakfast with understandably poor attendance especially in winter; the straw-plaiters at the end of a hard day's work when both they and the teacher were tired. Girls often left the Institution temporarily to go into service and forgot everything they had previously learned by the time they returned. The boys spent seven hours at their books each day, with the result that the older boys could read, write and had advanced as far as multiplication in their arithmetic, and the junior class could read and write, with even the simplest two or three in the class learning to read, write and spell, whereas the girls were not near this standard. To remedy this situation, it was decided that the girls should spend a longer period in the schoolroom at a more reasonable time of day, and that separate schools would be established for boys and girls with hours similar to those in outside schools when new premises were obtained for the Institution.[62]

Although a room was set aside in 1820 for children under school-going age and a woman was employed to supervise them, the premises at Copper Alley were too small and cramped for this to be carried out effectively and the project was soon relegated to the attic where the children ran wild, often unsupervised.[63] One of the priorities on moving to Usher's Island was to establish a proper infant school, the management committee having come to the conclusion that children were never too young to be trained, and that good behaviour, manners and simple rules learned at an early age give even such poor children a good start in life. A special fund raising drive was initiated for this purpose.[64]

Several years later, the managing committee described the beneficial results of infant education in the Institution.

1. Infant children were removed from physical evils and neglect to which they had been exposed;
2. Parents were relieved of caring for their children and could work for them instead;
3. There were also moral benefits:
   a. useful and important knowledge was impressed on the mind

> at a most susceptible age;
> b. children were removed from the view of vicious habits;
> c. they learned habits of cheerfulness, order, regularity and cleanliness;
> d. they could bring their new knowledge home to give good example to their parents;[65]
> e. they would go on to further education and become useful members of society, capable of working for their own support, and anxious to raise themselves above the class of pauperism.[66]

The managing committee were also eager to improve the minds of the adult mendicants. A lending library was established in the Institution in 1829 and the committee were amazed to find that, although the 'Irish poor have often been taunted, and stigmatised as some of the most ignorant and uncultivated among the nations, laying claim to the title of civilized', 600 out of 1,400 adult mendicants examined could read very well.[67] The managing committee thought it unlikely that a similar level of ability would be found among English mendicants. The books chosen for the library were partly of a religious character, recommended by clergymen of different persuasions, or else combined a moral precept with amusement. Another improvement was the provision of two hours education daily for young spinners who had not been educated previously. Only well-behaved girls were given this opportunity and received an allowance for the earnings they lost during the two hour period.[68]

The mendicants were also encouraged to better themselves and earn a little extra by taking posts of responsibility in the Institution. Bridget Pyke lost her job as superintendent of the spinners because she could not keep account of the flax yarn and other materials, being unable to write. The managing committee recommended that she should be replaced by a male mendicant at a wage of five shillings a week, without rations.[69] Mrs Pyke must have been highly regarded: a month later, she was appointed superintendent of a smaller department at one shilling and sixpence a week plus her rations.[70] A 'proper person', who was to receive one shilling and sixpence a week with rations, was sought for the very responsible position of door-keeper at the front door of the Institution, and a mendicant named Magee was allowed one penny a day to act as a messenger to the different sub-committees.[71] Another male mendicant was employed to keep idlers out of the spinning room.[72] Mary Lawless was paid five shillings as a 'douceur' for her trouble in sweeping the committee room. Having proved her worth looking after the children during the Annual General Meeting in the Rotunda, Anne Judge was appointed superintendent of the straw-plait school at five shillings a week.[73]

Many mendicants in the Institution attempted to get more than the rules entitled them to, but the managing committee worked equally hard to devise ways to counteract their efforts. When some elderly and infirm mendicants sold their provision tickets, it was decided to stop issuing tickets and have them carried into the dining hall for meals.[74] Some of the oyster shell pounders illegally claimed sick and infirm allowances of money and rations while they were earning wages.[75] When some people on the sick list sold their rations, as the food did not agree with them, the managing committee offered them a choice of four pence a week in lieu of rations.[76] Some home spinners were suspected of having other means of support, while working for the Association. As a result, home spinners were never allowed to work for the Association for more than a three-month period after December 1820, unless they could prove that they were unable to support themselves without the Association's help.[77] The overseer of the oat bruisers, Hamilton, was dismissed from his post and sent to pound stones for cheating the workers under his supervision.[78]

Although locks were purchased for all property belonging to the Institution, a certain amount of theft took place.[79] When articles of clothing were stolen from the storeroom, thirty shillings was offered as a reward for their return or ten shillings for information concerning their whereabouts.[80] A female mendicant named Brady was charged with stealing bones from the stores.[81] The superintendent was robbed of £1 5s 8d and a livery coat. The money was in small coin paid in by the mendicants for their rations; although the managing committee considered him careless in leaving money in his office, he was repaid the loss, but warned that it was not a precedent.[82] A reward of three guineas was offered for information when the books of the Institution were stolen. The books were returned and the clerk of the yard, the store-keeper, and a former mendicant each received a guinea.[83]

When charges were laid against the women who worked in the dining hall relating to the sale and distribution of food, every tub of food leaving the kitchen in future was weighed and padlocked and the weights recorded in a special book.[84] One of the women, Mary Eustace, who maintained her innocence, was dismissed from her position and put to pounding oyster shells. To make an example, her demotion was publicly announced. There were mitigating social circumstances in the case of another woman, Mary McGrath, who repented during an illness following the incident and confessed her crime to a clergyman. On returning to the Institution she endeavoured to make restitution. She was sent to spin for a short time, and was then apppointed overseer in the dining hall with a warning not to offend again.[85]

The label men employed to carry placards advertising the Institution around the city and the cart women who collected food scraps were fined if they did not ring their bells as they went about their work.[86] Adults were fined one penny and children one half-penny for non-attendance on Sundays.[87] When two women, dismissed from the woollen yarn department in Brunswick Street for bad work and negligence, were discovered working in the spinning room in Copper Alley, it was decided that mendicants dismissed from one department in this way should no longer be allowed to spin but would be put to a more laborious form of work.[88]

Having male and female mendicants working together in the Institution proved very disruptive. To improve discipline, it became necessary to separate the sexes, and several rooms in Copper Alley were cleared of spinning wheels, reels and oakum to provide this 'indispensable' separate accommodation in 1823.[89] Separate accommodation also had to be found for idle mendicants who distracted industrious workers from their tasks.[90]

Some younger clients also caused trouble. The minutes of 30 December 1823 record that two of the boys, Campbell and Kavanagh, sold part of the clothing lent to them on Christmas Eve. [91] Thomas Hennessey, aged eleven, was sent to pound stones for a fortnight for serious misconduct, as was Hugh Healy, not quite fourteen, for stealing a quantity of merit tickets from several of the other boys.[92] On another occasion, there was a complaint of 'improper and riotous conduct' against the usually well-behaved straw-plaiters.[93] A more serious affair occurred when the schoolmaster, Mr Lowry, reported Matthew Hughes, the son of the porter in Fleet Street, for breaking the school-room window and damaging the desks by scratching the words 'Mr Lowry tatler and lyar' on them with a nail. The boy's father called the teacher 'a parish-reared brat', challenged him to fight, and used other abusive language.[94] Two of Matthew's fellow school-mates gave evidence against the him and, when a sample of his writing was found to match that scratched on the desk, the case was proved and his guilt confirmed. Hughes senior complained that his son had been driven to such acts by Lowry's jealousy, and again called the schoolmaster insulting names. He was warned that the whole family would be dismissed if his son gave any more trouble. Two months later, the sub-committee for education reported young Hughes to the managing committee for 'maltreating four of the girls belonging to the straw-plait school', and recommended that the father should be removed from his post and 'some decent man' appointed to replace him as hall porter in Fleet Street.[95] However, the managing committee decided that Hughes could stay on condition his son was sent away and did not return.

The managing committee discovered that peer pressure was a more effective force among the girls in the Institution than any punishment they could administer. One girl who returned to begging 'was punished by her more independently-minded companions with the contempt which they considered due to one who had exposed herself to so unnecessary degradation'.[96]

Clients left the Institution for various reasons. The Institution found jobs for many of them; others left independently, confident of finding work for themselves now that they had some training. Some died. Some were asked to leave. Women whose husbands were not dependent on the Institution, and who had slipped through the admissions procedure, were dismissed when discovered. Those who later married men not supported by the Institution were required to leave.[97] The minutes of 3 September 1822 record the expulsion of 'several women of infamous character who never work and evidently support themselves by means unconnected with this Association.'[98] Those who refused to work although declared fit by the dispensary doctors were also dismissed.[99] Four women, who were sent to work for Mr Reilly in Blanchardstown Mills and returned to the Institution unsatisfied with their payment, were not readmitted to the Institution.[100] Mendicants absent for three days without reporting sick were presumed to have got work or relief elsewhere, and were struck off the books.[101] If they wished to return they were required to go through the entire admission procedure again. Children had to leave when their parents left, except in very exceptional circumstances.[102]

Table 3 shows the numbers of mendicants in the Institution at the end of each year and the average daily attendance during each year for the period 1818 to 1826. The initial impact of the Association's efforts is reflected in the decrease from the high figure of 2,930 in 1818 to 689 in 1822. The subsequent upward swing was due to a number of factors. The increasing problem of unemployment in Dublin; the many labourers who went to work in

Table 3: Number of Clients in the Institution at the End of Each Year and the Average Daily Attendance 1818–26

Year	Adults					
	Males	Females	Total	Children	Total	Daily Average
1818			2,248	682	2,930	2,624
1819	62	635	697	353	1,050	1,584
1820			870	91	961	1,050
1821					742	836
1822					689	691
1823	62	678	740	188	928	753
1824	125	1,031	1,156	442	1,598	1,184
1825	78	904	982	224	1,206	1,335
1826	150	1,068	1,218	261	1,479	1,288

Note: Information is not available in all categories for all years.
Source: Annual Reports of the Association for the Suppression of Mendicity in Dublin, 1818–6

England, leaving wives and families behind; the great increase during this time in the price of food; the establishment in other towns of Mendicity Associations which returned Dublin beggars to the city; the many English widows of Irishmen returned penniless to Ireland were all contributory reasons for the continuing increase to more than twice the 1822 figure over the next four years.[103] Controlling mendicity was a very difficult, if not impossible task: the annual report for 1826 noted that 'the state of street begging nearly compares to before the Institution opened'.[104]

The staff of the Institution was headed by the superintendent and included the assistant secretary, the sub-treasurer, the storekeeper, two clerks, two street inspectors, four collectors, a cook, a wheel-wright, a schoolmaster, an apothecary, the lace and straw-plait mistresses. In 1820 the managing committee had difficulty in finding a responsible person for the post of superintendent. When a complaint was made about superintendent Wilson, a sub-committee was appointed to investigate the matter. There is no evidence as to what the investigation revealed, but the minutes of the managing committee meeting of 14 December 1819 tersely record 'the post of superintendent is vacant'.[105] James Elliot, a member of the managing committee, offered to supervise the institution gratuitously until a suitable man could be found. In February 1820, Elliot resigned from the managing committee and was appointed to the post of superintendent at an annual salary of £80.[106] He remained in the position for ten years, giving loyal and devoted service to the Institution. A good idea of the daily working procedure in the Institution can be found in the list of general duties laid down for him that year:

1. To attend from the first opening of the gates at 6 am until the mendicants were dismissed in the evening at 6 pm;
2. To visit the different parts of the establishment in Hawkins Street during the day, and see the respective officers did their duty; to take care that the food prepared for the paupers was of wholesome quality;
3. Under the control of the honorary secretary, and subject to the regulations of the general committee, to order or procure such articles as might be needed for the use of the establishment and to take care that the orders given by the secretary and the different committees were carried into effect;

4. To issue working materials to the usual departments, and to receive the several returns of labour made to the store; to give out provision tickets to the clerk of the spinning room and others, and to attend at the dining hall to receive them again from the paupers as they came to dinner;
5. No mendicant was allowed to go out of the gates before 6 pm without a pass from the superintendent.[107]

Later accounts illlustrate the breadth of the superintendent's responsibilities. He sent any yarn that was not privately sold to the Linen Hall to be sold by the factors of the Association and was the officer responsible for all other sales and purchases. His most important task was to buy and sell to the greatest possible advantage. The clerks made their returns to him. He also reported to the managing committee on the work of the subordinate officers of the Institution during the year.[108]

The store-keeper and inspector of the yard was in charge of the premises and was the only person allowed to remain there at night. He opened the gates at 6 am and weighed out provisions for breakfast. He issued junk to the oakum pickers and weighed in the oakum to the store in the evening. He saw all the mendicants off the premises in the evening and locked the gates and doors.[109]

The number of blatant frauds persisting among the mendicants, women whose husbands had pensions, and those with other means of support, forced the managing committee in 1821 to replace the sub-committee of investigation, whose members could not give the time required for this work, with an investigation inspector. He was paid fifteen shillings a week, a rate the managing committee considered sufficiently high to ensure his respectability, as it placed him above the temptation to fraud or neglect of his duties. He attended every morning at the House of Industry where twenty four cells had been allocated for sturdy beggars in 1820. He identified people arrested for begging during the night who were on the books of the Institution. He received directions from the honorary secretary about admissions or other matters. He also attended some of the principal places of worship on Sundays, again to identify beggars who were receiving help from the Institution.[110]

When the Association began, many sturdy beggars left the city thinking the Association had extensive funds and powers. When they discovered that neither the Association nor the police had effective powers against them, they returned, 'having too little to fear from the Police, and everything to hope from the mistaken benevolence of the Dublin people'.[111] Their loud and bitter complaints that the Institution 'starved, overcrowded and ill-treated the poor' were believed by many of the public who resumed the habit of giving alms in the streets and at the doors of houses.[112] Until October 1819, beggars were invited or urged to go to the Institution. Placards advertising the facility were carried around the streets by mendicants from the Institution and notices were placed in hotels, bars and shops encouraging the public, if approached by beggars, to direct them to the Institution. Towards the end of the second year the managing committee decided to employ 'peace officers', or constables, to take up everyone they found begging on the streets and bring them to the Institution. At first, the constables each received one guinea weekly for this work; later, as an incentive because of the increasing number of beggars on the streets for which the Association was held responsible even by some of its own members, the constables received two pence for every beggar they brought in who was admitted to the Institution. The managing committee also paid twenty watchmen one shilling each per day to help the constables by pointing out beggars. All were directed to focus their attention around the churches on Sundays and around the market area as these places were 'greatly infested with beggars'.[113]

The expected influx of beggars during the imminent visit to Dublin of King George IV in August 1821 caused the managing committee to re-examine this arrangement. Following consultation with the police, it was decided that the constables presently employed by the Institution were inefficient and that they would be replaced during the royal visit by six more suitable men, to be selected by the police and paid by the Association. These constables were instructed to take up beggars, but to try to frighten the very old and infirm from the streets.[114] A proposal that the mendicants in the Institution should be allowed to view the royal procession from 'a quiet position between the Park and the City', under the supervision of officers of the Institution and the constables, was rejected by a majority of four of the managing committee.[115] The satisfactory outcome of these arrangements was reflected in a letter received following the King's visit:

> Dublin, August 25th 1821
>
> Gentlemen,
> When I, some years ago, contributed to the establishment of your society, I did not venture to hope that it would be so successful as I now find it. The City of Dublin is now as free of Mendicity as any other capital city I have visited—perhaps I might say that it is the *freest* from that unhappy practice. In acknowledgement of the good you have done and in the expectation of a continuance of your charitable and enlightened exertions I beg leave to offer you the enclosed draft.
> I have the honour to be, Gentlemen,
> Your obedient servant,
> J W Croker[116]

The Association also received a generous donation of £200 from the King. The supernumerary constables were then discharged.

At the end of the year the managing committee decided that any further connection with the appointment, superintendence or payment of constables would be inadvisable for the Association as it had led to 'abuse, loss and censure'.[117] A deputation from the Association explained the reasons for this decision to the Chief Secretary and asked his help with the problem of arresting beggars. The Chief Secretary instructed the police to arrest beggars in future and directed the governor of the House of Industry to increase to forty the number of cells provided for beggars in the House of Industry, sixteen extra cells at a cost of £400 to the Association.[118] Despite the appointment of patrols from each police station, the number of beggars on the streets continued to increase and there were many complaints about the inefficiency of the Association.[119] The police magistrates then placed eight constables 'in daily perambulation of the city' and two to each chapel on Sundays, all under the guidance of an officer of the Association who would point out the most obstinate and offensive sturdy beggars.[120] Two inspectors were appointed by the Association for this purpose on a month's trial.[121] They were required to give the following notice to any persons they found begging for the first time:

Friendly Notice to All Beggars

> If you are found Begging in the Street after this notice, you will be taken up and punished according to Law, therefore, if you really have no other means of subsistence, go to Copper Alley, where, in the Mendicity Asylum, you will get Work, Warm Food, and Shelter, if you are unable to work, you will be supported, and where, if you have Children, they will be Fed, Clothed and Educated. Then, why disgrace yourselves, or cruelly expose your children, to misery and ruin, by continuing to Beg.[122]

These inspectors also supervised the label men who carried boards on the streets publicising the Institution's work.[123]

The apothecary attended between 11 am and 4 pm daily at the Institution and visited the extern sick in their homes at other hours. If he visited a fever patient, he was required to report the case to the managing committee and to make sure the patient was removed to hospital. Each morning he visited all the departments in the Institution and examined mendicants who complained of illness. If he thought it necessary, he sent them to the dispensary to be seen by the doctor. He also attended on Sundays from 10 am to 12 noon.[124]

The clients were not alone in breaking the rules of the Institution, and problems with the staff were also dealt with firmly by the managing committee. Clerks not on duty by 10 am were fined one shilling each and clerks who were late with their returns for the weekly abstract were each fined five shillings.[125] One of the clerks, William Murphy, who admitted stealing £36 2s 10d, was allowed to repay £9 2s quarterly. His brother-in-law paid in £36 to the Institution as security for him, which he would recover if Murphy kept up the payments. If he failed to do so, he would be arrested and charged.[126] The cook was fined five shillings for every unlocked tub of food found leaving the kitchen.[127] Mrs Roche, the lace mistress faced three charges:

1. Leaving the children locked up without supervision and with candles lighting;
2. Allowing an orphan under her care to sleep in the Institution

3. Absenting herself from the Institution on Sunday. [128]

The managing committee were so impressed by her explanation that she was helping some of her ex-pupils to further their careers outside the Institution by teaching them new patterns at night in her own time and at her own expense as she had paid for candles herself, that they accepted her plea that the child in her care was always fed, washed and well cared for, and had only been sent to sleep in the Institution as a 'well-deserved punishment'.[129] Her absence on Sundays was also overlooked. Before long, fresh complaints from the lace-makers about her irregular attendance at breakfast time and during classes, resulted in Roche's dismissal.[130] Her replacement, Mary Dunn, was also reprimanded for bad attendance and 'other misconduct'.[131] Dunn's behaviour could have been related to a reduction in her wages as a result of a fall in the number of girls in the lace school. She was allowed to stay on for a month until a satisfactory replacement was found.[132] Eliza Kenny obviously proved satisfactory. After a year, she was placed in charge of the new premises at 13 Fleet Street. She was also chosen to care for a female orphan, and was given the front garret room in Fleet Street for this purpose.[133]

When Corcoran, the wheel-wright, was reported for neglecting his duty by not attending to all the wheels needing repair, a special committee was appointed and concluded that the reason for his unsatisfactory work lay in the manner in which he was paid. He was required to provide the materials needed for his work from his wages. The managing committee agreed with the recommendation that Corcoran's wages of fifteen shillings per week should be reduced to twelve shillings, and the Institution should pay for the necessary materials, provided that he worked full-time in his position. However, as his work had shown no improvement a month later, Corcoran was dismissed and the superintendent was asked to look for a replacement for him.[134] When the superintendent reported Mr Lowry, the schoolmaster, for 'improper and disrespectful behaviour', the managing committee decided a severe reprimand would suffice, as Lowry apologised and promised he would not repeat the offence.[135] On a later occasion, another schoolmaster was dismissed when he admitted selling two shirts belonging to the Institution. An entire school suit, six shirts, six jackets and five trousers were also missing but Gibbons stated that he had issued these to the children as usual but had not recorded them as required. Following this incident the managing committee decided that any schoolmaster appointed should give security 'for the faithful discharge of their duty'.[136]

Inspector Ferns was suspended because he was absent from duty, but reinstated when he explained that his absence was due to illness. However, he was not paid for the time he was absent because he had not reported his illness. Shortly afterwards, the police committee of the Institution, who liaised with the police about the taking up of beggars, recommended that Ferns should be dismissed from the time of his suspension because of his bad conduct while on duty and because he had refused to attend a meeting with them to explain his behaviour.[137]

A charge of cruelty and illegal conduct in arresting a street beggar, brought against another inspector, was the cause of some bad publicity for the Institution. A pamphlet was published accusing inspector Molloy of 'conduct calculated to fix a stain on the annals of any country'.[138] As far as the Institution was concerned, Molloy's error lay in identifying a notorious beggar to the police constables, although the woman was not actually begging at the time. She had used abusive language to him and made scurrilous allusions to his job. He was reprimanded and both inspectors were reminded that, as representatives of the Institution, they were required to be discreet and cautious, and must be prepared to put up with abuse and threats when on duty. They were instructed to take care only to have beggars arrested while in the act of begging.[139]

Another source of trouble for one of the staff was a live pig donated to the Institution by the Lord Mayor. The pig arrived late in the day and was confined in the pantry during the night. Following its release into the yard next morning, it was stolen. The thief's identity was unknown but the cook was reprimanded and fined five shillings for letting the pig into the yard.[140]

Four collectors called to households in the city on behalf of the Association. When they lodged the money collected in the bank, each was paid a percentage of the amount he had collected.

Archibald McDonald was reprimanded when he deducted the amount due to him before lodging his collection in the bank. This would mean the accounts were inaccurate and, if continued, the practice could lead to abuse.[141] Collectors were required to be very responsible people. A special committee was appointed to investigate charges against another collector, John Hughes; finding the charges partly proved, they recommended his removal from 'so important and responsible an office as that of Collector'.[142] On examination of his case some time later, the committee found that although he had not been dishonest, his reputation still did not make him fit to be employed as a collector.[143] In January 1823 all four collectors were warned to be more attentive to their work as householders had complained that they had not been approached for their subscriptions. The collectors were threatened with dismissal if more complaints of this nature were received. From that time on, the collectors were required each Monday to make a return of the householders they had approached during the previous week.[144]

One of the collectors was brought to court to explain why thirty copies of the annual report for 1829 that were supposed to be in his charge had been sold by Mary Connor as waste paper. Connor said that Miss Forrestal, a dressmaker in Bishop's Street, had employed her to sell them. Thirty more copies were found in Forrestal's possession, who said she had been given them as a present from the wife of an officer of the Institution named Fox. Michael Fox swore before a justice of the peace that he had no knowledge of his wife's activities. Mrs Fox had done this on two previous occasions. Fox was proved innocent, but cautioned to be more careful with the property of the Institution entrusted to his care. Mr Sharpe, a chandler, who had reported Mary Connor to the police, kept one of the reports for himself, complaining that he had not received a copy that year.[145]

The managing committee seriously investigated the references of all applicants for positions, even if they were already employed in the Institution. When an employee called Wade applied for the position of clerk in the central department, a query was raised about his drinking habits. The superintendent testified unequivocally to Wade's 'sobriety, regularity and diligence', and Timothy

Keeffe, foreman to Mr Green, the Castle Street publican, stated that 'Mr Wade was not in the habit of drinking in his employer's house, nor in going security for any person who did, nor running any score for more than one shilling at a time, and that but once, and when his business for the day was over'.[146] The managing committee were satisfied and Wade was appointed to the position.

Staff members were occasionally given bonuses for satisfactory work, but gratuities were never to be taken as a precedent. The superintendent was given £30 'in consideration of his very zealous and efficient exertions' during the move from Hawkins Street to Copper Alley.[147] Mr Collins, the sub-treasurer who lodged the daily receipts in the bank, received a gratuity of £10 for 'the faithful discharge of his duty' and his very accurate work which 'balanced to a fraction'.[148] The schoolmaster's salary of fifteen shillings per week was raised to £1 for being present before the boys 'begin to collect until they have dispersed'.[149] Adam Oliver was employed in May 1820 at eight shillings per week to teach the boys how to make toys. He received one guinea as a bonus in January 1822 as toy-making had become quite a profitable occupation. However, he was discharged two months later with a parting bonus of five shillings as he was no longer needed.[150] Sick officers were often paid a small sum to help during illness, but again no precedents were set and each case was judged on its merits.[151]

As was common practice in charitable institutions throughout the nineteenth century, the managing committee required letters of guarantee as security from the superintendent (£100) and the other officers of the Institution: the assistant treasurer (£100), the assistant secretary (£30), the three collectors (£100 each), the store-keeper (£200), the clerks (£30 for one and £20 for another), and the yard-keeper (£15).[152] Jobs in the Institution were highly valued and changes in personnel were rare.

CHAPTER FIVE

Financial Problems for the Institution 1824–1838

THE PLEASURE AND RELIEF AT obtaining the new premises for the Mendicity Institution at the end of 1823 were diminished by the deteriorating financial situation which delayed the 'final establishment of the Institution upon a permanent basis' at Usher's Island for almost two years.[1] 'The ruinous state of the old building and the very marshy condition of the ground' caused problems for the new tenants.[2] Their architect, Edward Parke, advised that the top storey of the old building should be removed entirely and a wing added to make it secure and habitable.[3]

Forming the front part of a square and the front of the Institution, this building would house the spinners, the schools, offices, a Committee room, and the dispensary in the upper part. The lower part would be occupied by applicants for admission, the laundry, and the stores. One side of the square would be formed by a large building where the stone pounders would work on the ground floor and the 130 foot long upper room would be allocated to the oakum pickers. The dining hall, where 500 could dine at one sitting, would be opposite this building; and the kitchen would complete the square. In the upper yard on the other side of Island Street, a long low building would be adapted for the infirm elderly and women with infants. This was the first part of the project to be undertaken. However, the Institution was unable to meet the expense of the extensive renovations even 'in the very plainest manner' as the building fund established in 1821 was not sufficient for the purpose.[4] A substantial legacy was received from Surgeon Leake, but only the annual interest on the bequest was available to the Association.[5] Eventually, the major repair and building work commenced late in 1824 when a generous legacy due from the estate of Rev Dr Barrett was used as collateral for a bank loan.[6]

The Institution's funds came from a number of sources: donations from householders, from visitors to Dublin, from servants, and from groups of factory workers. Collection boxes were placed on bridges, in taverns, hotels, lodging houses, and at most church doors when the clergy agreed. Charity sermons and occasional balls and concerts all raised money for the Institution. The courts sent money received from fines as did some householders who punished servants by withholding part of their wages. Sums found and unclaimed were often forwarded to the Institution. As its work became more appreciated, legacies large and small formed a considerable part of its income. Eventually, the managing committee decided to invest every donation of £10 and over for the future benefit of the Institution.[7] Table 4 shows the substantial sums required to maintain the Institution each year.

Following the first two difficult years, a reasonably comfortable position was reached during 1820–22, when prudent management allowed the managing committee to invest some of the Association's funds in government stocks.[8] Subscriptions fell in 1823 as some of the Dublin public began to take the Association's work for granted. Many shopkeepers, who had once paid beggars to stay away from their premises, now refused to support the

Table 4: Annual Income and Expenditure of the Institution 1818–27

Year	Income	Expenditure
	£ s d	£ s d
1818	9,151 0 9	9,594 18 9
1819	10,477 7 10	9,088 11 1
1820	5,722 6 10	4,380 1 8
1821	5,167 5 5	3,785 12 5
1822	4,320 14 8	3,524 17 9
1823	3,544 14 10	4,540 18 6
1824	5,278 15 7	6,302 11 10
1825	6,055 6 1	6,848 5 11
1826	6,249 3 6	5,852 13 0
1827	7,764 18 3	6,923 12 5

Source: 10th *Annual Report*, App 7, pp 76–7

Institution. Only about 600 of the 5,600 businesses in the city contributed to the Association, despite the fact that their tax burden had been lightened with the recent repeal of the window and hearth taxes.[9] The increase in the number of beggars in the streets, discussed in Chapter Four, encouraged alms-giving which diverted funds away from the Association. A disappointing loss occurred in 1824 when the Association joined with Cork Street Fever Hospital to bring an action for the recovery of part of a legacy from James Flood, to which both parties had been informed they were entitled. Their claim was lost and, despite the efforts of the advocates, the judge refused the charities their costs from the funds of the will. The Association's share of the costs amounted to £363 6s 8d.[10]

The managing committee complained that the Association's most loyal supporters were those who benefited least from its work—the wealthy who spent only part of the year in the city and the poor 'who have experienced least annoyance from the nuisance'.[11] In 1823 it was estimated that one penny each week from one-fifth of the citizens of Dublin would defray the annual costs of the Institution.[12] An account of donations received was published in the newspapers each week with a notice of the time that beggars could apply to the Institution each day. From 1821 onwards, the names of all the year's subscribers were published in an appendix to the Association's annual report. The managing committee were divided about how the donors' names should be listed. Some wanted them listed according to the streets where the donors lived, in the belief that omissions from the list would be more noticeable that way. Eventually, it was decided to publish the names alphabetically.[13]

While the Institution 'struggled onwards to maturity and vigor' [sic] during the 1820s, income often fell short of expenditure.[14] For most of the next two decades, successive managing committees operated under the threat of ruin and the imminent failure of the Institution. It would have been forced to close in 1824 without the help of its most loyal supporters, who continued to dig deep in their pockets whenever the funds reached a critical point.[15] A huge rise in the price of potatoes, from two guineas per ton in 1823 to five guineas in the early part of 1824, drove many of the poor to seek help from the Institution for the first time. This influx heavily affected the Institution's expenditure as the consumption of potatoes by the mendicants during the first six months of the year exceeded the entire amount used during 1823. The number of meals issued from the kitchen in 1823 more than doubled to 705,447 in 1824, of which only 127,455 were sold, the balance being given free to the mendicants.[16] By 1824 none of the occupations carried on in the Institution made any profit, although their role in instilling orderly, steady habits in the mendicants was considered worthwhile and better than handing out money for nothing.[17]

Adverse publicity in 1824 about the cost of repairs to the new premises at Usher's Island caused the managing committee to ask the newspapers to print the following paragraph:

> We are requested to contradict, in the most unqualified manner, a report which has, we understand, got abroad of a most injurious tendency to that valuable institution, the Mendicity Association. As to the fund from which the expenses on Usher's Island are to be drawn—not one sixpence has been, or will be, drawn for that purpose from the general fund. The whole will be defrayed from subscriptions raised already for that special object and from a grant made by the trustees of the late Dr Barrett which can only be applied to the purposes of the proposed buildings.[18]

Another cause for concern in 1824 was the lack of support for the provision carts. Frequent donations of bread, meat, vegetables and fuel came to the Institution through the Lord Mayor, but the provision carts were the most important regular source of food for the mendicants, as the quality of the stew they received daily depended on the bones and meat collected by the cart women.[19] Although the Association's income in 1824 was higher than in the previous year due to the extra donations from generous friends, the expenses were so high that the managing committee were compelled to use the entire bank reserve of £2,100 saved by previous committees, and still had to borrow from the bank to survive the last month of the year.[20] Various measures were taken to deal with this situation. The paid collectors were ordered to make lists of householders who were not subscribing; then volunteers, known as 'gentlemen collectors' and usually neighbours of the non-subscriber, solicited help for the Institution.[21] This was only moderately successful. Another tactic was to change the date of the next Annual General Meeting from January to May 1825 in the hope of attracting a larger attendance at that time of year.[22] This arrangement continued for two years when the date of the meeting reverted to earlier in the year. The decision to record the names of subscribers alphabetically was reversed and the names of streets where there were no contributors during 1824 (Little Britain Street, Little Mary Street, Little Strand Street, Blackhall Parade, Walker's Row, Waller's Row, Water Row, Beef Row, and Royal Row) were highlighted in the annual report that year.[23] The practice of recording subscriptions by streets continued until 1841, by which time the poor law was in operation and all householders were liable for poor rates. The Institution had been established and survived during times of heavy taxation with trade 'at its lowest ebb'. In 1824, 'in the hour of returning greatness', with less taxation and an improvement in trade, the managing committee considered that the outlook for the Institution should be brighter.[24] Anxiety about the future was evident in the committee's final plea of the year for funds when the probable closure of the Institution was mentioned: 'although they have not, up to the present day, been compelled to close the doors of the Institution, their funds are actually in the lowest state of exhaustion short of that necessity'.[25]

Distress throughout the city due to a huge rise in unemployment caused a further increase in the number of applicants for admission to the Institution in 1825.[26] Many manufacturing workers in Dublin were seriously affected by the removal of the protective duty in the silk industry, the erection of extensive silk mills in England, and the general adoption of improved and expensive machinery. Factories that had given employment to 'multitudes' in Dublin now laid off workers or closed down altogether. Many women and children had been employed in these factories. Some emigrated to England to find work, but many remained in the city deprived of their usual means of employment.[27] A Manufacturers' Relief Committee, set up to help these unemployed members of the working classes, aroused great sympathy but again diverted funds from the Institution.[28] The managing committee warned the public in 1825 that the Institution would be in serious trouble if subscriptions did not improve: 'in a Christian country the Poor cannot be permitted to starve'. The failure of the voluntary efforts of the Association would almost certainly be followed by a compulsory poor rate.[29] Turning their attention to the internal affairs of the Institution, the managing committee noticed that many skilled workers were encouraged by the high wages they could earn in the Institution to remain on the books and not look for work elsewhere.[30] The managing committee acted quickly: they stopped charging the workers for their rations and gave free food to all mendicants. When the workers no longer had to pay for food, the managing committee felt justified in cutting their wages considerably. As a result several of the best spinners and almost all the male stone-breakers left to find more remunerative work elsewhere.[31]

The managing committee had to investigate an allegation made by the General Board of Health that the Institution was responsible for an increase in fever in the Fishamble Street area. The Board condemned most of the rooms and tenements in Copper Alley, Fishamble Street and Court, Pembroke Court, Barrow Court, and Michael's Lane as being 'exceedingly crowded, filthy beyond description and badly ventilated', adding 'in Michael's Lane, Barrow Court and Copper Alley, fever at all times prevails more or less'.[32] The Institution's dispensary sub-committee refuted the allegation, pointing out that there were fewer cases of fever in the Institution that year although the number of mendicants was almost double that of the previous year. They argued that no mendicants from the Institution lodged in two of the houses mentioned by the Board, and there was only one mendicant in hospital from the other houses mentioned. They also reminded the Board that the Institution accommodated mendicants by day and could not control nor interfere with them in their own homes. The sub-committee added that the statement from the Board of Health was not borne out by the facts and complained that the tenor of the report could reflect very seriously on the Institution.[33]

Despite the grave financial situation, an infant school was opened in the Institution following the move to Usher's Island late in 1825. Recent research by Samuel Wilderspin, 'Master of the London Central Infant School and Travelling Teacher for the Infant School Society', had confirmed the managing committee's opinion that even very young children needed more than supervision and could benefit from basic education.[34] The managing committee were very satisfied with this initiative as the Institution now provided 'paternal and fostering care over the destitute mendicant in every stage of life'.[35]

The Institution had approximately £21 in the bank at the beginning of 1826, an especially difficult year in the city.[36] Confined at first to some of the manufacturing classes, fever soon spread throughout 'the entire mass of the poor'.[37] The managing committee claimed that the Institution helped to check the spread of fever by keeping 'vehicles of contagion' off the streets, giving the poor the chance of regular work, food and also

> 'many comforts of humble life, the want of which, if not the primary source of fever amongst them, must certainly render their constitution more susceptible of its attack, and subdue their powers of resistance to its awful visitation'.[38]

Financial assistance from the Mansion House Fever Committee enabled the Institution to help many of their sick mendicants, who otherwise would have died 'from the combined pressure of disease and destitution'.[39] There were so many other demands on the public in 1826 that subscriptions to the Institution continued to be low just when they were especially needed. Although church wardens in every parish co-operated very cordially when asked to help with the collection of subscriptions and other 'active and respectable individuals' also helped in this 'truly laborious and unpleasant duty' on the Institution's behalf, 'every week there was a likelihood of failure'.[40] Another consequence of the fever epidemic was the withdrawal of sixteen of the forty cells reserved for beggars in the House of Industry. These cells were reallocated to lunatics whose accommodation in a house beside the Hardwicke Fever Hospital was required for fever patients.[41]

In 1827 there began the most stressful period for the Institution since the first months of its existence in 1818. Fever continued to affect the poor and the price of potatoes rose sharply. The

Manufacturers' Relief Committee ceased operation and many unemployed workers turned to the Institution for help, increasing the numbers from 1,479 in December 1826 to 2,156 in May 1827. At a meeting in the Mansion House on 7 May 1827 called to discuss the best means of relieving the distress of the manufacturing poor, it was reported that 736 of this class were now supported by the Mendicity Institution. The meeting decided that, if the Institution was properly funded, it could deal adequately with the distress of the Dublin poor. However, as only 1,594 houses out of 11,419 solvent houses in the city were contributing to the Institution at the time, a special committee was appointed to raise funds. Church wardens were asked to encourage parishioners to contribute to this new fund, and owners of factories and shops were urged to start collections among their staff "in aid of their suffering brethren in the Mendicity Institution".[42] The outcome of this meeting enabled the Institution to survive during the summer of 1827, but by the end of September the funds were almost exhausted once more. A parade of mendicants was suggested, but the managing committee were reluctant to take this step as long as they had enough money to keep the Institution open for one week. Instead, they published an address to the large number of citizens who benefited from the Institution without subscribing to it, warning them that the only way of averting a poor law was to show the government that it was possible to support the poor by voluntary contributions.[43] This powerful address warned of the imminent closure of the Institution and described the consequences in vivid language:

> A torrent of the most loathsome, squalid, and often pestilential, outcasts, will soon again choke up your streets as heretofore—accumulated filth will again engender typhus fever, whose ravages will again extend through every class of inhabitants—strangers, disgusted and terrified, will hurry through your city; and opulent visitors will cease to give life and energy to your manufactures, by taking up their residence there...your ill-advised niggardliness will assuredly be the means, if persevered in, of bringing down upon Dublin the weight and the disgrace of a compulsory Poor's Rate.[44]

The press, 'ever active and zealous in diffusing whatever may tend to promote the interests of humanity, or of society at large', publicised the Institution's dilemma widely, resulting in many new subscribers, some generous donations and offers of help.[45] The first profit for some years to come from an occupation carried on in the Institution was made when four men bruising oats earned £26 15s after payment of their wages.[46]

The free rations and lower wages system that had been introduced two years earlier in 1825 to prevent stone-breakers and spinners remaining in the Institution when they could get work elsewhere, was now abandoned for the stone-breakers in order to target many of the idle factory workers and force them either to work or leave the Institution. It became necessary to raise wages that had been reduced under the free ration scheme.[47] Although the Institution suffered an initial financial loss from this manoeuvre, the managing committee thought it worthwhile to get rid of the idlers, who 'turned out for higher wages' and refused to work, throwing the whole Institution into 'a state of inconceivable confusion'.[48] Order was restored when the ringleaders were expelled and arrested by the police. Many others departed voluntarily, leaving only 25 of the original 131 in that department. This was the Institution's first encounter with industrial action. The spinners continued to receive free rations as the women worked well and did not abuse the system.[49]

The Mendicity Institution was now ten years in operation. During that time, a daily average of 1318 mendicants had been supported at a total cost of £56,660 5s 9d, an average annual cost of £4 6s for each mendicant or just under three pence per day. Taking into account the buildings at Usher's Island, the expenditure was £62,596 8s 4d for the 10 years: £4 15s for each mendicant per annum or just over three pence per day, and the Institution had fine extensive buildings on hand 'available for public service'.[50] During this period, 5,328 mendicants were returned to their homes by the Institution at an average cost of one shilling and seven pence each.

During 1828, the effects of the fever epidemics of the two previous years continued to disrupt the lives of the poor and impinge on the Institution. The death of some heads of family and the long convalescence of others affected the poor very badly. In addition, it took time for many of the manufacturing poor who had gone to search for work in England to send for their families. The managing committee reported:

> In the mean time the ordinary means of support are cut off, the prolonged absence of the father or the husband exhausts even that kindness to the destitute which is an honourable and distinguishing characteristic of the Poor of this Country; and the circle of dependents with which even the humblest is surrounded is now thrown upon public sympathy for support, and cold and hunger leave no alternative but street begging or an appeal to your Institution.[51]

Many usual subscribers reduced their subscriptions in 1828, considering it unfair that the burden of supporting the Institution should fall on a few, and hoping that their action would encourage reluctant subscribers. This ploy was unsuccessful: by September subscriptions were £1,500 less than at the same time the previous year and the Institution was once more on the verge of failure.[52] When it learned that the Institution might close, the public were greatly alarmed at the thought of 1,600 of the poorest people in the city roaming the streets. The Lord Mayor held a public meeting on 16 September at Morrison's Rooms where it was resolved, in order to support the Mendicity Institution and to avert the introduction of Poor Rates:

> 1. That the managing committee should seriously consider parading the mendicants through the streets;
> 2. That parish meetings should be held to fix a certain rate of subscription to the Institution for each householder, related to the rent of his house;
> 3. If these measures were not successful, that a general meeting of all the citizens of Dublin would be convened in November, to consider petitioning the Government to authorize a compulsory assessment for the support of the Institution.[53]

The meeting also decided that a forceful statement entitled *Threatened Poor's Rates—Mendicity Association*, published in that day's edition of *Saunder's Newsletter*, should be circulated throughout the city.[54] This statement, written by 'An Enemy To Taxation', linked the closure of the Institution with the introduction of a poor rate, which would deal the 'finishing blow to this declining city'.[55] It argued that the Institution had kept a poor law from the city and warned that a poor rate would be higher than any tax previously imposed, perhaps equal to all other taxes combined. The writer urged that the only way to avert this catastrophe was to subscribe more liberally to the Mendicity Association and to avoid giving alms in the streets, and concluded by urging citizens not to be 'a penny wise and a pound foolish'.[56]

The managing committee had hoped to avoid holding a parade fearing that the mendicants might be humiliated by walking publicly through the streets. However, when the situation was explained and they heard some committee members would accompany them, the mendicants agreed to take part.[57] The procession was well conducted, trouble-free, and the police did not have to interfere. As the managing committee reported to their members: 'a great multitude of your extreme Poor proceeded in a body through the streets with a decent tranquillity and a patient resignation of manner that spoke not in vain to the feelings of an Irish Public, who treated the parade with respect and kindness'.[58] Parochial meetings opposed the idea of levying a fixed sum on each house, considering it would be too much like a tax. They wished to encourage voluntary subscriptions, so the amount to be given to the Institution was left to people's generosity. Indeed, people were very generous: in several parishes many offered to give a regular amount to the Institution each year which allowed the managing committee to rely on a certain income. Others volunteered to become members of an auxiliary group to aid the managing committee, who were now fairly confident that the improvement would be permanent. There was no need for a further public meeting that year, which ended in an atmosphere of hope, if not actual prosperity.[59]

Also in 1828, the managing committee received the proceeds of a ball given in London by the Duke and Duchess of Clarence 'for the promotion of Infant Education in Dublin, and *more particularly* for the Infant School attached to the "Mendicity Institution"'.[60] The managing committee kept £300 for the Mendicity infant school and disbursed £400 among other infant schools in the city. Later in the year, a fancy ball held at the Rotunda solely for the support of the Mendicity infant school raised £700, making a total amount of £1,000 which became known as the Clarence

Fund. The original plan was to build a separate infant school in the upper yard, 'with a complete and well regulated playground and ornamental plots attached thereto'.[61] Instead, a room in the front building and front yard was cleared of adult mendicants and fitted up for the infant school, at a small expense which was charged to the fund. This decision caused quite a lot of dissension and debate among the managing committee. Some members wanted to spend the money invested for the infant school on extra accommodation for the adult mendicants whose conditions were very crowded.[62]

The great goodwill generated in 1828 by the Association continued the following year, but in practical terms the increase in subscriptions did not last, and once more income fell far short of expenditure.[63] Although business people benefited most by the removal of beggars from around their premises, they were still very reluctant to support the Institution, which once again only survived because of very liberal extra subscriptions from its most loyal supporters. Very unusually, the managing committee drew attention to particular donations: the first, an imaginative one by 'our long tried friend and supporter, Mr Robinson', the contractor for building King's Bridge over the Liffey, who fitted up a foot-passage over the bridge at his own expense and gave the Institution the profits from a toll of one half-penny charged to each passenger.[64] In 1829 the toll produced a sum of £89 9s 9d and the Institution received the net profit of £65 5s 3d. The second generous donation was from a group of workmen whose voluntary penny-a-week collections produced a sum of £102 8s 11d for the Institution.[65] Again 'stagnation in trade' caused many unemployed persons to apply for admission to the Institution, resulting in the highest summer numbers ever, despite the departure of those who left at this time every year to garden and sell fruit.[66] The managing committee attributed high numbers in the Institution to the general low state of the poor of the city and pointed out to the members of the Association 'the simple and well-ascertained fact that your numbers fluctuate in exact agreement with the demand for labour and the price of provisions'.[67]

For the previous four years all mendicants except the male stone-breakers had received free rations. While this enabled the managing committee to keep wages low, it also removed any incentive to work. Very few articles were manufactured in proportion to the numbers employed, and many mendicants did no work at all.[68] Now it was decided to return to the previous system of selling food to the majority of the mendicants. Two rations, each weighing two and a quarter pounds, could be purchased daily by each mendicant for one half-penny. The rate of wages was raised for those who could work and the rate of allowances for those who could not. The mendicants were now reclassified and their rates of payment graded accordingly. (See Appendix D.) Payments were calculated on the basis of a mendicant's estimated weekly expenditure: Food: 6 pence: lodging: 4 pence; straw: 1 penny; clothing (average): 3 pence, making a total of one shilling and two pence.[69]

An experiment to re-introduce knitting as an occupation for mendicants had begun in 1828; by the following year there was a very large and profitable knitting department in the Institution. An enterprising businessman, who gave employment to several charitable institutions, provided materials and paid a certain sum per pair of stockings knitted. With the success of the experiment, there was a distinct class of knitters in the Institution, formed from women who were incapable of harder work, and women with young children who had not worked previously.[70]

A new clerk was employed in 1829 to deal with the additional numbers. One had been needed for a long time but, due to the financial situation, the managing committee had been reluctant to increase the number of paid officers. As a result, the only clerk had been over-burdened and daily payments had been entrusted to some of the mendicants. That 'evil' was now stopped and the work was more evenly divided between the clerks. The new officer, a pay and check clerk, became responsible for the entire duty of payments. His accounts were examined daily by the superintendent and audited weekly by a member of the managing committee.[71]

On the verge of ruin again in 1830, the Institution was only sustained by support from the Lord Lieutenant and various public bodies.[72] The number in the Institution rose during the year to 2,821, was never lower than 2,124 and the daily average was

2,517. Once again, an extraordinary rise in the price of food during the year 'increased in a two-fold ratio the expense of supporting the Institution; it increased the number of objects of relief and augmented the cost of maintaining the individual'.[73] In February 1830 advertisements were published in the press drawing attention to the troubled state of the Institution's finances and reminding the public that it would close if cash on hand fell short of a fortnight's expenditure. Two months later, the continuing increase in the numbers in the Institution and the lack of response to the appeal caused the managing committee once again to call a public meeting in Morrison's Rooms.[74] Although to their 'mortification' this meeting was badly attended, it was decided to re-establish parochial committees to assist with collecting subscriptions, and to contact many absentee ground landlords for help.[75]

Despite the formation of parochial committees, the strenuous efforts of a few loyal supporters, and a donation of £100 from the officers' performance in the garrison amateur theatricals, 'public apathy, almost as general as it was unaccountable and distressing,' prevailed.[76] The decline continued until the managing committee decided to call a special meeting of the entire committee on Friday 11 June to discuss closing the Institution.[77] This meeting was publicised and clergymen were requested to urge support for the Institution at services on the following Sunday.[78] At the special meeting, attended by the ex officio members and chaired by the Lord Mayor, it was decided that the Institution would close on the following Friday, unless subscriptions improved, along with some assurance that any improvement would continue.[79] As £300 was subscribed in response to the appeal, the Institution was kept open for another week.[80] For several months during the summer of 1830, the Institution continued to operate on a week to week basis. As well as the usual Tuesday meeting of the managing committee, an extra meeting was held each Friday to monitor the financial situation and the funds received during the week.

In the middle of this financial crisis, the managing committee appointed a sub-committee to deal with a serious complaint from a neighbour, Thomas Byron of 7 Usher's Island. Pipes from the Institution were emitting smoke to the detriment of his garden and his family's health, and washing could not be put out to dry. One of the Institution's windows overlooked his yard, which he was unable to let as a result.[81] The matter was speedily dealt with: the window overlooking Byron's premises was blocked up and another made in the wall overlooking the lane; the pipes were extended up to roof to remove the problem with the smoke. This further increased the expenses of the Institution.[82]

The Lord Lieutenant, the Duke of Northumberland, who had very generously supported the Institution with donations amounting to £600 during his term of office, expressed his 'extreme regret' on hearing of the possible closure, but offered further help only if the citizens were prepared to support the Institution on a permanent basis.[83] Westminster was also interested in the Institution at this time. An order from the House of Commons Select Committee on the Irish Poor, chaired by Thomas Spring-Rice MP, 'That there be laid before the Committee copy of the last report of the Mendicity Society of Dublin' was forwarded to the Institution by the Under-Secretary of State for Ireland, William Gregory.[84] The order was complied with immediately and copies of two recent annual reports were also sent to Gregory for his attention.[85]

As the Institution was 'now upon the very precipice of extinction', the managing committee reluctantly reduced the mendicants' wages and allowances.[86] Since before the reduction few received more than one shilling and twopence per week from which they paid for food, lodging, straw and clothing, this could only be a temporary measure. The public was alerted to the crisis and the parochial committees increased their efforts. As many of the wealthier people were out of town during the summer, subscriptions were not plentiful; and the Institution had to rely on the generosity of public bodies, societies and some wealthy individuals to remain open during these months. Notice of a generous donation of £300 from the Benchers of the King's Inns was published in the press and several musical societies promised their support.[87] Trinity College gave £100; the Religious Society of Friends, £211 2s and the society of law clerks, known as the Friendly Brothers of St Stephen, five guineas.[88] The managing committee applied for help to the trustees of the fund established in 1822 to aid the poor of Ireland and also recommended the establishment of Houses of Industry all over the country to look after the incurable and infirm poor.[89]

Potatoes were scarce and expensive during 1830, at one stage costing the Institution £30 a day. Stirabout and milk replaced stew for breakfast while potatoes remained at a high price.[90] The mendicants liked stirabout, but an experiment of replacing oatmeal with rice was not popular. The managing committee were pleased by the relish with which the mendicants returned to the exclusive consumption of stew once the price of potatoes dropped, but they discovered that the reason some mendicants preferred stew to stirabout was that stew was more easily carried out of the Institution. In periods of scarcity, mendicants were often asked by friends to buy food cheaply for them from the Institution's kitchen.[91]

A special meeting was called at the beginning of September to consider 'the melancholy and alarming state' of the Institution's funds.[92] It was decided to notify the Lord Lieutenant that the number of mendicants in the Institution was 2,700, nearly double that of previous years, and that there was no longer enough money to pay for another day. The Duke was also informed that £1,693 had been collected for the Institution since his letter of 12 June, indicating the level of interest among the citizens in maintaining the Institution, and this was received during the worst time of the year for collections when the city was largely deserted during the summer months.[93] The Duke immediately sent £100 and promised to give £1,000 to be invested on behalf of the Institution as soon as an equal sum was collected from the public and similarly invested.[94] Although they considered the likelihood of success remote, the managing committee appointed a special fund-raising committee, of which Daniel O'Connell was a member, to attempt to achieve this target. They also decided to parade the mendicants through the streets of the city on the following Monday. Despite the dreadful financial situation, new linen blinds were ordered for the board-room windows before the next committee meeting.[95]

The proposed parade was postponed 'as it met with the decided disapprobation of the government', and the Lord Mayor was also opposed to it.[96] The managing committee accepted the postponement, although previous parades had been both 'harmless and beneficial', but warned that the Institution might close within a few days.[97] For a change there was some good news when the Paving Board offered to take all the shingle the Institution might provide, and agreed to accept larger sized gravel at the same price per ton as previously paid for fine gravel, which would produce a greater profit for the Institution. Consequently, as many mendicants as possible, both male and female, were set to breaking stones. Two weeks later, the Paving Board reduced the price of the larger sized gravel by sixpence a ton; however, the work was still very welcome.[98] The managing committee were also grateful when a baker from North King Street, Mr Rogers, donated money to the Institution instead of giving his usual presents of Michaelmas cakes to his customers. In the troubled financial state of the Institution, some members of the managing committee wanted to revert to the original rule which restricted admission to beggars and the infirm poor with at least six months residence in Dublin, but the majority of the committee thought that all in distress who could be reduced to begging if they did not receive the Institution's help should be admitted while the Institution remained open.[99]

An acrimonious meeting took place when a deputation led by the Lord Mayor visited the Chief Secretary, Sir Henry Hardinge, to explain the Institution's financial situation and to give the government notice of the probable discharge of the mendicants and the closure of the Institution. The Chief Secretary expressed surprise that the citizens of Dublin would allow such a valuable establishment to be closed and suggested that the Lord Mayor should ask them for a commitment to pay an annual amount to the Institution. They might give the coming reduction in paving tax to the Institution. He also mentioned that he had learned that the managing committee increased the number admitted whenever their funds improved. The Lord Mayor replied that the committee did not need any advice from the government. It was a matter for the Dublin citizens themselves to suggest an assessment for the support of a voluntary organisation. The deputation insisted that it was necessary to relieve every case of poverty to prevent mendicity and complained about the lack of accommodation for beggars in the House of Industry.[100] Within a few days of this meeting, Lady Emily Hardinge, the Chief Secretary's wife, sent a donation of £5 with a promise of a similar amount weekly for next six months. Notice of this generous donation was published in the newspapers.[101]

The managing committee decided to publicise the visit of the deputation to the Chief Secretary and also some resolutions that were passed at the subsequent committee meeting:

> 1. That the Lord Mayor should be requested to ask all the clergy to solicit support for the Institution among their respective congregations;
> 2. That a statement of the Institution's finances should be sent to all the clergy;
> 3. That the public should be informed that the Institution had £15 on hand to support 2,700 mendicants, but that the managing committee would try to keep the Institution open until the New Year when subscriptions customarily came in.[102]

The Institution continued to struggle on precariously, often without enough for one day's expenditure and only by borrowing from committee members.[103] In November 1830, the 'warmest thanks of the committee' were sent to Rev W B Mathias for the very timely sum produced by his eloquent appeal in Bethesda chapel on the previous Sunday.[104] Collections were also received from other churches and chapels. Circulars asking for assistance were forwarded to those who had not yet made collections for the Institution. Some gentlemen donated their fee of £13 for serving on a special jury in the court of common pleas.[105] When the citizens of the city of Charleston, South Carolina sent a generous donation to be divided between institutions for the poor in Dublin, Cork, Belfast and Galway, the Dublin Mendicity Institution received £84 2s 6d.[106] Despite a loan of £1,000 from one of the committee members there was only £18 18s in the bank at the end of the year.[107]

The managing committee decided to publish an appendix to the forthcoming annual report listing the names of all householders in Dublin, specifying the sum given to the Institution and also the names of non-subscribers.[108] Before doing so one thousand copies of the following circular were printed and distributed to non-subscribers:

Suppression of Street Begging

To the inhabitants of this House

By direction of the Managing Committee of the Mendicity Institution we beg leave respectfully to solicit your contributions to the funds of the Institution before the first of January next.

It has been determined to print complete lists of the subscribing and non-subscribing Householders in every street and the Committee are anxious to give the fullest notice of the resolution, the object of which is to render the subscriptions as general as possible, and, by dividing, lighten the burden and duty of supporting those of our fellow creatures, who but for this Institution would be compelled to beg in the streets.

The Collector of this District [name and address of collector] is directed to wait upon you and to give the proper receipt. Subscriptions are also receivable at the Bank of Ireland, at all the private banks and at the Mendicity Institution, Usher's Island, (which you are requested personally to visit), all the departments of which, together with all the books, plans, accounts etc. of the Committee are open daily to public Inspection.[109]

Chiefly through the efforts of one committee member, Thomas Wright, the fund-raising committee raised the required sum of £1,000 just before the Duke of Northumberland's retirement in December, when as promised, he gave his 'princely parting gift of One Thousand Pounds' towards the establishment of a separate fund, the interest on which would benefit the Institution.[110] Many other noblemen followed his example and their contributions brought the total amount to £3,150, which was invested in government stocks and named the Northumberland Fund.[111] The investments were then passed to the Commissioners for Charitable Donations and Bequests to comply with the Duke's wishes that they should be guardians of the fund.[112] On his departure from Ireland the Duke gave an additional £100 to the general funds of the Institution. In a letter of appreciation for his generosity during his term as Lord Lieutenant, the managing committee told the Duke that 'among the splendid honours of your illustrious family it will be recorded that your Grace was the friend of the poor'.[113] A bust of the Duke was placed on a pedestal in a conspicuous part of the Institution. The Duchess of Northumberland expressed her delight at the parting gift of a piece of lace made by the children in the Institution and assured the managing committee: 'I shall always remember, with pleasure, the excellent arrangements of their Institution which are so well calculated to relieve the unfortunate victims of want, and I trust it will continue to prosper in their hands'.[114]

At the Annual General Meeting of the Association in 1831 the members decided to send a petition to parliament asking that either or both the House of Industry or the Foundling Hospital should provide space for beggars as they had been established to do at the expense of the people of Dublin. The petition also pointed out that legislation was needed to allow magistrates to commit beggars of every description there.[115] During the early months of the year, the Institution's funds suffered because of another public subscription raised for the labouring poor of Dublin, and also because of appeals made for the poor in the west and south-west of Ireland, who were 'in a deplorable state' at that time.[116] Subscriptions were also affected by the unsettled state of public feeling on the introduction of a poor law, now constantly discussed as a possibility.[117] By April 1831 the number on the books had 'increased alarmingly' to 2,800, the Institution was in debt, and the managing committee resolved

> that under the existing circumstances of the Association it is the opinion of this Committee that they would be only deceiving themselves and the public if they did not avow their conviction that without some manifestation of a proper and active feeling being excited throughout the now inert mass of householders who have not yet subscribed, such as their experience of the past can justify but little hope of their witnessing in the future, it will not be practicable for them to carry on the business of the Institution through the ensuing summer, relying on voluntary contributions alone.[118]

This increase in numbers in the most difficult year for the Institution since its foundation was due to a particularly harsh winter and the abolition of another Manufacturers' Relief Committee which had been established in September 1829. The Association did not approve of these committees: it believed that giving money and asking for no work in return created habits of pauperism and dependence. When these relief committees ceased, people expected the Institution to give similar help.[119]

A public meeting in April was attended by a large number of wealthy and respectable inhabitants of Dublin who expressed shock and regret that barely one quarter of householders now supported the Institution. A fund raising committee was appointed and the managing committee were implored to remain on, although it was acknowledged members would be fully justified in resigning.[120] In spite of door to door collections 'in the opulent parts of the city' and appeals in all the churches, sufficient funds could not be generated to support the Institution.[121] Although they considered the action 'defective in principle and otherwise objectionable', the managing committee were forced to limit the amount of stones broken by the stone-pounders in order to keep their wages down.[122] The number on the books rose to 2,900 in May and the situation continued to deteriorate. The trustees of the fund established in 1822 to aid the poor of Ireland refused the Institution's application for help.[123] Fines from the courts, previously sent to the Institution, were forwarded to the Meath Hospital instead.[124] As funds were now exhausted, the managing committee requested another public meeting, at which 'many inhabitants of this City, most respectable for character and rank, undertook the painful and laborious office of soliciting subscriptions from those who had hitherto refused the paid collectors of the Institution'.[125]

The managing committee's preferred source of funds was direct voluntary contributions, as balls or concerts offended some members of the Association. However, when there was no choice but to leave nearly 3,000 mendicants destitute on the streets, it decided to hold a fancy ball at the Rotunda.[126] Although it was an unsuitable time of year, the Lord Lieutenant, the Marquess of Anglesey, attended as did a few wealthy people who had remained in the city during the summer. The managing committee were grateful for the sum of £238 8s 10d raised by this event, although it did not cover the expenses of the Institution for even one week.[127] The sub-treasurer, Mr Collins, submitted his resignation, partly due to illness but mainly because he felt unable to take his salary when the Institution had no funds.[128] A third public meeting that year, held at Mansion House in June, decided to send a deputation to the Lord Lieutenant to inform him of the alarming state of the mendicant poor of Dublin.[129] The Lord Lieutenant received the deputation 'most graciously' and was told that the Institution was £800 in debt, that the weekly expenses were nearly £250, and that it could no longer be supported by voluntary contributions.[130] It was a serious and significant admission.

The deputation did not ask for a grant of public money, but for a loan of £2,000–£3,000 to cover the expenses of the Institution until the government decided the question of the future support of the poor. It suggested that the buildings and other property of the Institution could be used as collateral for the loan. The Lord Lieutenant had no funds from which to make such a loan but sent the application to the Chief Secretary, who did not even acknowledge the request.[131]

'Thus deprived of almost every hope, disappointed in every quarter', the managing committee decided, by a vote of six to four, to discharge every person who was fit to work from the Institution on 5 July 1831: only the aged, the infirm and children remained.[132] A gradual dissolution was thought best if the Institution was to close. The destitution of even some of the mendicants might encourage non-subscribers to contribute. It was also important to keep the Association in existence. As long as it remained in any form, it could benefit from annual dividends from a capital sum of about £17,000 donated over the years and invested on behalf of the Institution. These would be lost for ever if the Association ceased to exist even 'for a moment'.[133] The Sunday allowance was stopped and new admissions were restricted to the mendicant aged and infirm and to orphans and women with babies.[134] The inspector was suspended until further notice and was finally granted £4 compensation because his discharge was due 'to the partial failure of the Institution'.[135] Most of the mendicants behaved very well when discharged and reflected 'that quiet endurance of misery, that "patience of despair", by which the conduct of the labouring classes in Ireland, in periods of famine and disease, has been in many instances distinguished'.[136] Only a few persons of notoriously bad character caused any trouble when discharged. Although many shops in the city were broken into and robbed at this time, it was mainly common thieves who committed these crimes, knowing that the starving mendicants would be blamed.[137] On 19 July, with the numbers down to 2,100 and a fall in the price of potatoes by more than half to 24 shillings per ton, the managing committee were able to discharge the debts of the Institution. Immediately, they resolved to provide two meals a day for every mendicant who applied for help. This resolution re-established

> 'that immense benefit, which was amongst those originally contemplated by the founders of the Institution, viz.: *that so long as the Mendicity Association existed, no human being need perish from hunger in the metropolis of Ireland*'.[138]

Mendicants were allowed to leave after breakfast and return to the Institution for dinner.[139] The funds continued to improve and every mendicant attending on 2 August, who had formerly been on the books, received lodging money. On 9 August the managing committee, anxious to return to the principle of giving no help without work, put all who could labour back to work in return for their food and lodging money.[140] Mendicants were no longer allowed to leave after breakfast. Spinners were required to spin at least two hanks of yarn; stone-breakers to pound at least eight bushels of gravel; and oakum workers to pick at least two pounds of oakum, entitling them to four pence lodging money and free rations.[141] However, on 16 August, the superintendent reported that there was 'no such thing as order among the mendicants'.[142] The stone-breakers and spinners joined together and refused to work until they received their former rate of pay. The lodging allowance was increased to sixpence, and the ringleaders of the disturbance were dismissed from the Institution.[143]

The managing committee spent the next few months attempting to return the Institution to its former state. The Mendicity Association co-operated with the Society for the Relief of Sick and Indigent Roomkeepers, an organisation established in 1790 for the relief of the Dublin poor, in promoting the Dublin Musical Festival. The

Institution received £200 as a donation from the receipts of this event.[144] In September, the Paving Board agreed to take all the shingle the Institution could produce.[145] Stone-breakers were now paid one half-penny for a bushel of shingle, without rations. The mendicancy condition was removed and admission extended to all the infirm and aged who applied to the Institution.[146] However, funds were still limited and the managing committee asked for time to pay a bill due to the Committee for the Relief of the Poor in the West of Ireland, who had sold potatoes at a very low price to the Institution during the summer.[147]

The managing committee were dissatisfied with this limited operation as they wanted to admit all who were in need of help.[148] Finally, in November 1831, the admission restrictions imposed in July were lifted. The clergy were asked to hold collections for the Institution on the occasion of its re-opening.[149] Two inspectors were employed to assist the police who agreed to resume arresting beggars.[150] Knitting was started again, the knitters receiving their rations and three pence per pair of plain stockings, four pence per pair of ribbed stockings, and two pence per pair of children's stockings knitted. The Paving Board employed sixty mendicants as street sweepers, paying the Institution three pence per day for each sweeper, who was given two pence daily and his rations by the Institution. These mendicants had their breakfast at 8 am each morning so they could be on duty by 9 am.[151] However, only one week later, after Christmas, the Paving Board sent thirty of the sweepers away, incapable of work; of the remainder, seven refused to work at all and five more gave up during the day. Only eleven reported for duty the next morning and the Paving Board decided to discontinue employing mendicants from the Institution.[152]

During the last months of the year the threat of cholera, which had already reached England from the east, made the public aware how easily disease could spread if mendicants were free to roam the streets. It was recalled how the Mendicity Institution had helped prevent the spread of disease in 1826, and how, during the typhus epidemic prior to its establishment, many wealthy people had been infected by beggars, who crowded around their carriages and at the doors of shops begging because they had no other source of relief. Strolling beggars, wandering from house to house, had also passed on the virus 'which was generated in the abodes of poverty'.[153] In this way, families were affected who otherwise would never have come into contact with the disease. The advantages of an establishment such as the Mendicity Institution were obvious: 'an Institution which prevents the resident beggar from wandering about the city, and, (what in the present instance is of equal importance), prevents the country beggars from entering into it'.[154] The public realised that the Institution would be invaluable 'in arresting the progress and diminishing the fatality of the disease' should it come to Dublin.[155] Cholera usually made its first appearance among the poor, and the disease could only be treated successfully if caught in the early stages. Consequently, there was a great advantage in keeping people in such a high risk category together where they could be examined daily by doctors and the disease detected immediately it struck, and from where they could be sent to hospital at once. The patient's chance of recovery would be increased and the risk of contagion reduced for the community. Knowledge of where the sick person lived would enable the source of the disease to be instantly known and immediate disinfecting to take place.[156] Although officers of health were appointed in many parishes and money was allocated for whitewashing, disinfecting and cleansing the dwellings of the poor, there was no legislative provision to make assessments for food, clothing or lodging for them. The managing committee did not wait for subscriptions to come in but made the admission policy 'as wide and unrestricted as formerly'.[157] This faith was justified when money poured in, and before long the Institution was restored to a more secure financial footing.

The managing committee 'gratefully accepted' a grant of £100 at this time from the Commissioners for the Education of the Poor in Ireland. The Institution qualified for this grant because of the non-denominational nature of its schools.[158] Seven members of the Association objected to this grant as being contrary to principles of the Society of the Protestant Friends of Education to which many members of the Association also belonged.[159] However, the managing committee insisted that the system of education had remained the same since the foundation of the Institution and had always been approved by the membership.[160]

During the cholera epidemic of 1832, preventive measures recommended by the Institution's dispensary medical officers—the disinfecting process adopted throughout the establishment, the improved diet that included more meat, and the transfer of many mendicants to lighter work—resulted in very little cholera within the Institution.[161] As the epidemic in the city worsened, the Institution provided a temporary hospital for its sick mendicants in a nearby building, for which a grant of £100 was received from the Board of Health. Only ten of the seventy-nine patients treated in this hospital died, which was considered an exceptionally low figure in such a virulent epidemic.[162] The hospital also prevented the panic of previous epidemics when carriages transporting the sick to hospital were thrown into the river or attacked in the streets. The mendicants appreciated the treatment and attention given to their sick peers who were not brought to hospital through the public streets.[163] The Institution also provided a convalescent hospital where sick mendicants recuperated. This helped to prevent a relapse and other mendicants were encouraged by how quickly former patients returned to the Institution.[164]

Many of the young women from the Institution worked as nursing attendants in the temporary hospital. The managing committee recommended some of the best to the Board of Health and fifty were employed in cholera hospitals throughout the city and elsewhere in the country.[165] The Institution also received £500 from the Mansion House Fever Committee to provide new clothing for mendicants, not only for those recovering from cholera for whom new clothes were essential as their old clothes had to be destroyed, but also for the other mendicants, most of whom were badly in need of new clothes. As 'want of clothing was an evident pre-disposing cause of cholera', this was a very important donation.[166] Nevertheless, the managing committee distributed the clothing gradually, as they knew from experience that too rapid a distribution could cause fraudulent applications. They received permission to spend £100 of the donation on flooring certain parts of ground floor where a large crowd of mendicants sat daily. This gave them immediate comfort, provided a permanent improvement and also fulfilled the terms of the grant by helping to prevent disease.[167]

The Institution survived during 1833 and 1834 through good management of the funds, although subscriptions were not generous and the managing committee were forced to spend too much time in soliciting them.[168] The Association continued to complain about the lack of accommodation for beggars in the House of Industry and the futility of arresting them when the majority were released immediately and others could be held for only one night. Table 5 shows the number of beggars convicted and committed to the 24 cells in the House of Industry between 1827 and 1833. The Governor of the House of Industry was unable to increase the number of cells for beggars, but agreed that two children could be placed in the same cell with a parent.[169]

In 1835, regular subscribers were notified that early payment of subscriptions would be greatly appreciated. However, the amount subscribed fell £600 below the previous year's level. The Institution now had only 1,900 subscribers, which meant that 13,000 householders did not support it.[170] The shortage in funds prevented the managing committee from purchasing at the best prices as they could not take advantage of fluctuations in the price of coal or potatoes.[171] The Institution always sold kitchen waste, and £51 earned by the sale of potato peels was particularly welcome that year.[172]

The managing committee received so many complaints about

Table 5: Return of Beggars Convicted and Committed to the 24 Cells in the House of Industry 1827–33

Year	Number of Beggars
1827	2,804
1828	2,223
1829	2,132
1830	2,967
1831	1,775
1832	2,550
1833	3,287

Source: 16th *Annual Report*, App 5, pp 61–2

the number of beggars on the streets, particularly children, that they decided to investigate some specific cases and publish the results:

> No. 1. J S This man, who writes a beautiful hand, and had a good situation as a clerk, which he lost by drunkenness, has for several years exposed himself and his infant children, almost naked in the streets; he is frequently drunk, and uses violent and blasphemous language, although when it suits his purpose he is a well spoken man; he has sometimes a written scroll before him, purporting to contain a true statement of his condition; occasionally kneeling on one of the bridges at night, with his shivering children beside him, he endeavours to extort money from passengers, by threatening to throw those poor infants into the river; he has been with his family in the Mendicity Institution, where he was employed as an assistant in taking down the names of applicants for admission, and his children were fed, clothed, and educated. He has often been committed from the Police Office to the House of Industry, and on *more than ten of those occasions*, was drunk when taken up.
>
> No. 2. Mary M lives in Vicar-street, from whence she sends out her three little children, the eldest a boy eight years old. She has them placed sometimes near the Bank, more frequently on Carlisle-Bridge; they are left there rather late in the day, and mostly until ten or eleven o'clock at night, uniformly so in bad weather. The Mendicity Inspector has more than once called at her lodging, and induced her to withdraw them—of late she has not exposed them.
>
> No. 3. Mary H. lives in Rainsford-street. This woman exposes three very young creatures by leaving them the whole day in various places, more particularly next the wall of the Royal Dublin Society's lawn in Merrion-Square. This is their regular post during rainy or severe weather; she does not stay with them; the Mendicity Inspector has often called on her; and for the present, her children are withdrawn from at least any conspicuous place of exhibition.[173]

The committee publicised these cases to illustrate their efforts and difficulties with recidivist beggars. They added:

> there are now daily in attendance there [the Institution]—and for the present, orderly and well behaved—two of the most remarkable and troublesome men in their line, one of them a man who has been for

years in the habit of begging through the city, half-naked, and shaking in a peculiar and distressing manner. He has now the candour to admit that it was a mere artifice.[174]

Not all contributions received at the Institution were money. In the Annual Report for 1835 the managing committee published a list of some welcome non-pecuniary donations received during the year:

Contribution	*Donor*
400 loaves of bread	Lord Mayor
36 rolls and 21 loaves of bread	Mr Jackson of Nassau St
A carcass of mutton	Mr Weldon
A carcass of mutton	Mr Barlow, Sybil Hill
A leg of mutton	Magistrates of 4th Div
One cask of raisins	Messrs Boyce
10 lb of raisins	A Lady
Sundry articles of clothing	Anonymous
2 shirts, 2 vests, 1 pr trousers	A half-pay Captain
7 pair of small clothes, 2 hats, 2 vests, 4 pairs leggings	Rev. Mr Cooper
12 pair stockings, 12 cravats, 2 shirts, 2 handkerchiefs	George French Esq.,K.C.
48 yards of calico	Miss Nunn, Holles St.[175]

The Institution now had its own pensioners: eighty elderly and very infirm mendicants who no longer could attend daily. Although it was against the strict application of the rules, the managing committee refused 'to desert in their worst extremity, those who have previously exhibited so decent an example of quiet resignation, and so becoming a determination to maintain some degree of respect for their character, under the most trying and adverse circumstances'.[176] A special donation also enabled the Institution to clothe these pensioners.

The three-year period before the enactment of poor law legislation in 1838 was yet another difficult time for the Institution during which funds frequently ran out as both the number of applicants for admission and the cost of food continued to rise. The general committee, which included the managing committee, the vice-presidents and ex-officio members, met frequently to discuss the grave financial situation. At the end of March 1836, the managing committee were forced to sell £100 of 3 per cent stock to meet the expenses of the current week.[177] The Association accepted that the low level of support was due partly to the public's annoyance at the great numbers of beggars on the streets, and partly to the expectation of compulsory provision for the poor. The managing committee asked the public to stop giving alms to beggars and to support the Institution, stressing that they had learned from the government that poor law legislation would not be introduced that year.[178] However, in May 1836, when the price of oatmeal and potatoes had risen by 50 per cent since February, the managing committee's patience was exhausted. They asked that a public meeting should be held to either accept the resignation of the committee, 'or adopt some measure to save the Institution from *ruin*'.[179]

The attendance at this public meeting consisted, with a few exceptions, of members of the general committee of the Institution. At this display of public apathy, the meeting adjourned for a week in the hope of achieving a higher attendance so the committee could make a last appeal for the Institution which would 'inevitably close its doors unless pecuniary assistance is immediately afforded'.[180] Ministers of all denominations and church wardens of every parish were invited to attend the next meeting, at which an auxiliary relief committee was appointed to help the managing committee raise funds. It was reckoned that as the weekly cost of running the Institution was presently £184, a sum of £5,152 would be needed to maintain it until the end of year.[181]

The efforts of this relief committee kept the Institution open during the summer months.[182] They raised £1,800 in nine weeks; but only £455 came from new subscribers, the old reliables once again provided the larger part of this sum.[183] All the money subscribed was absorbed by the daily needs of the Institution and no improvements could be made. A parade of mendicants was planned, but cancelled at the request of the Chief Secretary.[184] Week after week, the managing committee debated reducing the mendicants' earnings and allowances or dismissing all the stronger ones, three-quarters of whom were women, to beg on the streets.[185] At the end of September when the balance in the bank was less than £1, the managing committee placed a notice in the newspapers warning that the Institution was about to close. During this stressful period a gentleman wrote on behalf of his gardener's wife, who had put a crown piece into the Mendicity box on Carlisle Bridge instead of a penny; he was sure her statement was correct as she was a very decent person. The Institution repaid her the money.[186]

The Institution struggled on until the end of November 1836 when the public was informed that it was over £200 in debt with 2,300 mendicants to support.[187] By the following week the debt had risen to £407 and the Institution was unable to buy materials for its workers, who were asked to return any flax or materials they had as there was no money to pay for their work. Once again the managing committee called for the help of the auxiliary relief committee.[188] On its recommendation, they rented part of a shop in Parliament Street as a central collection office for a month, during which a sum of £116 6s 1d was received.[189] Fortuitously, the executor of the Honourable Sophia Ward's estate advanced £500 of a legacy she had left to the Institution. Although the customary procedure was to invest all legacies, this and a smaller one received during that year went to meet the current expenses.[190]

Unemployment was very high in Dublin in 1837, as the very long winter curtailed outdoor employment. The high price and poor quality of potatoes led again to an increase in the numbers in the Institution. Disease was widespread throughout the poor of the city.[191] Many artisans and their assistants, a class which did not usually seek relief, applied to the Institution for help. 'A timely and munificent contribution from an amateur society' was received when a concert by the Dublin Choral Society raised over £100 for the Institution.[192] However, the Poor Law Bill had been introduced in parliament in February and the expectation of its enactment continued to affect subscriptions. At the Annual General Meeting that year citizens were urged to continue their subscriptions until the law came into force.[193] A letter was received in March from the private secretary to the leader to the House of Commons, Lord John Russell, stating that there should be no need for the Mendicity Institution once the workhouses were established, but it was vital it should continue until the unions were formed and could provide for the destitute.[194]

At a special public meeting called in May, the Institution joined with the Society for the Relief of Sick and Indigent Roomkeepers and the Strangers' Friend Society to draw the government's attention to several unsatisfactory clauses of the Poor Law Bill currently going through parliament, and to request temporary support until the provisions of the act took effect. This request was refused.[195] At the end of May the Lord Lieutenant, the Earl of Mulgrave, sent £20 in response to notice of the imminent closure of the Institution.[196] However, on learning from a deputation of the Association that the Institution would be out of funds in two weeks as the weekly expenditure was £250 and the weekly income only £50, he agreed to put its request for a loan to the government.[197] Meanwhile, the managing committee wrote to the Chief Secretary, Lord Morpeth, asking for his support and enclosing an account of the deputation's conversation with the Lord Lieutenant.[198] Lord Morpeth sent £30 on his own behalf but explained that the Chancellor of Exchequer would need evidence of substantial local support for the Institution before he could agree to a loan. The managing committee decided to try to meet the Chancellor's requirements and asked regular subscribers to increase their usual subscriptions for this purpose.[199] Once again, many loyal supporters did not fail the Institution. A collection of £45 was made by some friends of Henry Grattan, MP, his own contribution being £10.[200]

The passage of the Poor Law Bill through parliament was delayed by the death of King William IV; however its future implementation continued to militate against subscriptions to the Association. People believed they should not have to support the Institution as well as pay a compulsory assessment. The managing committee was forced once again to spend legacies on current expenses instead of investing them.[201] In a constant state of anxiety as to whether the Institution could continue, the managing committee arranged to have charity sermons preached on the same day in all places of worship of every denomination. These charity sermons raised £1026 9s and alerted the public to the general state of distress of the poor as well as giving them an appreciation of the value of the Institution and the danger that threatened it. A sum of £7 14s was also received from 'those few Jews who reside in Dublin'.[202] The Religious Society of Friends, which had a worship structure without sermons, forwarded a sum of £132 9s through Samuel Bewley, one of the founder members of the Institution and a loyal and generous supporter for nearly twenty years.

Any subscription raised in Dublin for the poor brought a huge number of paupers to the city from the country. On this occasion so many remained in the city that a sub-committee was appointed to deal with them. Many were sent home and £25 was allocated to the sub-committee so a small sum could be given to each one who left the Institution to obtain work elsewhere.[203] The Institution continued to operate as widely as possible under its restricted financial circumstances. Although the Paving Board did not usually want stones at that time of the year, in the circumstances it offered to take a small quantity for repairing the streets. Later in the year, the Board agreed to take all the shingle the Institution had on hand if it could be delivered to wherever it was needed. The Institution arranged to have the shingle delivered at a cost of sixpence per ton.[204]

1838 began badly for the Institution with many subscriptions remaining unpaid.[205] A generous donation from Robert Fannin was timely. He presented £600 to trustees of the Association for investment in government stocks, with the interest to go towards meeting the current expenses of the Institution.[206] Several concerts given in aid of the Institution raised a total of £162 11s 6d.[207] These donations were the exception, however; fewer than one seventh of householders were currently subscribing and with so many in the Institution there was continuous pressure on the funds.[208] Headed by the Mendicity Association, a number of charities drew up a petition to parliament concerning the worsening situation of the Dublin poor. The Duke of Leinster was asked to present it to the House of Lords and the City MPs, Daniel O'Connell and Robert Hutton, to the House of Commons.[209]

At the beginning of May 1838, the number on the books rose to over 3,000, and the Institution notified the Chief Secretary that there was only sufficient money to feed this number of mendicants for three days.[210] When the Chief Secretary replied that, although anxious to support the Institution, the government had no funds available for this purpose, the general committee decided to appeal to the citizens at a public meeting when a final attempt would be made to devise ways to prevent the closure of the Institution. If this failed they would close the doors and admit no more beggars.[211] This appeal targeted traders in the principal streets who benefited most from the Institution. Some of the most loyal subscribers were again asked to solicit non-subscribers in their own streets, and church-wardens and clergy were also recruited for this purpose. This time the strategy of using gentlemen collectors was successful; £100 was collected in eighteen streets and other regular subscribers were asked to do likewise in their own neighbourhoods.[212]

Friends of the Institution occasionally devised unusual ways of giving help. Mr Gibbons suggested charging a fee of sixpence to everyone who came to see the furniture on sale in his establishment, with the proceeds going to the Institution.[213] Similarly, the loyal Mr Robinson of the Phoenix Park Iron Works offered to open his foundry to the public for a fee which would benefit the Institution.[214]

During the summer months of 1838, the managing committee met from day to day in an attempt to keep the Institution open. They asked noblemen assembled in London for Queen Victoria's coronation, particularly those with a connection to Ireland, for their help.[215] Another auxiliary relief committee was formed and met at least twice weekly at the Mansion House. An address to the public warned of the consequences which would follow the closure of the Institution if the usual subscribers continued to withhold their subscriptions and the rest of public refused its support:

> When the Gates of this Asylum are closed against the multitude of hungry expectants, they will crowd about your shop doors, repelling your customers by their squalid wretchedness or gather in groups before the halls of your private houses, frightening and appalling yourselves and families upon every in coming and out going by the very aspect of their miseries and imprecations that must be wrung from them by their sufferings and despair. They will infest every street and square and public place in such a manner as to expel from the City every one

who can possibly live out of it.[216]

The address also warned of the danger of a typhus epidemic if over 3,000 destitute mendicants were let loose on the streets and told those who might be withholding their subscriptions because they thought the poor rate would be levied immediately the act was passed, that the poor law could not possibly come into effect for some time, as:

> Before one penny of Rate is actually levied on the Public the boundaries of the Union must be traced out, the boundaries of the Electoral districts must also be traced out, the valuation of the assessment must be made, the applotment upon that assessment must be held over for Inspection, the Guardians must be elected, and finally the Workhouse must be built . . . nearly a full year must elapse before they will be have to pay any poor rates.[217]

The public was also advised that this was the last year it would be asked to support the Institution as the burden of supporting the poor would be shared in future by 'those miserable defaulters' to whom the Institution now appealed for the last time 'to place upon record but one redeeming instance of a free will offering upon the shrine of charity'.[218]

The funds of the Institution had been helped in 1837 when the Paving Board took all the available shingle.[219] The Institution now had 1,000 tons ready for sale which would deteriorate if left, and again the Board was asked to give preference to this shingle as the Institution's funds were in such a bad state. The Institution also advertised that 'a superior material for avenues or gardens and shrubbery walks' could be delivered to householders at a very reasonable price.[220] As breaking limestone was the only profitable occupation now carried on in the Institution, all the young and fit women were put on this work, bringing to over 100 the number employed at stone-breaking. Over 200 women worked at spinning and over 50 at knitting. Neither of these occupations made a profit, but they saved the Institution sixpence lodging allowance for each worker. However, even the most hardworking could earn no more than one shilling per week, the majority making only enough to pay the rent.[221]

The managing committee proposed substituting a collection

for the Institution in lieu of the plan to have the city illuminated for the coronation of Queen Victoria.[222] As the arrangements for the illuminations had already been made, this could not be done. Instead, collections for the Institution were taken up in each street on the day of the coronation: 'A more acceptable compliment could not be offered to the feelings of a Young and Interesting Queen than to make the occasion of her coronation an opportunity for exciting the charitable feelings of her subjects.'[223] One of the early pieces of legislation to receive the assent of the newly-crowned queen was an *Act for the More Effectual Relief of the Destitute Poor in Ireland,* otherwise known as the *Poor Relief (Ireland) Act* 1838.[224] The passage of this act was to affect the future work of the Mendicity Association profoundly and irrevocably.

CHAPTER SIX

The Institution, the Poor Law and the Famine 1838–49

IN 1804, A SELECT COMMITTEE of the House of Commons on Legislative Provisions for the Poor of Ireland reported:

> the adoption of a general system of provision for the poor in Ireland by way of a parish rate as in England, or in any similar manner, would be highly injurious to the country and would not produce any real or permanent advantage, even to the lower class of people who must be the objects of such support.[1]

During the next thirty years, while poverty and destitution increased in Ireland, numerous commissions and committees investigated the condition of the Irish poor, making some recommendations but with little practical result.[2] It was not until 1834, when the Elizabethan Poor Law was replaced in England by the new and harsher workhouse system, that the Government seriously considered extending the poor law to Ireland.[3] In 1833, a Royal Commission, chaired by the Church of Ireland Archbishop of Dublin, Dr Richard Whately, was appointed to inquire once more into the condition of the poorer classes in Ireland. Following a wide-ranging investigation into many aspects of the lives of the poor and the institutions caring for them, the Commission advised that a poor law based on the workhouse system, such as that recently introduced in England, would not be appropriate for Ireland, and proposed, instead, 'a broad plan of economic development' and a wide range of social services.[4] In a bid to counteract the Royal Commission's report, the government sent its own emissary, the English Poor Law Commissioner, George Nicholls, to produce a report that would strongly advocate the establishment of a workhouse system in Ireland even stricter than that in England and Wales.[5]

Although one of the objections to the establishment of the Mendicity Association was that it would be 'the groundwork of taxation on the inhabitants of Dublin for the support of the poor', successive managing committees argued that, on the contrary, the successful operation of the Institution would prove the efficiency of the voluntary principle and obviate the necessity for such a law.[6] They believed that 'the timely application of relief to temporary poverty may have the effect of preventing it from becoming fixed indigence' and that the Institution could suppress street-begging without giving the poor any right to relief.[7] When, in 1829, there was a 'vague though pretty general report' about the introduction of a poor law, the managing committee decided that until this happened, they would continue to operate and improve the Institution to the highest degree possible, believing that the poor should not suffer while the debate went on.[8]

For many years, the Association also rejected the idea of compulsory support for the Institution, believing that this would attract idlers and people dissatisfied with their jobs to the Institution, which would then really be a poor house by a different name.[9] The managing committee considered that a bill introduced at Westminster early in 1831 proposing the compulsory support of the Dublin Mendicity Institution, reflected both the esteem in which the Association was held and recognition of the value of its work. Nevertheless, the committee strongly believed in the voluntary principle, if it could be made to work.[10] Therefore, their admission later that year to the Lord Lieutenant, the Marquess of Anglesey, that the Institution could no longer be supported by voluntary contributions was a watershed in philosophy and a dramatic change in policy.[11]

Nor did the Association agree with a combination of voluntary and compulsory provision for the poor, as suggested by a majority of the Irish Royal Commissioners in their 1836 report. Like Daniel O'Connell in the debate on the Irish Poor Law Bill, the Association argued that voluntary donations were only plentiful when the poor had no other means of support or to avert compulsory provision, giving as an example how voluntary contributions to the House of Industry had dwindled in the previous century 'when allied to a contribution from the national purse'.[12]

Managing committees of the Mendicity Association had always refused to comment on the merits of a poor law, feeling it was not the committee's business to promote or oppose it. Once it was certain that the introduction of a poor law was inevitable and issues of the amount and the kind of poor relief were being widely discussed, the committee were concerned about the welfare of the poor they had looked after for so long and considered it correct to offer opinions based on almost twenty years' experience.[13] Their Statement on the Poor Laws in 1835 to the Commission for Enquiring into the Condition of the Poorer Classes in Ireland reflected the principles governing the Institution.[14] If these principles were incorporated into the legislation, the committee agreed with the English Poor Law Commissioners that

> a compulsory Provision for the relief of the Indigent, can be generally administered on a sound and well-defined principle; and that under the operation of this principle, the assurance that no one need perish from want, may be rendered more complete than at present, and the Mendicant and Vagrant repressed by disarming them of their weapon—the plea of impending starvation.[15]

However, George Nicholls' idea of what Ireland needed was far different from the Mendicity Institution's generous principle 'that no one need perish from want'. During his brief time in Ireland, Nicholls visited the Mendicity Institution; but

> after a careful examination of the Dublin Mendicity Association, which has with difficulty been kept in existence by the great exertions of the gentlemen constituting the committee, and by the threat of parading the mendicants through the streets,

he reported that he did not consider voluntary contributions could support all the Dublin poor, and pointed out that if this was the case in the capital, the difficulty would be greater elsewhere in the country.[16] Although he conceded 'the Dublin Mendicity Association has certainly done great good, and it must be admitted that the sudden closing of its doors would be productive of much suffering', Nicholls considered that it encouraged vagrancy by providing a safety net for beggars to rely on when they did badly on the streets, 'thus operating, in fact, with respect to vagrancy, as a kind of voluntary labour-rate'.[17] He argued that the chief reasons for its existence had been the absence of any system of relief for the destitute and concluded: 'The Dublin Mendicity Association therefore affords no precedent for general adoption as a medium of relief in Ireland.'[18]

When a copy of the Poor Law Bill was forwarded from London for the comments of the Association in February 1837, a sub-committee appointed to examine the bill reported: 'its proposed enactments are well calculated to ensure the wise and benevolent objects of a law designed for the prevention of mendicancy and vagrancy and affording relief to destitute poor in Ireland'; but the committee had reservations about the workhouse being the sole source of relief, as many of the poor would need outdoor relief.[19] Unless workhouses were quickly erected throughout the entire country, the first ones built, presumably in Dublin and other large towns, would be over-crowded and pressurised. The sub-committee were all too correct in this prediction. They also pointed out the need to provide immediate temporary and easily accessible accommodation for the elderly and infirm.[20]

The financial difficulties experienced by the Institution prior to the enactment of the poor law were discussed in the previous chapter. A 'trying transition period between the outgoing of the voluntary, and the incoming of the compulsory system of providing for the poor' followed the passing of the *Poor Relief (Ireland) Act* in July 1838.[21] Ignorance of when they would be liable for a poor rate continued to deter subscribers and a rumour that all the Institution's funds would become the property of the Poor Law Commissioners inhibited legacies.[22] Determined to keep the Institution open as long as required, the managing committee made weekly appeals to the public, through the generosity of the newspapers. As the numbers in the Institution continued to increase, help in superintending the schools was also urgently required. Ladies were asked that 'an occasional hour or so, snatched from the gay and fashionable scenes around them, be bestowed in looking after the improvement of these poor, but truly deserving, objects of their own sex'.[23] In August 1838, when subscriptions were £905 less than those of the previous year and the Institution was again threatened with closure, a special meeting was held to consider the dire financial situation.[24] An address, explaining the financial problems and warning of the imminent closure of the Institution, was printed cheaply and distributed widely round the city headed by a short note

Crisis!!!

The Mendicity committee ask the Inhabitants of Dublin what is to become of the Poor in the Institution? as the funds are completely exhausted.
Usher's Island, 21st August 1838.[25]

The outcome of this appeal was evident a week later when the managing committee once more addressed the public:

> The inhabitants of Dublin are respectfully informed by the Managing Committee of the Mendicity Institution that there is at present but
>
> £3 11s 9d
>
> in Bank to provide sustenance for near 3,000 human beings this week and that the Committee must inevitably close the doors of the Institution, a casualty which the Public cannot be surprised at, when, notwithstanding their last appeal the Income of the week was but £31 2s 4d to meet an Expenditure of £220.[26]

Members of the Association helped at each venue when simultaneous charity sermons were once again given in all chapels and churches in September and a sum of £729 0s 10d was raised for the Institution.[27] An appeal to the bakers of the city to give a donation to the Institution in lieu of the usual custom of providing their customers with Michaelmas cakes, raised a very satisfactory £122.[28] An appeal to grocers did not achieve such a result 'which might well have been expected from so wealthy and influential a class of traders'.[29] The Mendicity Association shared the outcome of this appeal with the Society for the Relief of Sick and Indigent Roomkeepers, each receiving approximately £40, after advertising costs of £30 had been deducted. By November the Institution was £500 in debt and by 15 December was penniless. Its drafts could no longer be honoured at the bank.[30] At the request of the managing committee, the Lord Mayor summoned the directors of all charitable institutions in Dublin to Usher's Island on 21 December 1838 to discuss the best way of providing relief for the poor in the interval before the Poor Law Commissioners began operation. At this meeting, the charities stressed the importance of continued public support for all institutions assisting the poor, as the poor law would not be put into effect for at least a year, and also the need for increased subscriptions because of the rise in the price of oatmeal and potatoes on which the poor depended. A motion, proposed by Alderman West and seconded by Daniel O'Connell, warned that, unless non-subscribers supported the Mendicity Institution and regular subscribers increased subscriptions, it would be forced to close, 'which would be a most deplorable calamity at this particular period of the year'.[31] A week later, O'Connell wrote to the honorary secretary of the Institution:

> Merrion Square,
> 31st Decr 1838
> My Respected Friend,
> I beg to enclose to you £10—being double my annual subscription to the Mendicity. It is absolutely necessary to have the most active exertions made to prevent the unfortunate persons who now are relieved at that Institution perishing from utter destitution in the Interval between this and the coming into operation of the poor Laws. One of my reasons for opposing that Law was the belief that its enactment would inflict a torpor upon voluntary charity and that the effects of such torpor would be felt with increased mischief in this interval between the passing of the Law and the levying of the poor rate. My prophecy has, I fear, proved too accurate but my anxious hope is, that the generosity of the Inhabitants of Dublin will prevent its being true to the full extent. I wish to defeat my own prognostic. It is quite true that the poor rate cannot be operative sooner than one year and a half from this period, that is not until June 1840. Alas, what are the poor to do in the meantime if the coming of the poor Law dries up the sources of present relief. It is absolutely necessary that the most active steps should be taken to prevail on those who have not hitherto subscribed now to contribute and as to those who have already subscribed to double their subscriptions.
> I owe to myself to add, that my opinion upon a poor law is unchanged, but I am only the more bound to obviate all its mischiefs.
> I have the honor to be very respectfully, my dear friend,
> Faithfully yours,
> Daniel O'Connell[32]

The publication of this letter in the newspapers and the publicity generated by the meeting of all the institutions serving the poor attracted sufficient subscriptions to keep the Institution open. In addition to his annual subscription, the Lord Lieutenant, the Marquess of Normanby, had provided every mendicant with a substantial dinner of beef, bread and beer on the day of the Queen Victoria's coronation. On Christmas Day 1838, for the third year in succession, he sent half a ton of beef and two tons of potatoes for the poor, while Robert Fannin Junior sent two sheep 'to aid in rendering them somewhat comfortable on this happy and holy festival'.[33]

As the cost of food continued to rise, numbers in the Institution were again very high in 1839. A public meeting was called in April when the Institution's debts were £870, there were 2,563 mendicants on the books, and only three shillings and five pence in the bank.[34] A *fete champetre*, held in the Phoenix Park lodge of the Chief Secretary, Viscount Morpeth, raised £482 7s 9d, but by the end of July the Institution was again £700 in debt. The managing committee reluctantly paraded the mendicants through the streets in August. Charity sermons on behalf of the Institution were not as successful as formerly because of so many other calls on people's charity, but a public meeting called by the Lord Mayor at the end of September generated a great response, which temporarily eased the Institution's financial problems.[35]

However, many people withheld subscriptions to the Institution in 1840, believing the Poor Law was already in operation and the workhouses were open. The Institution had £347 6s 11d in the bank on 24 March, debts of £245 14s 4d and 2,883 mendicants to support.[36] The managing committee appealed in vain to the public and to the government. At a meeting in the Mansion House in April, although it was agreed that they would be fully justified in closing down and releasing nearly 3,000 destitute people onto the streets, friends of the Institution asked the managing committee to persevere until the workhouses opened.[37] Finally, the South Dublin Union workhouse opened its doors on 24 April 1840, followed on 4 May by the North Dublin Union.[38] When the managing committee discharged 1,000 paupers from the Institution on 7 May 1840, a new and very different era began for the Mendicity Institution.[39]

Looking back in the Institution's Golden Jubilee year, the managing committee remarked that the introduction of the Poor Law in 1840 'modified very materially the working of the Institution'.[40] The number of mendicants in the Institution fell dramatically from 2,753 in April 1840, just before the Dublin workhouses opened, to 403 in June, only two months later.[41] As the Mendicity Institution was now comparatively empty, it was time for the managing committee to make a plan for the future. The first step was to reduce the scale of the Institution, dispensing with the services of six of the nine officers and many of the servants who had been instrumental in the successful running of the Institution in the past. There would be few extern sick to visit in the future, as the committee believed these people were now entitled to accommodation in the workhouse; so the dispensary was discontinued, and arrangements were made with a neighbouring hospital to treat any of the poor in the Institution who became ill.[42] Only forty children of school age remained, most having gone with their parents to the workhouse. The large schools of the past were no longer required and the annual grant of £100 from the Board of Education was terminated. Boys now attended schools in the adjacent parishes of St Audoen or St Paul, according to their religious affiliation; only a small school for girls and infants staying open in the Institution.[43] School-children were given a suit of clothes two months after admission and were entitled to another suit every eight months afterwards.[44] A meeting of the general committee on 4 August 1840 decided to admit any deserving case recommended by a subscriber as the poor law was not yet fully operational. It was decided to sell tickets to the public at 1s 6d per dozen which they could distribute if approached by beggars, who would then be entitled to a free meal in the Institution.[45]

The managing committee were very pleased that all citizens were now compelled to share the burden of supporting the poor.[46] However, they had to determine the appropriate role for the Institution when the poor law was fully operational. It did not take long to ascertain that 'in large cities there are always casual poor who do not come within the scope of the Poor Laws'.[47] The managing committee eventually concluded that the Mendicity Institution would still have heavy and responsible duties to perform: it would be required to give occasional relief to the poor until admitted to the workhouse, to the Irish poor sent back from England on their way to their homes in the country and to English paupers seeking help to return home.[48] Although the Dublin workhouses contained over 3,700 paupers by the end of 1840, the huge number of beggars still on the streets showed the value of the Institution as a 'useful adjunct to the Poor House'.[49] It was clear that an establishment was still necessary where all beggars could be directed to apply for relief.[50]

The Institution needed the public's support to supply 'the perhaps unavoidable omissions of the Poor Law system', by giving relief to the destitute who for one reason or another did not go to the workhouse.[51] In addition to dividends, the managing committee estimated that the Institution would need about one third of the previous amount subscribed annually to carry out this task.[52] However, they reminded the public of the space available in the Institution and offered, if sufficient donations were received, to open its doors widely once again.[53] A new source of funds became available when, due to the fall in numbers, the managing committee were able to let part of the premises to 'respectable tenants' who paid rent.[54]

In order to curtail expenses, the managing committee tried to get as many poor as possible into the workhouse and continued to adapt their system of relief to meet the needs of those not catered for under the *Poor Relief (Ireland) Act*.[55] However, the Irish poor detested the workhouse and would not enter it unless they were absolutely desperate. The number of beggars on the streets was an indication that many preferred to take their chance there than to endure the harsh conditions in the workhouse. Others preferred to remain in the Institution. The 1842 annual report records:

> Alicia Meehan, a delicate girl of about 12 years old, having been in hospital for a few weeks, was discharged therefrom somewhat relieved, though still delicate; she was recommended strongly to enter the poor house, and all its advantages accurately portrayed as peculiarly befitting her state; she entreated to be still continued in the Institution. She was brought before your committee the following Board day, and the

> committee concurring in opinion with that previously recommended to her, she feelingly entreated them not to remove her from her nurse, whose maternal kindness she eulogised in a most feeling manner and with tears of gratitude in her eyes, and concluded by saying 'that she well knew she would recover under the nurse's care' but that her heart would break if obliged to go to the poor house.[56]

Admission to the Irish workhouses was totally at the discretion of the poor law guardians and there was no right to relief. When questions were raised about the continuing existence of the Institution, the managing committee pointed to the people who could not gain admission to the workhouse for various reasons: shortage of accommodation, some peculiarity in their case, or not coming within the meaning of the Poor Law Act. When it was suggested the Institution prevented the full and effective operation of the poor law, the managing committee argued that the Institution only gave relief for one day before putting all able-bodied people to work.[57] Those who did not pass this work test were dismissed and received no further help. The Institution also proved to be 'a most useful auxiliary to the working of the poor law', when rumours about the bad treatment received in the workhouse deterred many of the poor from seeking admission.[58] The Institution admitted a number of poor women with delicate children who were unwilling to enter the workhouse, perhaps because of the rule that would separate them from their children or because of the extremely high death rate of children there. The Institution supplied food and lodging money to these women until their prejudice against the workhouse lessened.

During the 1840s several founder members of the Association died. Henry Cole was 'among its foremost and most active friends' for a period of twenty-two years, and the loss of his constant attendance at the weekly meetings of the committee was severely felt by his fellow committee members following his death in 1840.[59] William Lunell Guinness, 'a gentleman whose heart was ever warm to the wants of his fellow creatures', died in 1842; and Dr Thomas Orpen, 'a kind friend to the poor' and one of the trustees on the Institution's move to Usher's Island, in 1845.[60] William Keartland, who 'when advanced in age continually attended an Institution which he had nursed, fostered, and cherished', died in 1846.[61]

Several vigorous members died young: among them Robert Fannin, Junior, one of the Institution's most generous benefactors, who died in 1840.[62] His widow continued to support the Institution by providing 'three fat sheep' for dinner every New Year's Day until her death in 1865.[63]

Most of those who received help during the early 1840s remained only for a brief time in the Institution, while they were waiting for admission to the workhouse, on their way home from England, or while they were temporarily unemployed. Those who remained longer than one day were employed breaking stones or at knitting.[64] Robins says that orphans were generally cared for in the workhouse after the introduction of the poor law, nevertheless, twenty-eight of the orphans admitted to the Institution before the law was introduced remained at Usher's Island, 'the residue of 21 years accumulation'.[65] Working mendicants paid for their food; the remainder got free rations and lodging money. Stirabout and milk frequently replaced stew in the daily rations during these years, as donations of meat were not as plentiful as before.[66] Each mendicant attending on Sunday received five pounds of whichever food was available without charge. The Lord Lieutenant, Earl de Grey, continued the custom begun by his predecessor of providing a beef dinner for all in the Institution on Christmas Day, when an allowance of four pence was also given to each mendicant. The Institution was now the only place in Dublin where 'those persons in actual want can and do receive a meal of food as an act of charity, on the solitary representation of being in want of it'.[67] The managing committee admitted all paupers who applied for relief in order to try and take away every excuse for begging.[68] Table 6 gives an interesting picture of the mendicants in the Institution in the last week of the years 1843 and 1844.

Although the managing committee encouraged all mendicants who were residents of Dublin to apply for relief to the poor law authorities, they continued to stress the advantages of the mendicity system over that of the poor law. When working by day in the Institution, the poor could go home at night where they had the opportunity to be with their family and hear of any available work. They wore 'no badge of poverty' as did the poor in

The Institution's first home was in Dublin Society (later the RDS) House in Hawkins Street (Courtesy National Library of Ireland)

The gate (now incorporated into a hotel) marks the entrance to Copper Alley, off Fishamble Street, the Institution's home from 1820 to 1824 (Courtesy Old Dublin Society)

The Mendicity Institution in the 1940s, from across the Liffey (Courtesy Old Dublin Society)

At the formal opening of the present building in 1954, the Chairman, W. H. Tennant and the President's wife, Mrs Sean T. O'Kelly, examine the old minute books

Many of the Institution's clients came from Dublin's notorious tenements. Above: a lane off Francis Street. Below: A tenement room in the Liberties. (Courtesy Old Dublin Society)

Dubliners endured extreme poverty such as this as late as the 1930s. The bottom picture shows an outdoor privy, which would have been used by several families. (Courtesy Old Dublin Society)

James Boydell, Trustee and Committee Member 1898–1920

William C. Boydell, First Annual Chairman, Trustee and Committee Member 1920–1963

Derek Boydell, Trustee and Committee Member 1963–95

Richard G. Tennant, Chairman 1991–96

In Mendicity House, Usher's Island

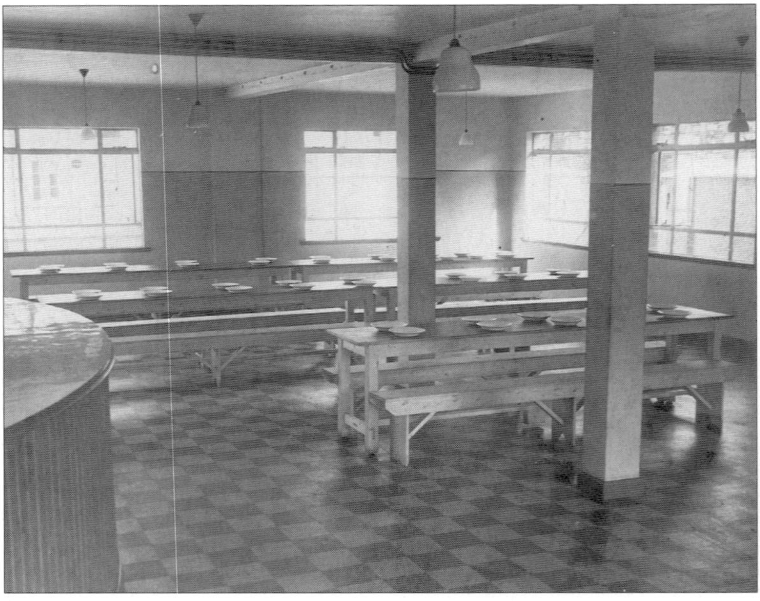

In the new building (1954)

The present dining-room

More than 130 free meals a day are prepared and served from this bright kitchen

The Management Committee in 1987: Standing (l–r) Richard Tennant, James Hudson, Dorothy Browne, Percy Scott, John Smiley Seated (l–r) Charles Smith, Archbishop Donald Caird, Derek Boydell

The Management Committee in 1998: Standing (l–r) George Sheppard, Canon John Crawford, Patrick Bewley, Timothy O'Leary Seated (l–r) Anne Coffey, Richard White (Chairman), Dorothy Browne, John Smiley

the workhouse, but clothes they bought for themselves.[69] The Institution also gave help to all who asked for it, whereas the poor law authorities often refused help, even to many who assumed they were entitled as residents of Dublin to enter the workhouse. The Institution had also taken on the transmission of paupers from one union to another: duties that were undertaken by parishes in England.[70] The limited accommodation in the workhouses and the fact they were open only two days a week for general admissions were also disadvantages highlighted by the Institution. On one occasion, the Institution sent 150 people to apply for admission to the South Dublin Union; although the applicants were elderly and infirm and women with infants, only about seven were admitted and the remainder had to return to the Institution.[71]

A Night Asylum, a charitable institution for the houseless poor, had been established in 1838 in Bow Street, Smithfield to provide destitute homeless people with shelter. It consisted of a large hall, two staircases and eight rooms: each thoroughly ventilated, washed

Table 6: Classification of the Institution's Clientele in the last week of December 1843 and December 1844

Occupation	1843		1844	
	Males	Females	Males	Females
Knitters		21		57
Stone-breakers	26	21	20	21
Label holders	2		2	
Carters, potato cleaners		6		6
Employed in kitchen & dining hall	1	2	1	3
Gate and door keepers, fire man	8		7	
Sweepers, scourers		4		4
Oat bruisers	2		2	
Applicants for admission	7	12	7	18
Waiting for admission to workhouse	3	9	22	46
Children in school	9	27	11	21
Children below school age	2	7	4	6
Total	60	109	76	182

Source: 27th *Annual Report,* p 11

out every morning, well warmed by fires at night, and lighted with gas to enable the inmates to read or work. An average of ninety-five poor people attended this shelter each night. During 1844, of the 1,472 applications for admission to the Institution, almost half came from the Night Asylum, which thus cooperated with the Institution in providing round the clock care for many of the poorest people in Dublin.[72]

In 1846, when the failure of the potato crop caused great hardship for the poor, so many applied to the Institution that most of its former functions were resumed. More staff were required and some of the previous officers were re-employed. The dispensary service was resumed and proved very useful, especially for mothers with young children and during the frequent fever epidemics. Dr O'Flaherty, who had been apothecary to the Institution for many years before the opening of workhouses, returned as medical officer. The boys' school was re-opened, and a schoolmaster appointed. Religious services and instruction, suspended a few years earlier, recommenced on Sundays.[73] The managing committee had laid in a store of provisions, having anticipated a rise in price when food became scarce. When this was used up they bought rice and Indian meal at the same price as potatoes had been formerly.[74] The poor gradually became accustomed to the change in food. Each person now received two and a quarter pounds of oatmeal stirabout and a half pint of milk for breakfast. Dinner was rice and turnips or rice and Indian meal with a half pint of soup made from beef heads. Nursing mothers received milk in place of soup and an extra half ration at each meal.[75]

The numbers in the Institution continued to rise as the situation in the country worsened and famine became widespread. The average daily attendance of 597 in January 1847 gradually increased until the Institution helped 2,298 people daily during the first week in May.[76] The schoolmistress had 250 children under her care.[77] Donations of Indian meal were received from both archbishops of Dublin, the Religious Society of Friends, and the Dublin Parochial Association for the Relief of the Poor of all Religious Denominations.[78] O'Connor says that the famine pinpointed the fatal weakness of the workhouse system. Confining relief to the workhouses was disastrous in a country with as many poor people as Ireland, when the number of places available was a mere 110,000.[79] The widespread public concern aroused by the catastrophe in Ireland caused the British Government to change this policy in February 1847, first by the introduction of soup kitchens, followed in June by the provision of 'outdoor relief' which meant that the poor could receive help outside the workhouse.[80] The managing committee encouraged the poor in the Institution to apply for outdoor relief and became stricter in their own admissions policy, as they did not believe anyone should get relief from both sources. The average daily attendance fell to 925 in June 1847 and continued to decrease until the number seeking help daily from the Institution in December 1847 was 417.[81] However, in a letter to the editor of *Saunder's Newsletter*, the honorary secretary, Daniel Kinahan, suggested that the poor law could be better and more cheaply administered under the principles of the Mendicity Institution, stressing that giving outdoor relief alongside the workhouse system would certainly increase the poor rate. He pointed out the advantages of the mendicity system of confinement by day with paid employment over the poor law system of confinement by night and day with unpaid employment:

> The Mendicity Institution may be regarded as a branch workhouse to the Dublin Union Poorhouses; a labourer and his wife and family apply for relief and are admitted, the man is put to break stones, the wife to work, and the children are sent to school; they have an opportunity every evening of hearing of employment; they have the opportunity to become independent labourers.[82]

From August to November 1847 the managing committee assisted the North Dublin Union by feeding some of its poor on outdoor relief. These people, who also received medical relief from the Institution's dispensary, remained in the Institution during the day, which had the advantage of keeping them off the streets. The daily average number helped in this way was 411 in August, 555 in September, 657 in October, and 296 in November.[83] Once again, the Institution had proved to be a useful auxiliary to the poor law authorities. Table 7 describes the mendicants in the Institution around this time.

A more evocative picture of the Institution's clientele is derived from a poem written by the joint honorary secretary, William Nugent Skelly, and published in pamphlet form as an appeal for funds in 1847. Although the language seems excessively flowery to the twentieth-century reader, it does give a vivid account of the people in the Mendicity Institution during the time of the Famine.

THE MENDICITY

If you desire the truth to know
Of human misery and woe
And piteous want and deep distress
In all their frightful nakedness;—
And if you have a heart to bear
Scenes that are rarely met elsewhere,
Then come, ye healthy, come with me
And visit the Mendicity!

Enter the mansion, and behold
Two thousand creatures, young and old— *

Table 7: Classification of the Institutions' Clientele in Week Ending 1 January 1848

Occupation	Males	Females	Total
Knitters		67	67
Male stone-breakers	33		33
Female stone-breakers		38	38
Women with children in arms		47	47
Oakum pickers	3	6	9
Employed in kitchen and dining hall	2	4	6
Gate and door keepers	25		25
Oat bruisers	2		2
Applicants for admission	5	6	11
Children in schools	43	46	89
Children too young for instruction	38	40	78
Total	151	254	405

Source: 30th *Annual Report,* p 14

The infant—adult—many too
Of four score years, now meet your view—
Driven from their last resource—the street,
To get a morsel here to eat,
Their sad existence to sustain,
Hopeless of work they've sought in vain!

What but Religion's holy sway
Can make them drive despair away?—
She whispers to the aching breast
That God doth love the poor man best,
And for his sufferings here below
That heaven's best treasures He'll bestow
On such as for His sake will share
The cross His son vouchsafed to bear!

You cannot picture to the mind
A case of woe, but you will find
Its parallel within these walls
Where wretchedness on pity calls!

See the admitted here today,
And what I state you'll not gainsay,
That here within these precincts we
The most distressed of mortals see,
As all who seek relief may come—
The lame, the blind, the deaf, the dumb,
Whose tales of suffering and of woe
Which patiently they undergo,
Might chill the bravest heart with fear,
And from the sternest force a tear!

That aged man whom you see here,
Had once six hundred pounds a year,
But spending at too fast a rate

* In May 1847 the numbers on the books exceeded 2,500

He had to sell his old estate,
And now his tide of fortune out,
His only meal is stirabout!
There's an old widow, ninety five,
Par'lytic and but half alive,
Bent by infirmity and grief,—
'Tis death alone can bring relief
To her who now has nothing, save
The hope of bliss beyond the grave!
As if from out the clouds he came
Here's a poor foundling none will claim
Whose looks but too well indicate,
His sad, forlorn and helpless state!

There's a poor cripple from his birth
Without a relative on earth,
A fellow full of fun and wit,
Who from his cradle begged his "bit".
He's one of hundreds whom I've seen,
Who for some thirty nights have been
Without a single change of dress,
So that his state of—you may guess!
Your perfumed lord or lady might
Shudder at one in such a plight.
A poor abandoned orphan child,
A maiden lone, but undefiled,
Who pawned each article of dress
Sooner than tell her deep distress,
And now her only coverings these—
Some tattered rags—but no chemise!

A pale emaciated form
Of one, like you, most nobly born
Who little thought that she should be
A skeleton from poverty!
Her silken robes now turned to rags,—

Her bed of down now changed for flags!—
A nobler form could scarce be seen
To grace a duchess or a queen,
And many a drawing room you may pace
Nor see such lineaments of face!

A female with a child comes in,
And promises no more to sin,
Since by starvation she was driven
To feel how she offended heaven!
For sometimes God by such means tries
The sinner's heart before he dies.

Upon a door a boy is borne,
His famished cheeks are wan and worn,
Without a friend on whom to call,
He slept as usual in a hall,
Where frozen by December's frost
The use of all his limbs he lost!

And now two dying babes are brought,
Who with their—now dead—mother sought
A place of refugee for the night
In a dark entry where they might
Avoid the snow and piercing cold,
Their mother's cloak around them roll'd,—
But when the wretched three *were found,*
The mother could not leave the ground,
The infants lived, but life had fled
From the poor mother who was dead!

An infant just come into life,—
The mother—a deserted wife—
Whose fortune by her husband spent,
The villain off to England went,
And there enlisted in a corps,

That may be twenty years or more
On foreign service in the East,
So, that this monster, worse than beast,
Has here *escaped, but knows full well*
For such a crime he merits hell!

But worse than all that came before,
A maniac rushes to the door
With rolling eyes—dishevelled hair—
Muttering a curse—and then a prayer!-
Frantic with rage, she wildly shrieks—
Nor has she slept for ten long weeks,
Since, of misfortunes, the most sad,
Starvation drove the creature mad!

How many from the typhus bed—
By parching thirst and hunger led,—
Come here with gaunt and ghastly look,
As if a moment's time they took
From death—Death's triumph just to show
Ere to the other world they go!
Nine *of such cases* now *are here* *
Who unlike living things appear!
The doctor comes,—the pulse he feels—
A typhus case the pulse reveals.
"Away", the secretary cries,
"To Cork-street, or the poor man dies!"

Enough!—appalling scenes like these
Affright the eye that seldom sees,
Only a beggar whom we meet
When passing through the crowded street,
And whom so hastily we shun,
Lest what Christ taught us might be done!

* During this past year, for several months, the average number of fever cases daily admitted, and sent from thence to hospital was *ten.*

O God of mercy, who could be
A witness of such misery,
Nor feel how few these are who know
The full extent of want and woe
Among the wretched of mankind,
Such as within these walls we find!
And oh! ye wealthy, proud and vain,
If by this picture *you should gain*
One moment's thoughtfulness of heart,
Oh! let your selfishness depart,
And exercise your charity
To aid the good Mendicity.

In the late 1840s the Institution continued to feed all who applied for help before 9.30 am, although those who were starving were given help at any time during the day. Applicants continued to receive relief if they had no other means of support. The policy, although not always observed, was to refuse admission to any person the Institution believed was entitled to help from the poor law Union.[84] However, in practice, residents of Dublin were permitted to remain until they were admitted to the workhouse; persons from the country were sent to their homes; the casual poor and people returned from England remained until they could get work or help from their friends; and English paupers were returned to England if they passed the work test imposed by the Institution.[85]

The Institution was still finding it difficult to make ends meet during these hard times. The minutes of 24 August 1847 mention the need to sell much of the stock on hand because subscriptions were so low.[86] In December 1848 such a large number applied for help that a special meeting of the general committee decided to limit admission to those in the greatest distress, if funds did not improve.[87] This was a major decision: apart from the partial closure of the Institution in 1831, the Association had never refused help to any eligible person unable to get aid elsewhere. Once again the managing committee blamed the inadequacy of the poor law system of relief. As the South Dublin

Union did not readmit people until a month after they left the workhouse during the Famine, the only place for them was the Institution. The managing committee suggested that a small sum should be given to each pauper for his work and kept for him until he left the workhouse; in a short time he could earn enough to support himself outside the workhouse for a month while he looked for work. There was plenty of work available for stone-breakers in Dublin, as 58,000 tons of gravel were required for the city streets. This plan could also have the advantage of reducing the poor rate.[88] By the winter of 1848 there was only one weekly admission day to the workhouse, and the managing committee queried what would paupers do if the doors of the Mendicity Institution were also closed to them. An address, headed *Mendicity Institution—Alarming State of the Funds*, drew attention to the situation in the hope that it would generate sufficient subscriptions to keep the Institution open on its former principles. The public was informed that every shilling contributed went to the relief of the poor, as interest on the permanent investments (shown in Table 8) were more than enough to pay the rent and the expenses of the staff.[89]

In 1849, stone-breaking was still the test of poverty for an able-bodied person to gain admission to the Institution. The other occupations carried on were oat bruising and knitting stockings for contractors and the trade in general. The forty knitters were mainly unemployed servants. Only five orphans now remained

Table 8: Funded Property of the Institution Yielding Interest

Name of Fund	Principal £ s d	Fund in which Invested	Yearly Interest £ s d
Dr Barrett's	8010-10-0	3˘% Stock	260-6-10
Surgeon Leake's	3876-10-0	Ditto	126-0-0
Hon Sophia Ward's	1598-10-0	Ditto	51-19-0
Clarence School	1000-0-0	Ditto	32-10-0
Mr Fannin's	600-0-0	Ditto	19-10-0
Northumberland	5184-1-7	3% Stock	155-9-2
Hon Sophia Ward's	259-17-10	Ditto	7-15-10
Rev Samuel Davis's	55-16-4	Ditto	1-13-6
Total	20,585-5-9		£655-4-4

Source: 31st *Annual Report* p 14

in the Institution. Lack of funds made it necessary again to reduce the numbers of officers in the Institution. Dr O'Flaherty offered to attend without remuneration, and the valuable dispensary service continued. When cholera struck the city that summer, there were only two bad cases in the Institution, one of whom recovered; the other was an old man who did not seek help in time. That the diarrhoea so prevalent among the poor during that summer did not develop into the fatal form of the disease, was attributed to the prompt treatment given by the Mendicity Institution's dispensary.[90]

The Mendicity's principles were fully tested during the Great Famine when the workhouses were full. At the height of the distress the number in the Institution did not exceed 2,500. The system worked well. Those who could get temporary work left for a short while and then returned 'cheerfully' to the Institution.[91] The managing committee were still concerned by the under-use of their extensive premises, and ever optimistic, despite the uncertain financial situation, were considering the introduction of an innovative project for the benefit of the Dublin poor and once again a new role for the Institution.[92]

CHAPTER SEVEN

The First Public Baths in Dublin 1848–1909

SINCE 1842 WHEN Edwin Chadwick's *Report on the Sanitary Condition of the Labouring Population of Great Britain* high lighted the link between disease, poverty and environmental factors, the sanitary improvement of crowded cities had become a widely held aspiration throughout the United Kingdom.[1] Fever was rampant in Ireland during the Great Famine. When Dr Harty, one of the founder members of the Mendicity Association, proposed that the Institution should erect a bathing and wash-house establishment for the benefit of its clients, a sub-committee was immediately appointed to investigate his proposal.[2] It was the far-sighted Dr Harty who had been reluctant to dispose of the outdoor shower bath in 1820, following the accusations of cruelty discussed in Chapter Three.[3] Several new bathing establishments had recently been erected in some English cities and in Belfast with reportedly beneficial results for the health of the inhabitants. When the sub-committee learned in 1847 that Dublin Corporation had no immediate plans to provide public baths in the city, they recommended that the Institution should erect the proposed establishment for the immediate benefit of its clients, but in such a way that it could be opened at a later date to all poor people who had no such facilities available to them.[4] The managing committee agreed to proceed with the project and decided to establish a special fund in order 'to accomplish so great and so obvious a good'.[5] An architect estimated that £500 would be needed to adapt and fit out one of the buildings in the Institution. Dublin Corporation agreed to supply water for the project.[6]

Money came in very slowly to the baths and wash-house fund, despite a contribution of £20 from the Lord Lieutenant who said that the inhabitants of Dublin should be among the first to introduce such useful establishments in Ireland.[7] Every avenue was explored to raise money for the project. The Commissioners of

Charitable Donations and Bequests refused the managing committee's request to release £1000 for the baths from the Clarence Fund (the fund established for the infant school).[8] An application was made to the Archbishop of Dublin for portion of the money donated to him for charitable purposes by Jenny Lind.[9] A disappointing sum of £180 was raised by the time of the Annual General Meeting in 1849, when the threat of a cholera epidemic caused Dr Harty to remark:

> that at all times, and under any circumstances, it is highly expedient for the promotion of cleanliness, and of moral and industrious habits, as well as for the prevention of dangerous and contagious diseases among the poorer classes, to encourage the establishment of bathing and washing Institutions, and that such Institutions are now the more indispensable under the threatened visitation of epidemic cholera.[10]

Dr Harty urged the incoming managing committee to continue the effort to raise the balance of approximately £300 then needed to complete the project.[11]

The managing committee assured the public that the poor would use the baths, citing the substantial use by Irish people of a recently established baths and wash-house facility in East Smithfield, London, where the nationalities of the clientele were classified as shown in Table 9.

Although Queen Victoria responded to the Association's appeal and gave £50 to the baths fund when she visited Ireland in 1849, the amount collected was still not enough to begin the project. The architect's original estimate having been revised, the

Table 9: Classification of People using Bathing Facilities in London in 1848

Nationality	Bathers	Washers
English	12,849	16,555
Irish	13,441	16,644
Scotch	786	1,178
Welsh	232	404
Foreigners	354	499

Source: 31st *Annual Report*, p 9

amount now required was £700.[12] An appeal was also made to the Bank of Ireland, the Benchers of King's Inns, and other public bodies.[13] Long-time supporters of the Institution, the Benchers promised £50 for the baths as soon as the rest of the required amount was collected and also sent one hundred guineas as a donation to the general funds.[14] A full-dress subscription ball was held to raise funds for the project.[15] Fortunately, as the general funds of the Institution were 'in a prosperous state as compared with last year', the managing committee were able to transfer £250 to the baths fund in May 1850. Three years after Dr Harty's original suggestion, a sub-committee was appointed to erect the baths and the project finally got under way.[16] It is evident that the Institution's finances had indeed improved as arrangements were also made at this time to have the front of the Institution painted, the windows glazed and painted, and the walls 'properly coloured'.[17]

Having examined several suggestions made by the architect, John Bourke, as to the best building to use for the baths, the managing committee asked him to draw up a detailed plan for the conversion of the present dining hall into the washing and drying department, the dispensary and the infants' and girls' schoolrooms into the bathing department, with the smoothing or ironing room in the upper story. When the sub-committee for the project received another architect's opinion of the difficulties that could arise if Bourke's plans were adopted, they advised the managing committee to advertise for alternative plans. These were to be sent in within three weeks, with a prize of five guineas for the best.[18]

Five architects submitted plans under assumed names: *Veni Vidi Vici; Fair Play and No Favor; Candidatus; Thermae*, and *Rufus*.[19] The prize was awarded to 'the gentleman named '*Rufus*'' whose plan for the baths to go in the east wing of the Institution was selected as the most suitable.[20] *Rufus*' identity was revealed as John Sterling Butler and he was appointed architect to the project. His fee was agreed at five per cent of the expenditure, which was not to exceed £500.[21]

Butler and superintendent Cottle inspected bathing and wash-houses in Liverpool, Manchester and London.[22] In the light of the visit to London, where he considered the baths were the finest he had seen, Butler amended his plan for the project at Usher's Island.[23] He recommended the installation of slate baths and timber washing and steam tubs, the drying closet to be heated by steam and to have timber drying horses. He also favoured the newest method of heating the hot water cistern by means of a metal ball fixed in the centre of the cistern, with the steam passing in at the top.[24] His estimate of £860 for the work was accepted, and the completion date was agreed as 1 June 1851.[25] John Bourke, the original architect consulted by the committee, was paid £15 10s for his work and told the managing committee that he regretted that he had not entered the competition.[26]

Although the baths fund had not quite reached £600 by January 1851, the managing committee agreed to a further revised figure of £979 and appealed for donations to enable completion of the project 'which is so essential for the promotion of health and cleanliness, and of the moral and industrious habits of the poor'.[27] The general funds of the Institution were used again in April to pay a sum of £200 due to the contractors. The costs continued to rise. The builders recommended the erection of a second boiler for the exclusive use of the bathhouse at a cost of £42, leaving the existing one to serve the wash-house. On the advice of the architect and the sub-committee, the managing committee approved the installation of a second boiler provided it could supply both wash-house and bathhouse.[28] When the project was nearly finished, the Corporation agreed to enlarge the supply pipe for carrying water to the Institution, an arrangement that was to become a source of contention at a later date.[29] A ticket office was constructed, Robert Dalton was given a trial as stoker, and posters advertising the first public baths in Dublin were printed.[30] Finally, at the end of the year, the baths and wash-house were completed and a notice was published that the opening day would be 16 February 1852.[31]

The Lord Lieutenant and Countess Clarendon expressed their great pleasure at the opening of the baths, which were more elaborate than was originally planned. There were separate entrances for male and female bathers. Four first-class and six second-class baths were provided for male bathers and eight second-class baths for females. No first-class baths were provided for women at this time, and it is clear from the records that the wash-house was considered to be their province: it contained forty stalls, each partitioned off, 'so one female cannot look at another's clothes'.[32] The wash-house had a machine for extracting water, 'a drying closet with heated air', a mangle, smoothing tables and irons.[33] Since most poor people had only one set of clothing, each woman was given a loose shift to wear while washing and drying her clothes. She could then take a bath and leave the Institution 'clean in appearance and dress'.[34] The managing committee now saw their future clientele as not only the poor in the Institution and the surrounding neighbourhood, but also the working class throughout the city. Tickets were available for benevolent people to purchase and give to 'fitting objects who must conduct themselves with propriety while using the facilities'.[35] Householders were urged to encourage cleanliness in their houses by giving tickets to their servants. The Institution's clientele could use all the facilities free of charge.[36]

The baths quickly became very popular, being 'universally adopted by the various classes of society' as people from all over the city and even some from the country came to use the baths at Usher's Island.[37] Saturday nights were particularly busy when the week's work was over and in preparation for Sunday. Shortly after the baths opened, a letter was received from a commercial assistant who suggested extending the closing time to 9pm on week nights and to 11pm on Saturdays. This arrangement would allow him and many of his colleagues to use the baths as the business houses did not close until 7pm on week nights and 8pm on Saturdays.[38] The managing committee agreed to make this change, although crowding on Saturday nights remained a problem. On 11 May 1852 the minutes record that the Institution could not be closed until after midnight on the previous Saturday because of the huge number taking baths. Many had to wait an hour, and several had to leave without getting a bath although they had paid for tickets. To meet the demand, it was decided to build two more first-class baths and to put a second male attendant on duty on Saturday nights.[39] The new service now had five employees: a stoker, one female and two male bath attendants, and a laundry mistress.[40]

Towards the end of 1852, the managing committee allocated an additional sum of £350, received from the estate of Sophia Ward, for the installation of five additional bathrooms 'of a superior description'.[41] These rooms were spacious and warm, which was considered essential after a bath and until a bather had finished dressing. Eight pence was charged for these superior first-class baths, while the regular first-class ones cost sixpence.[42] The Institution now had twenty-five baths, five superior first-class, four regular first-class, and ten second-class for male bathers. Although two first-class baths were now provided for women, the overall number of female baths was reduced to four, most likely because of the lower use of the baths by women. In the first year, out of a total number of 19,807 baths taken in the Institution, only 2539 were taken by women. The pattern was repeated in following years as can be seen in Table 10. The remaining two second-class baths were used by the clientele of the Institution. When the additional baths were completed, there were more than enough for the demands of Dublin public, except for late on Saturday evenings, which was still a very crowded time, and which the managing committee conceded would remain a problem. The wash-house was not as popular as the baths, but the managing committee hoped that the working classes, for whom it was intended, would learn to appreciate it, as English workers had done. In the interim, it was extremely useful for washing and drying the towels and sheets used in the bathhouse.[43]

Before long the managing committee was forced to make the first of what was to be a long series of complaints to the Corporation about the lack of water on several evenings, which had resulted in many people having to go away without a bath. The managing committee blamed the size of the supply pipe fitted by the Corporation for the problem and requested an extra supply of water to meet the needs of their extra baths.[44] An additional water tank had to be installed.[45] There were other problems, too. Local residents complained about the soot from the bathhouse chimney and the architect was called in to make adjustments.[46] One of the bath attendants was dismissed when a complaint was made that he had been 'shamefully inebriated' on duty and had insulted 'several respectable people' who had come to bathe.[47] Having quarrelled with them and ordered them to leave, he told them their time was up and threatened to put out the lights. The superintendent was forced to apologise to two gentlemen who complained, and a new attendant was appointed.[48] Bad behaviour was not confined to the male staff. The female bath attendant, Margaret Clark, was reprimanded for using 'language unfit to be heard' when arguing with the stoker about an overcharge of steam in the wash-house.[49] The number of towels that disappeared from the bathhouse was another on-going problem. Despite orders that the box for soiled towels should be locked, a press with a lock and key provided for clean towels, and the bath attendants should be fined when towels were missing, the problem persisted.[50] Finally, the superintendent was asked to take stock of the towels and to report monthly on all matters relating to the stock of the bathing and washing department.[51] Following complaints by the laundry mistress about her treatment by the male bath attendants, the managing committee reprimanded them severely and promised Mrs McAllister that she would be protected in future.[52] McAllister was soon in trouble herself when she sold one of the bathing dresses belonging to the bathhouse. Shortly afterwards, she left the Institution, having secured a better position. The former schoolmistress, Mrs Wade, was appointed in her place.[53]

A 'remarks' book was kept in the bathhouse and every obser-

Table 10: Usage of Mendicity Institution Baths in 1854

Bath	Male	Female	
First-class baths	2,776	104	
Second-class baths	7,125	970	
Third-class baths	12,123	1,614	
Free baths (male and female)			115
Total	22,024	2,688	115

Source: 37th *Annual Report,* p 9

vation was brought to the managing committee's attention.[54] Many comments were very favourable:

> I visited the baths here and found the accommodation in every way good and very good attendance from all the servants connected. They are much cheaper than in Scotland and I do not see how you can give the same accommodation for half the price. Robt Ireland, Broughton Cottage, Edinburgh (near Bellvue Crescent)[55]

> I am very much pleased with the arrangements and cleanliness of the bathrooms. Would suggest a printed notice being placed in each bath room recommending persons to take a warm bath *twice* a week as highly conducive to health and a preventive against disease!! Surgeon G F Whitely from Richmond, Surrey.[56]

> The Count de Barruel Beauvert has visited this establishment and considers it as creditable to its promoters as useful to the community.[57]

The Secretary of Chester Public Baths also praised the baths at Usher's Island on his visit in August 1852.[58] However, not all the comments were good:

> The idea of calling the bath I have had warm is quite ridiculous paid for a first-class ticket. James Dillon, 19 Bachelor's Walk.[59]

> I think that the price of the first-class baths is too high for the difference of the accommodation. T E Gamble.[60]

> The water is exceedingly dirty and full of mud and sand in the first-class baths otherwise extremely hot and comfortable. I M O'Toole[61]

A note underneath this last comment explained that the dirty water on that occasion was caused by heavy rain.[62]

Although they turned down a request from the Mechanics' Institute to reduce the price of first-class baths for its members, the managing committee allowed boys from the Chancery Lane Ragged School Dormitory and the Shoe Black and Ragged School, Strand Street, to use the wash-house free and the baths at half price provided they came early in the week. The managing committee suggested that the schools should pay a gratuity to the attendant in the wash-house for teaching the boys how to wash their clothes.[63]

Despite their popularity, the baths were not very profitable, making £77 5s 2d after expenses were deducted in 1854, when nearly 25,000 baths were taken. The less favoured washing department, where 589 people washed 16,500 articles during the year, also made very little profit: 306 people from the Institution used the wash-house free of charge and almost 42,000 towels and sheets were washed and dried for the bathing department.[64]

The managing committee continually tried to upgrade their establishment and were very proud of their first-class baths, believing them 'worthy of any individual's attention'.[65] Two first-class and one second-class showers were added in 1854.[66] In the first-class category, warm baths and showers now cost eight pence, cold baths and showers, fourpence; second-class warm baths and showers cost sixpence, cold baths and showers, threepence. There was also a third class where warm baths cost threepence, and cold, one penny. Particular attention was paid to cleanliness. In the first and second classes every bather got clean water and two towels; third class bathers got clean water and one towel. Use of a bathing sheet cost one penny; a bathing cap, one half-penny; a bathing shift, one penny; and a square of scented soap, one half-penny.[67] In the wash-house the charge was one penny plus soap. Everything else was free.[68]

The Institution had some distinguished visitors. During the Royal visit to Ireland in 1853, Prince Albert inspected all the facilities provided for the clientele and was very impressed with the baths and wash-house. The Institution received £75 from money donated by Queen Victoria for charitable purposes. The Lord Lieutenant, the Earl of Carlisle, also commented favourably on the neatness and cleanliness of the project when he visited two years later.[69] In November 1855 an inscription was placed on the plinth of the Institution:

The Usher's Island Public Baths and Wash Houses Mendicity Institution Open for the Street Beggar and Poor of Dublin.[70]

The baths and wash-house service was one of two unique services provided by the Institution. The second, the transmission service, is discussed in Chapter Eight. However, some of the original services were no longer provided. Both the schools and the dispensary closed in 1852.[71] All children of school-going age entering the Institution were now sent to local parochial schools to which the Institution paid an annual contribution of £2.[72] Under the Medical Charities Act, 1851 clients of the Institution were entitled to use local dispensaries, with the result that so few patients remained for Dr O'Flaherty that he queried the usefulness of continuing the dispensary service and finally retired from the Institution at the end of 1852.[73] The Institution continued to feed the casual poor of the city and a small number of regulars as social conditions slowly improved during the 1850s. The average number attending daily was rarely over 200 and for the most part remained around 150. Some received food for just one day and did not return. Others worked in the Institution until they could obtain work elsewhere or were admitted to the workhouse.[74] The managing committee still gave occasional assistance to the poor law authorities. In response to a request from a guardian of the South Dublin Union to admit poor people from the Union for one shilling and sixpence each weekly, the committee agreed to feed them for two shillings weekly. The Union also paid for an overseer.[75]

Senior staff members now coped with several jobs in the Institution, each of which had formerly been the sole responsibility of one person. Only three officers were employed by the Institution after 1854; the five workers in the baths and wash-house, a cook and sixteen servants comprised the rest of the staff.[76] Many staff members had a long family connection to the Institution. If they were ill, they had to find their own replacement, and family members usually stood in for them. If they died, those who had helped out were often made permanent in that position or given another job in the Institution in recognition of the long and faithful service given by their relative. This was a common practice in the workhouses and charitable institutions in the nineteenth century. Wives of staff members were also employed when a suitable job became available.[77] Charles Hale, now the resident officer, store-keeper and clerk of the knitting department and stone yard had been with the Institution since the beginning. His wife was appointed laundry mistress in 1855. Their son, Henry, became assistant clerk in the ticket office on Charles' death in 1860 and succeeded to his father's position the following year. Unusually, the gratuity that would have been due to Charles Hale at the end of the year was paid to his widow, reflecting the high opinion in which he had been held.[78] When Mrs Hale died in 1864, her sister received a gratuity of £3 to pay the medical and funeral expenses and an additional £1 for working as laundry mistress during Mrs Hale's illness.[79] Sons usually succeeded their fathers, but on one occasion when the resident officer resigned on the grounds of ill health, his wife was allowed to take over his position while retaining her own duties as laundry mistress. This was because her husband, although incapacitated, remained on the premises. On his death some time later, a male resident officer was appointed.[80]

After five years, the managing committee evaluated their bathing and wash-house service for the benefit of other towns that might be considering building similar establishments. Although there were now thirty-four baths, nine first-class, fourteen second-class, and eleven third-class, the demand was still so great at certain times that many applicants for second-class baths could not be accommodated. The managing committee concluded that the baths had contributed to the health and comfort of the inhabitants of Dublin, although the wash-house had not been used to any great extent. Neither service was self-supporting, as rent was not charged for the premises, and the staff involved also worked elsewhere in the Institution.[81] Any profit went to pay interest on the money borrowed to complete the project whose total cost was £2000. The baths had also saved Dublin Corporation from the expense of providing a similar facility for the public.[82]

Financially, the 1850s were good years for the Association, and the managing committee invested in government stocks whenever they had money to spare.[83] Rents proved to be a very lucrative source of income. Every yard and shed not required by the Institution was rented, and even waste ground found a tenant.[84] Wool, hay, cattle, old rags and iron were stored in the rented areas, the only stipulation being that no shed could be used as a slaughter house.[85] Although several of their oldest subscribers died in the 1850s, among them Lord Plunkett, Lady Elizabeth

Alexander, Luke White and C T Webber, the managing committee were very pleased with the support now received from the public.[86] The whole Institution was thoroughly repaired and the exterior dashed and painted in 1855. The dining hall was subdivided, one half remaining for diners, while the other half accommodated the applicants for temporary relief.[87] As it was thirty years since the opening of the premises at Usher's Island, this refurbishment was both necessary and timely.

The managing committee considered that the clientele was in good health and condition and content with the treatment given in the Institution. The committee claimed to feed the poor more cheaply than the guardians in the workhouses. They published economical and nutritious recipes as a guide for other institutions and prisons. (See Appendix E.) It is evident from Table 11 below that the amount of work undertaken by the Institution's clientele had decreased considerably by 1856. The continuing high number of women that had been a feature since the early years is also reflected.

In 1857 the Institution had a lucky escape. A resident on the opposite side of the Liffey saw flames through the old schoolroom window and raised the alarm before serious damage could be done. The police fire service put out the fire within an hour.[88]

Table 11: Classification of the Institution's Clientele in Week ending 9 August 1856

Class	Male	Female
1. Stone-breakers		4
2. Knitters		15
3. Nurses		4
4. Children of 2 and 3 above	6	6
5. Children at school	14	6
6. Yard department		10
7. Casual cases	16	83
Total	36	128

Source: Minutes, 12 August 1856

During the early 1860s the baths at Usher's Island were often closed because of lack of water. The supply was particularly bad at weekends when the baths frequently had to shut at 9pm, leaving many dissatisfied customers. The Institution lost money and good-will on these occasions. The managing committee continually complained to the Corporation who first attributed the shortage to a lack of water in the Grand Canal, although the Inspector of Water Works admitted that corporation workmen had cut off the water by mistake on one occasion.[89] Following further complaints, the water main in Marshall Lane that supplied the Institution was opened, but the problem persisted.[90] Eventually, a system of rationing was introduced. No third-class tickets were issued for cold baths on Saturdays during the summer as these took water away from the second- and third-class warm bath ticket holders.[91] John White was appointed plumber to the Institution to look after and report on all the pipes in 1868. Nevertheless, the Corporation complained of 'a fearful waste of water' in the Institution due to a lack of proper fittings and warned that if the situation did not improve the Institution would have to pay threepence for every hundred gallons of water used.[92]

Occasionally, there were other problems with the service. On one occasion the bath attendant and a lady taking a bath at 8.50pm were locked in the bathhouse in darkness and had to knock on the door for a considerable time before they were let out. The lady was very alarmed and threatened to write to the committee about the matter. The resident officer, Henry Hale, was warned to be more careful in future when he admitted that he had completely forgotten that someone was still bathing. There were also complaints about the colour of the water. A doctor who had recommended the baths to many of his patients reported that one of them found the water so dirty that she would not use the baths again. The attendant was reprimanded, and the baths were closed for two days while the tanks were cleaned.[93]

Ó'Grádá believes that the position of women, relative to men, improved in post-Famine Ireland. This may be reflected in a striking change that occurred in the gender profile of the Institution's clientele during the 1860s and 1870s. Whereas the number of both men and women using the services declined during the period, there was a significantly larger fall in the female clientele. In 1867, the number of men attending daily nearly equalled that of women for the first time; by 1875 the proportion of men to women in the Institution had risen to more than 2:1. Two events within the Institution in the early 1870s may have accelerated the pace of change: the superintendent's death in 1872 after forty years in the position; and modern experience suggests that women may have been more inhibited than men by the Committee's decision to distribute tickets to the public promising careful investigation of people applying for help from the Institution.[94] The higher proportion of men remained a permanent feature.

The Association now found it almost impossible to get people to serve on the managing committee. In the early years, it was considered a problem when between fifteen and twenty members of the sixty-strong managing committee attended weekly meetings, the quorum being set at seven. During the 1850s, membership gradually fell until there were only forty-three committee members elected in 1860, and this number had further decreased to thirty-six by 1865.[95] The last direct link with the founders and the early committees was broken when Surgeon Wright died in 1851 and George French in 1860.[96] Family members of those dedicated men continued to support the Institution, and new generations of La Touches, Orpens, Kinahans and Bartons served on the committee. However, meetings frequently could not be held because of the poor attendance, despite the reduction of the quorum to three members. Eventually, regular attendance was confined to clergy from the local parishes and one or two other members. Loyal committee members were highly prized and every effort was made to retain them. A case in point was Charles Gaussen, who served as joint honorary secretary for many years. When he submitted his resignation in June 1873 at the age of seventy-seven, the other committee members begged him to reconsider and persuaded him to remain on the committee. Although the other honorary secretary, Thomas Vance, had promised to do all the work, Mr Gaussen was immediately asked to draft the annual report.[97] He again attempted to resign in 1876 when he was eighty, but the committee replied 'they could not think of accepting his resignation or losing his valuable services'.[98]

Charles Gaussen died eleven years later following an accident at the 'patriarchal age of 92', while still in office.[99]

The Institution had always been fortunate in having hardworking, dedicated men in the position of honorary secretary. The position was so onerous that most years two men were elected to share the work. Two men died from fever while holding the office: Thomas Abbott, who died in 1837, was noted for 'his everyday intercourse with the Poor of the Institution for 17 years; the deep seated affection and respect which they feel for him, was evinced by the gloom and grief which pervaded the whole establishment on the tidings of his death'.[100] A public subscription fund was set up to erect a memorial to him in Christ Church Cathedral, which can still be seen today. In 1855 two ornamental pedestals were placed in the hall of the Institution, one in his memory and the other in honour of William Nugent Skelly, the author of the poem, *The Mendicity*, recorded in Chapter Six, who died in July 1852.[101] These pedestals did not survive when the Institution moved to new premises in 1954, although plaques in memory of William Nugent Skelly and Daniel Kinahan are fixed to the wall of the present-day dining room. Daniel Kinahan succeeded his father, also Daniel, on the managing committee in 1820 and served for thirty-nine years, many of them as honorary secretary. On 26 April 1859, the minute book recorded his presence and the lack of a quorum for a meeting. A pencilled note was added: 'This day DK complained of a pain in his groin and never attended after'.[102] Daniel Kinahan died some weeks later, having spent his life 'in doing good, relieving the poor and destitute, the aged and infirm'.[103]

The managing committee received a considerable shock in 1872 when a discrepancy was found in the accounts, following the sudden death of Mr Cottle, who had been superintendent of the Institution for over 40 years.[104] The firm of Craig Gardner and Co. who were called in to examine affairs found that a sum of £436 6s 8d was missing. Fortunately, considering his long service, the problem seemed to have arisen from carelessness due to Cottle's age and declining faculties, rather than to any lack of integrity. Nevertheless, the managing committee pursued his widow for the missing sum, eventually settling for £300 and payment of solicitor's fees.[105] However, the true financial status of the Institution remained uncertain, and the annual report for 1874 could not be published. A combined annual report for 1874 and 1875 noted the discovery of a serious fraud perpetrated by the office clerk, William Burke. It appeared that, for some time, he had been altering many of the cheques given to him for petty expenses and had stolen the balance.[106] A warrant was issued for his arrest, but he absconded and could not be found.[107]

The Lord Lieutenant, the Duke of Abercorn, suggested that a meeting should be held to discuss the rumours circulating in Dublin about the financial affairs of the Institution. Instead, the managing committee asked an accountant to audit the accounts for a three-year period from October 1872 to the end of 1875, to report any errors and to recommend a way of keeping books which would guard against such an occurrence in the future.[108] During this worrying period the organisational structure of the Institution was altered. Robert Purcell was appointed as secretary to the Institution and effectively became the secretary-manager and the most senior member of staff, with the superintendent as his second-in-command.[109] The accountant, Mr Hancock, discovered that a sum of £1,293 was missing during the period under review. A new set of books was opened and the method of bookkeeping he suggested was adopted.[110] This episode appears to have affected the Institution's relationship with the Lord Lieutenant and his successors: from the following year, they no longer subscribed to the Institution nor provided the Christmas dinner for the poor. Thanks to the generosity of the public who responded willingly to the managing committee's appeal, the traditional Christmas dinner continued to be enjoyed every year by over one thousand poor people. The rooms were always brightly decorated for this event and many visitors came to the Institution during the day, lending 'a cheery aspect to the surroundings'.[111]

In the 1870s when money was short some of the Institution's stock was sold to meet current expenses and the managing committee tried, once again unsuccessfully, to use the interest from the Clarence Fund for general rather than educational purposes.[112] Various economies were made in the Institution. Newpapers were discontinued as was the daily pint of milk for the committee, except on Tuesday. The resident officer's milk allowance was reduced to one quart instead of two. Clocks were no longer wound as the charge for winding them had been raised. The yardman was temporarily discharged as there was little work, and the salary of his wife, the cook, was reduced from seven and sixpence to five shillings weekly. Able-bodied people applying for relief were admitted at dinner-time only, except in bad weather; only destitute women with children and disabled people received two meals daily. Further relief was refused to any one who had already received help for fourteen days in a two-month period.[113] When it could not afford to help all those who applied, the Institution passed many on to other important Dublin charities such as the St Vincent de Paul Society, the Society for the Relief of Sick and Indigent Roomkeepers, or the Association for Distressed Protestants.[114]

Towards the end of the 1870s the financial situation of the Institution recovered, and the order excluding those who had received relief for fourteen days in two months was rescinded 'with a view to more extensively relieving the wants of the poor.'[115] The number applying to the Institution continued to be affected by the current economic and social situation in the country. Numbers rose steadily each year as 'the prevailing depression in the commercial world' caused many people to lose their jobs and apply for relief.[116] (Table 12) During the winter months, labourers were allowed out after breakfast to look for work. If they did not succeed, they returned to the Institution for dinner.[117] In 1879, the worst year for the country since the Famine, the Institution rose to the emergency and became 'a densely crowded lazar for many months', relieving 110,000 people, 45,000 above the previous year, 'very many being of the better class, and formerly able to maintain themselves and families in competence and respectability'[118] However, towards the end of the year when money was short because of heavy demand on the funds, it was decided to confine the help given to strangers to one day and to relieve Dublin people for one week in a thirty-day period. The 62nd annual report defined the role of the Institution for the members of the Association:

> The Poor House is generally the last resting place, next to his grave, for

> the miserable pauper; but the Mendicity Institution often intersperses midway in the dread descent, and by stretching out the hand of sympathy has saved many a one from sinking into a hopeless and helpless condition.[119]

The Institution received support during this busy period from the Mansion House Relief Committee, the Committee of the Dublin Charities' Fund, and the Richmond Fund, who were all involved in the enormous task of helping the Dublin poor.[120]

Table 12: Annual Clientele of the Institution 1877–1880

Yr	Men	Women	Children	Total	Daily Ave
1877	21,480	12,332	2,846	35,658	100
1878	42,022	17,745	4,452	64,219	176
1879	74,088	25,077	10,374	109,539	300
1880	71,903	21,938	9,454	103,295	283

Source: Annual Reports, 1877–1880

Although the baths at Usher's Island remained the only public baths in the city for many years, their popularity gradually declined. The managing committee considered closing them in 1871 when they were running at a considerable loss due to falling numbers and the high price of coal. Two years later the baths were still losing money, and the attendants were warned they might not be needed after 1 December 1873.[121] Thomas Dockrell made an informal approach to some members of the Corporation about the purchase of the baths, and the managing committee formally offered them to the Corporation in February 1874.[122] Despite an editorial and letters in the newspapers supporting this proposal, the Corporation declined to take this step.[123] The managing committee decided to keep the baths open because 'the poor have no such advantage elsewhere in the city and from a sanitary point of view these baths have proved eminently beneficial'.[124] During the 'commercial depression pervading the whole community' during the late 1870s and 1880s, the baths did badly, as few could afford even the reduced prices.[125] However, they were still highly valued by those who were working.

The managing committee described

> the feeling and satisfaction of the poor man, begrimed with the stains of his calling in forge or factory or workshop, after he has enjoyed a bath. He is all the better for the process, he looks better; he really is better, and he is enabled to bear his usual toil better.[126]

When other baths opened elsewhere in the city, the Institution's baths remained the only one in the vicinity of Usher's Island, and was 'a great boon to the artisan and working classes of that quarter.'[127] Eventually, the Corporation opened baths at the more centrally-located Tara Street, which took away many of the Institution's clients, including the Jewish community for whom a special bath had been provided at Usher's Island to comply with their ritual laws.[128]

The opening of other public baths and the introduction of bathrooms in modern buildings resulted in the baths at Usher's Island often operating at a loss at the turn of the century.[129] However, the managing committee persevered and installed new boilers for the baths in 1899 and new hot water pipes in 1905.[130] In January 1908, the weekly receipts of eleven shillings and two pence were the lowest on record.[131] A year later, in January 1909, it was decided to open the baths on Saturdays only, from 1-10pm, and two of the staff were let go.[132] The service limped on until the end of the year, when the receipts were four pence for the week before Christmas.[133] There was no formal proposal to close the baths. The service just petered out, bringing to an end yet another chapter in the history of the Institution and of the city.

CHAPTER EIGHT

The Mendicity Institution's Transmission Service 1818–1969

When the Association for the Prevention and Suppression of Mendicity in Dublin was established in 1818, it found that many beggars on the streets were non-residents of Dublin. Some had come with the hope of getting work in the capital, others because of the city's reputation for extreme generosity to beggars. There were also those who were stranded in Dublin unable to complete their journey home, having been returned from England by the authorities when they could not support themselves.[1] Often, entire families accompanied a sick member to Dublin from the country and had to beg in order to support themselves while the patient received hospital treatment. Children were initiated into begging in this way, and the Association strongly disapproved of national hospitals admitting patients from the country, 'who form no part of the poor of Dublin'.[2] The managing committee of the Mendicity Institution did not expect the citizens of Dublin to take responsibility for non-residents, nor did they think the Association's funds should be 'exhausted in the support of strangers'.[3] Their solution was to send these people back to their homes, and so the unique transmission service began.

Over 2,600 people were returned home by the Institution in the seven-month period from June to December 1818. Those fit for work were given paid employment for between one to four weeks, while their case was being examined. If they refused to work, their application for help was rejected.[4] Most of the non-national applicants were English, with just a few coming from Scotland.[5] In England, under common law, parishes had taken responsibility for their poor since the fourteenth century. The Elizabethan poor law of 1601 introduced the means by which relief would be granted, the origin of the rating system.[6] Under laws of settlement first introduced in 1662, a parish became responsible for supporting only the poor born within its boundaries and their dependants, and could remove and return to their own native place all those born elsewhere who might become a burden on the parish. During the eighteenth century many parishes joined with others to form a union of a viable size, which then took on the responsibilities of each individual parish.[7]

Once a person's right to support in an English union or parish was established, the Institution arranged passage to Liverpool for him and his family and gave them an allowance for food during the journey. The Dublin and Liverpool Steam Packet Co agreed to charge the Institution half fare for these passengers.[8] In later years, English people were sent to the port nearest to the place where they were entitled to live under the laws of settlement, again at a reduced rate. However, the Institution was unsuccessful in its attempt to get English railway companies to transport them cheaply for the remainder of their journey.[9] Those who came from further afield were sent to an English port where they could get a passage to their native country. France, Spain, Russia, Germany and America were among the final destinations of the many people helped by the Institution as the service expanded.[10]

Irish mendicants came from all parts of the country, but Ireland had no laws of settlement. Strictly speaking, the Institution's rule was that every one sent back to the country needed the guarantee of a householder to repay the fare to the Institution if he ever returned to beg in Dublin.[11] In practice, the Institution tried to ensure that people were known in the place to which they were going and had family or friends who could look after them if necessary. Irish steam packet and railway companies also transported Irish mendicants to their homes in the country at half price.[12] As few of these fares were ever repaid, the Institution bore most of the cost of returning strangers to their homes—a cost, the managing committee frequently pointed out, that was borne in England by the poor law authorities. Table 13 shows the pattern of transmissions and the cost of the service to the Institution between 1818 and 1832.

The Association's rota sub-committee, which was responsible for monitoring all applications to the Institution, could make recommendations regarding transmissions, but the sole responsibility for ordering them lay with the honorary secretary, 'as a check upon unreasonable or excessive expense.'[13] It was impossible to prevent fraud completely. As the managing committee regretted: 'money given to enable applicants to travel to the interior, has, too frequently, been applied to other purposes'.[14]

Once the initial large number of beggars was returned to their homes in 1818, the number of transmissions dropped considerably. The Institution refused to help 'many poor trades-people [who] applied to be sent to the manufacturing districts of England', and also refused women who wished to join their husbands already seeking work there.[15] The Association considered that its money would have been wasted if these people were sent home by the English poor law authorities when they applied for relief. In principle, the managing committee were reluctant to export destitute people who were unable to support themselves at home, although they felt this could be justified in the case of England

Table 13: Transmissions by the Institution 1818–1832

Year	Destination England	Destination Ireland	Total	Cost £. s. d	Amount repaid s. d
1818			2647	214 16 0	-
1819			526	49 15 0	-
1820			203	22 7 3	2 6
1821	37	48	85	9 7 6	10 10
1822			67	4 4 2	14 4
1823			323	33 5 6	13 4
1824	261	114	375	44 3 3	17 11
1825	78	67	145	16 13 9	7 6
1826	366	50	416	9 13 9	6 2
1827	386	216	602	54 12 0	16 0
1828	120	64	184	22 13 6	3 0
1829	260	214	474	53 19 6	10 6
1830	238	166	404	43 10 6	16 6
1831	65	47	112	16 6 0	4 0
1832	175	148	323	37 5 0	2 6

Source: Annual Reports of the Association, 1818–1832

where Irish labourers contributed so much to that country's growth.[16]

One of the persistent difficulties faced by the Association in trying to achieve its objective was the amount of alms-giving on the streets. The managing committee regularly asked the public to give up this custom and to support the Institution instead. The clergy preached frequent sermons on the evils of giving alms to beggars. In 1825 ten thousand bills were printed by the Association and distributed around the city requesting the citizens 'not to give alms in the streets as such only induces the country beggars to come into the city, and prevents those of the City taking advantage of the Mendicity Institution where all actual city beggars get food gratis, and work if able'.[17]

The scope of the service widened in the 1830s when it became evident to the managing committee that there was little hope of an improved future for many of their clients in the increasingly difficult economic climate in Ireland. When England's relatively new colony in Australia was seeking female immigrants, the committee conducted 'the most minute inquiries' into the demand for servants there, the usual wages for labour, the attention paid by the local government to immigrants on their arrival, and into the character of the person contracting to bring them out.[18] Having received satisfactory replies and 'having regard to the almost hopeless state as to *advancement in society at home*', the managing committee helped thirty of the best young women workers in the Institution to emigrate as servants to Van Dieman's Land (Tasmania) in 1833.[19] Most of these women had worked as nurses during the cholera epidemic of 1832. A special subscription fund was established to raise money for the venture as it was considered that the general funds of the Institution should not be put to 'procuring a *permanent* settlement for the poor.'[20] Many other female mendicants were interested in the idea of emigrating, but the managing committee could afford to send only seven more women in 1834.[21] Great care was taken to ensure the women would be well occupied during the voyage. They were given material to make clothes for themselves, some before sailing and the remainder while at sea. They also received religious and other instructive books to read on the journey and a 'respectable man and wife', passengers on the ship, were employed to look after them.[22] Letters of a 'very cheering, satisfactory and creditable character' were received in the Institution about these young women who had been

> *for several years* an *unwilling* burthen on the public bounty, and are now in the best spirit of honest independence, cheerfully endeavouring to better their own condition by seeking a livelihood by labour and industry, at the distance of many thousand miles from their native country.[23]

Two years later the managing committee co-operated with a tobacco manufacturer of Richmond, Virginia, in sending twenty-five boys, many of them orphans, to start new lives in America, having been told 'these boys will be well fed, get three suits of clothes in the year, a comfortable house to live in and every comfort they can wish for and when out of their time will be engaged at the least 5/- per diem. Can this be done in Ireland?'[24] The Catholic boys were given religious books and Protestant boys each received a bible and prayerbook at a cost to the Institution of £7 4s 1d. Richard Westmore, an orphan who had been in the Institution since he was four years old, wrote back frequently, relating the progress of the emigrants. His letters, the first from Liverpool, reflect the warm relationship many orphans had with the women who had cared for them and also with the staff in the Institution:

> Dear Sir,
> We take this favourable opportunity of writing to you to let you know we are all landed safely in Liverpool on Sunday morning last 21st instant. We are in the care of one Mr Langan who sees every thing done rightly for us. We get our 3 meals regular in the day, our breakfast at 9 o'clock, our dinner at 2 and supper at 7 o'clock. During our passage we were all used tolerably well by the Sailors. We slept in the Princes dock in the vessel called Governor Troop, in which we will sail to New York clean and comfortable. We made very good use of the money you gave us and did not leave it out foolishly. We will sail on Tuesday morning. We send our best thanks to Mr Cottle [the superintendent] and Mr Fullam [the clerk] for the trouble they took with us in seeing us out of Ireland. We most earnestly request you will send for all our separate friends and read this for them, viz, Mrs Dargan, Mrs Grundy, Mrs

> Ward, Mrs Maguire, Mrs Victory. Mrs Collins. John Collins requests you will let his mother know that he will write to his uncle in Philadelphia and we all request you will read this to the boys of our school to let them know how comfortable we are situated. Do not expect another letter until we land in Virginia when we will send you the full particulars. Tell our friends also not to fret, that if God spares our lives and gives us his grace we will return home prosperous men in the course of nine years. Dear Sir, I request you will tell Mrs Robinson not to fret for me for I will return please God home again and make her quite happy and comfortable.
> Signed: Richard Westmore
> I had not time to do it well so I pray excuse me.[25]

A second letter described the initial happy situation of the boys:

> My dear Sir,
> I take this favourable opportunity of writing these few lines to you, hoping you are in good health, as I am at present, thanks be to God for it, and to let you know of our good success. We had a very rough passage from Liverpool to New York of six weeks, sailing on the 24th August and landed on the 1st October during which we never expected to see Virginia, for our Captain was a very old man and he said as often as he went that voyage that he never saw such a rough sea. Our maintop mast was broken in two by the violence of the storm. We at length landed and on 6 September [October] we sailed from New York to Virginia, with a very pleasant passage of one week and landed on the 11th of September [October] where we are as happy and comfortable as our heart can wish us to be with Mr Allen in his Tobacco factory, who is a very good man and if we have good conduct we will come to be prosperous men in the course of 5 years. We are altogether in one factory, with numbers of negroes working around us. We also have all new clothes and get 2 meals in the day, but plenty of the very best he can buy, working 7 in the morning until 6 in the evenings twisting the tobacco and learning the art of the trade. We are so happy that not one of us would go back now for any consideration. I hope when you read this that you feel quite happy that we are so well off, after you taking such care of us. Read this for the following people Mrs Robinson, Mrs Grundy, Mrs Ward, Mrs Victory, Mrs Dargan, Mrs Reilly, Catherine Collins, Mrs Maguire—let her know that her son John Maguire ran away from us in New York and we know not where he is. Let the schoolboys hear this and Mr Herbert. Let Mr Graves know how well we are off. John Ward requests his mother to let his sister know how we

> are and if any more boys are coming let them not be dismayed but follow our example. We are quite sorry that Bernard Collins had such a misfortune as not to come and meet with such good luck, as we have. James Fox's thanks and best respects he sends to Mr O'Neill also Edward Power to Mr Fullam and I to dear Mr Graves for his kindness towards me in every thing that lay in the bounds of his power. I also send my thanks to Mr Cottle for his kindness to me. Let them all know how well we are. Let dear Mrs Robinson know especially how I am and send me word is she in good health. No more at present but send my love to you and her and all the other Gentlemen of the committee. I entirely forgot to let you know that Mr Allen is very well and has me in his office and says as soon as I learn the art of the trade he says he will make me an overseer of the factory.
> Signed: Richard Westmore
> NB Send me an answer by return of post as soon as is convenient to your honor how you are and all the other gentlemen of whom I write, also how all our friends are and especially Mrs Robinson. Send me an advice from under your hand and care directed as follows To the care of Mr Wallace Allen, Tobacco Factory, Richmond, Virginia, United States.[26]

Sadly however, two years later the picture was very different:

> Dear Sir,
> I hope you will excuse the liberty I now take in writing to you these few lines to let you know that the Messrs Allen treated us very bad, so much so that the Gentlemen of the City of Richmond out of mere charity towards us stated our situation before the Hustings Court, and had them summoned to answer for their ill treatment towards us. We were all taken away from him, and John Allen, Jun. was bound over to keep the Peace with us. There is a lawsuit now in the hands of Messrs Lusborough and Myers, two attorneys, who are suing Messrs Allen for damages for their horse whipping us so cruelly for merely speaking to them about the cruelty of their overseers and also of the bad feeding. Out of all that left Dublin the first time, better than one third are labouring in canals and such other places tossed about through the world without friends all through Mr Allen's means; a few in employment and the rest in none. For my own part, I had several comfortable situations engaged in writing and keeping Books, but as soon as Mr Allen came to hear of it he came and got me discharged on account of my keeping his Books for him the time I lived with him. Several others of us obtained services all of which through his means they were obliged to give up. We are now living every where we can for our boarding and

clothes alone. John Collins is learning the cigar making, James Collins, the Hatting, James Fox the same, these Mr Allen bound out himself being as he said too big and too old for him. I do not doubt but I and all of us could get very comfortable homes in other parts of the country but not having money sufficient to carry us we are obliged to remain where we are. The 2nd boys that came out are all living with a cotton Manufacturing Company, they are all pretty well to do, no regret, and are heartily sorry at hearing of Mr Thomas Abbott's death. But we still hope we have a friend in you and Mr Cottle. We wish Mr Cottle and Mr Fulham are well and in good health. We would be happy to hear of you getting your health and all the gentlemen that took trouble in our interest. We wish our friends and parents are in good health and hope to be remembered to them. I hope dear Sir if you think or find it no trouble to you that you will write a few lines letting us know if you received this letter for we have sent several but without any answer to them.

I remain your ever humble and obedient servant,
Richard Westmore

Direct your letter if you be pleased to write one, as we are not living with Messrs Allen now, to Richard Westmore, Richmond, Virginia, US. Tell Mrs Robinson, Mrs Dargan, Mrs Grundy, Mrs Collins, and Bernard to send letters and they will be received.[27]

Australia was again the destination for some young women from the Institution who were unable to get into the poor law workhouse in 1840. The managing committee were faced with a choice: 'to turn them adrift on the world or make some personal effort to save them from ruin'.[28] A fete champêtre to raise money for this purpose was held at the residence of the Chief Secretary, Viscount Morpeth, in the Phoenix Park. Unfortunately, the weather was bad and the event made little profit, but the Institution launched a special subscription fund that brought the total to within £3 of the cost of outfitting and sending the thirty-one young women to Australia at £4 18s 6d each. The following extensive list of new clothes and other articles was given to each young woman.

2 calico gowns	2 combs and a brush	Needles
8 shifts	4 caps	Thread
6 pairs stockings	2 wrappers	Tape
2 pairs shoes	Garters	Prayer-book
2 bonnets	Scissors	Bible and testament

2 flannel petticoats	A glass	Paper, pens and ink
1 black petticoat	Porringer	Pencils
3 aprons	Plate	Five shillings
5 towels	Can	Ten shillings for passage to Plymouth
2 sheets	2 spoons	
5 handkerchiefs	Knife and fork	
1 shawl	Bag to contain above	Knitting needles
1 stays	3 lbs soap	Pockets
1 coarse apron	1 lb starch	Black calico
1 bag	Blue	Smoothing irons
1 box	Pins	etc. etc. etc.[29]

In 1848, alarmed by the huge number of deserted and orphaned children being admitted to the workhouses, the government introduced a scheme to send suitable orphan girls to Australia where young unmarried women were urgently required. The managing committee arranged for five of the orphans remaining in the Institution to participate in this scheme. Jane Fitzpatrick, Jane Coote, Eliza Davis, Mary Anne Moloney, and Jane Gibney were outfitted by the Institution, each receiving the required 'trousseau' of six shifts, two flannel petticoats, two pairs of shoes, an appropriate bible, a psalm or prayer-book, and a wooden box made of good material with strong locks for her belongings. These girls sailed in August 1848 from the North Wall in Dublin in a steamer bound for Plymouth where their health, personal cleanliness and their possessions were subjected to close inspection before they were pronounced fit for the long journey ahead of them.[30] It is most probable that they sailed to Australia on the *Lady Kennaway* which berthed in Melbourne early in January, 1849. MacDonagh describes these emigrant passages to Australia as subject to a very high degree of state regulation and intervention. Consequently, immigrants usually arrived more disciplined and healthier than their North American counterparts. This was important as the initial weeks or even days after arrival were often decisive in the entire future of the immigrant; what happened or did not happen then was commonly determined by the character of the weeks or months at sea.[31]

Committees on which there were representatives of the Protestant, Presbyterian and Catholic churches were set up in Sydney, Adelaide and Melbourne, to look after the immigrants on arrival and care was taken that they would not be employed by persons of bad character. Robins says all the immigrants were rapidly hired, and many were later reported to be giving great satisfaction to their employers.[32] Although McDonagh says that Anglo-Saxon Australia did not regard immigrant orphan girls highly, it is to be hoped that the girls from the Mendicity Institution were among the great majority who, according to Robins, probably 'behaved well, gave satisfaction as servants, married and brought up their families in better and happier circumstances than mid-nineteenth century Ireland could offer them'.[33]

The managing committee continually highlighted the unfair situation of Irish people living in England for many years who, when they applied for relief from the authorities in the area where they were living, were returned to Ireland although there were no laws of settlement here. The managing committee complained that England was sending back 'broken down' labourers, having 'exhausted their strength and vigour'.[34] It was unfair that Irish labour had contributed greatly to England's wealth, yet Ireland, which had not benefited, had to support these labourers when ill, disabled or elderly. The managing committee described the horrific circumstances of Irish paupers in England:

> who were so constantly, and in many cases under circumstances of great hardship and cruelty, sent, even by force, from England; having been torn from their families, friends and home, to be thrown on the quays of Dublin, without any reference or regard to the excessively great misery and inconvenience resulting from landing a poor object at a central port, whose destination is frequently at either extremity of the kingdom.[35]

The managing committee condemned these 'cruel, if not illegal proceedings' and urged modification of the law that returned these emigrants back to Ireland.[36] Those who were not natives of Dublin were sent on to wherever the Institution had previously ascertained there would be some provision for them.[37] The committee claimed that, without this timely aid, hundreds of destitute and helpless people would have died on the streets of Dublin without food or shelter, unable to get relief at the workhouse.

This fact alone justified their appeal for the public's support, although the poor law was now in operation.

While thousands of Irish people travelled to England in search of work, the introduction of low fares on tramp steamers in the early 1840s encouraged unemployed English people to travel to Ireland with their families in the hope of finding employment. Many were unsuccessful and, having been reduced to 'the utmost possible distress', applied for help to the Institution.[38] Each case was strictly investigated. If genuine, the poor man and his family were transported to the port in England most convenient to their place of settlement, in as comfortable a manner as the Association could afford. The work test operated by the Institution proved effective in sorting out genuine cases for transmission. In 1845, 106 English people were transmitted but 118 other English applicants refused to work and therefore left the Institution.[39]

As the number of regular clients decreased once the poor law was in operation, the provision of food to the casual poor became the most prominent feature of the Institution's work with the transmission service second only in its usefulness, meeting 'a perpetual and continually recurring want.'[40] During the 1870s all applicants for transmission appeared before the managing committee, who were made aware of the changing needs of the poor. The transmission service took on a wider and more pro-active role.[41] After Catholic Emancipation the hospital service in Dublin expanded greatly with the building by religious orders of a number of modern hospitals. The managing committee now took particular satisfaction in helping destitute convalescents from the country, who could not afford the fare home when discharged from St Vincent's or the Mater Hospitals.[42]

During this decade there was a change in transmission policy. The Institution's transmission service now united families and helped wives and children to join their men who had gone to work in other parts of Ireland or abroad. It also helped people with a prospect of work elsewhere to take up the opportunity. The Institution undoubtedly must have facilitated the creation of dynasties of Irish working families in England in the nineteenth century. People who would never have entertained the idea of begging now applied to the Institution for help to improve their life chances elsewhere.

In the late 1870s, a great number of workers came to Dublin following the closure of mills and factories in England and Scotland. The number of transmissions rose significantly when many were unable to get the work they hoped for and applied to the Institution to help them return home.[43] England and Scotland were not the only final destinations for the Institution's clients in these years. Others were helped on their way to 'very distant homes', as Frenchmen, Spaniards, Russians, Germans and Americans applied to the Institution for help.[44] Some of these were shipwrecked sailors who 'begged their way to Dublin from the coast', and were sent to ports in England or Scotland where they would have some hope of finding employment.[45] Occasionally, foreign teachers unable to get pupils in Ireland and unemployed Irish teachers were helped to go abroad where their skills might be required.[46] The transmission service met a genuine need. As the managing committee remarked, 'no other institution in Ireland undertakes this kindly work'.[47] The Institution also saved many infirm elderly people from dying in the workhouse:

> Poor invalids form a touching and melancholy group. Their work is done, their days are drawing to a close, and instead of being confined to the infirmary or cheerless workhouse, they are sent to distant friends or relatives amongst whom there is good reason for believing they will find the needed sympathy and shelter.[48]

The transmission service became such an important feature of the Institution's work in the latter decades of the nineteenth century, that special books were kept to record the details of every applicant, whether successful or not. A bleak picture of a world without old age, widow's or disability pensions emerges from these books, which tell stories of destitute widows attempting to join sons or daughters for support in England or in other parts of Ireland. Having failed to get this support, some asked for help to return to their native place. One striking feature is the great amount of mobility among the poor; another is the number who applied to be sent to their birth place even after forty years away, in the hope that someone there would remember them and care for them; yet another is the number who went to join family members already established in America or Australia, many of whom sent money for the new emigrants. The Institution did not transmit people without investigation. Great trouble was taken to check details. Occasionally, people did not take up the offer of transmission, having secured employment or been offered help by relatives or friends in Dublin before the date of their passage. The transmission books highlight the importance of friendship among the poor who helped each other if at all possible, and confirm Burke's thesis that the tradition of spontaneous giving among the poor themselves ran deep in Irish society.[49] An extract from one of the transmission books shows the wide variety of applicants and their reasons for seeking help during two weeks in March 1885:

> Bridget Byrne, 33 and child aged 2 years are natives, she of Dublin. She was married some 10 years and went to England some time after. Her husband is a coach painter and was employed in different parts of England. She came from Loughborough last Saturday, her husband having sent her to his relatives—he had previously brought the child over and left her here with his brother. She is without any means and applies for transmission to Loughborough.
>
> Kate McDonnell, 22, is a native of Co Leitrim. She came from there some two years ago since when she has been at service. Her passage is now paid to America and she applies for transmission to Liverpool.
>
> Louis Borisov is a native of Poland. He came to Dublin some 3 weeks ago; he is a teacher. He is unable to get any employment and having no means he applies for transmission to Manchester.
>
> Catherine Gordon and child aged 3 years are natives of Scotland. She came from there some two months ago, expecting to find some of her relatives. Her husband died 12 months ago. She has been in the North Dublin Union since she came.
>
> Geo. Rogerson, 27, is a native of London. He is a seaman and was on board a ship from France to Galway; he met with an accident on board and was left in Galway. He is now on his way to London where his family are living.
>
> Mary Devlin and 2 children aged 3 years and infant are natives of

Dublin. She went to England some 7 years ago with her husband. He went to Glasgow to look for work. She came to Dublin 7 weeks ago thinking she would get work. She has no means and wants to return to Liverpool where she has a daughter living.

John Byrne, 28, is a native of Dublin. He went to England some years ago and was in the army for 9 years. He came to Dublin last week expecting to find his relatives. He finds they went to Australia and he now wants to get to London on his way to Natal having previously been assistant steward on one of the steamers running to South Africa.

James O'Shaughnessy and wife are natives, he of Limerick, she of London. They came from London a month ago looking for employment. They have no means and now want to return to London.

Patrick Byrne and 3 children, 10, 7, and 2 are natives of Kilkenny. He is a tinsmith. His wife went back there some time ago and he wants to go there.

Ellen Atherton, 19, is a native of Cork. She was married there to a soldier in the Rifles. His regiment is now quartered at Aldershot and is under orders for India. She has not the means to go to her husband and applies for transmission to Aldershot.

Martha Akin, 33, and 4 children, 9, 6, 3, and one year are natives, she of Ballymena. They have lived in Dublin for some years. Her husband who is a plumber went to Limerick last month and is now in permanent employment there. His family have not the means to go to him and they apply to be forwarded to Limerick.

Mary McGovern, 24, is a native of Wexford. She has lived in Dublin for some time. Her husband who is a bricklayer went to America some months ago and she has not heard from him since. She is a servant. Having a prospect of getting a good situation in London she applies to be sent there.

Sarah Bywater and 6 in family aged 16, 15, 13, 11, 7, and 5 years. She is a native of Co Wicklow. She went to England many years ago and was married there. They have lived in Dublin for 12 years. Her husband went to Cardiff last month and she wants to join him there.[50]

It is interesting to compare the early transmission books of the

1880s with those of the 1920s. An analysis shows that the number helped by this service had declined considerably by 1925 as had the proportion of children transmitted. In 1885 nearly one third of all transmissions were children, whereas children accounted for less than 15% of the total number transmitted in 1925. Persons classified as children were those travelling with a parent or guardian. On several occasions this category included persons of eighteen years of age. Of the women transmitted in 1885, 11% were described as deserted wives, nearly two thirds of whom travelled with children. Almost 5% of the women transmitted in 1925 were so described, one third being accompanied by children. Single women represented only just over one third of all women transmitted in 1885 compared with more than half of those transmitted in 1925. Interestingly, two single women were recorded returning home with their babies in the earlier period, but in 1925 there is no record of a single mother travelling with a new baby. Of the men travelling in 1885, nearly three quarters were single compared with just over one half in 1925. Table 14 describes and compares the pattern of transmissions in both years.

Dublin had a large floating population at the end of the nineteenth century. Any hint of available work in the city attracted workers to the capital from the country and other parts of the United Kingdom. Work began on the both the tramway and main drainage systems during this period and hopeful workers crowded into the city.[51] Those unable to get work applied to the Institution for help and the Institution did not fail them 'when no friend [could] be found to forward them on their way'.[52] During the early years of the twentieth century English and Scottish mechanics and labourers continued to come to Ireland when trade was slack at home, and many applied to be returned home by the Institution, if unsuccessful in their search for work in Dublin.[53] When the baths closed in December 1909, feeding poor people and transmitting strangers were the remaining services provided by the Institution.

During World War I all but one of the railway and shipping companies withdrew the half-fare concession and charged the Institution full fare for transmission cases. As many of these were going to well-paid jobs as munition workers in English and Scottish factories, the managing committee decided to pay only half

Table 14: Transmissions by the Institution in 1885 and 1925

	1885		1925	
	N	%	N	%
Gender				
Men	149	32.1	91	49.7
Women	164	35.5	65	35.5
Children	150	32.4	27	14.8
Total	463	100.0	183	100.0
Nationality				
Irish	378	81.8	154	84.1
English	67	14.5	22	12.1
Scottish	11	2.1	5	2.8
Other	7	1.6	2	1.0
Total	463	100.0	183	100.0
Destination				
Ireland	239	51.6	84	45.9
England	188	40.7	80	43.7
Scotland	36	7.7	19	10.4
Total	463	100.0	183	100.0
Marital status of all women				
Single	57	34.8	34	52.3
Married	66	40.1	20	30.7
Widow	23	14.1	8	12.3
Deserted	18	11.0	3	4.7
Total	164	100.0	65	100.0
Marital status of women with children				
Single	2	2.8	-	-
Married	46	40.1	8	88.9
Widow	12	16.9	-	-
Deserted	11	15.5	1	11.1
Total	71	100.0	9	100.0
Marital status of men				
Single	107	71.8	49	53.8
Married	38	25.6	37	40.7
Widower	4	2.6	5	5.5
Total	149	100.0	91	100.0

Source: Transmission Books of the Mendicity Institution

of the fare in future for these workers, but continued to pay full fare for all other transmission cases.[54] At the Annual General Meeting in 1921, it was decided to ask the railway and shipping companies to revert to the long-standing arrangement of carrying passengers from the Institution for half-fare as in pre-war days. Eventually all the lines agreed to this proposal. In March 1922 the Burns and Laird Line, which had continued to give the reduction throughout the war on the route to Glasgow, withdrew that concession owing to the depressed state of its business and the high cost of running expenses. When the situation improved for this firm in the following year, it generously renewed the concession to the Institution.[55]

The unique transmission service continued to be widely used. The Institution reported among the applicants many 'distressed persons of the better sort, teachers, governesses, artisans, foreigners and others of the industrial class'.[56] Other applicants came from the Iveagh Hostel and other hostels around the city. Societies such as the Central Mission, the Soldiers' and Sailors' Help Society, and the Protestant Orphanage Association sent people to the Institution for transmission. Clergy of every denomination also referred people in need of the service to the Institution.[57]

Occasionally, committee members asked that certain applicants should be treated as special cases, as when Rev Thomas Irwin recommended Bernard Hawkes, who received a sum of £28 14s towards the fare to Canada for himself, his wife and two children. Mrs Cooper of Foxrock received £7 towards her fare to America at the suggestion of Rev J Tobias. On Canon Monahan's recommendation, £5 was given to Mr Sherman towards his passage to America, the Canon offering to try to raise more.[58] Sometimes, the Institution paid the fare for people travelling from London to Dublin, as in the case of Agnes Fox, who was recommended by Mrs Ida Monahan of the Hotel Pelletier, Harcourt Street. In the case of Mr Cassidy, who was unemployed in London but had a chance of a job as sexton of Clontarf church, the managing committee asked the London Mendicity Association to help. However, the London Association replied that it was not in their province to pay the fare from England to Ireland.[59]

The service did not always run smoothly. Frequently, people

did not turn up at the boat and the Institution found it difficult to get refunds for the tickets. When the managing committee approved the transmission of the Hicks family to London in November 1926, Mr Hicks refused to go. Despite his wife's desire to go and a visit from Canon Monahan, Hicks remained obdurate, so the managing committee decided not to take any further action in the matter.[60] When the applications for transmission in January 1927 by Patrick Fegan and his son of Usher's Quay and Richard Canavan were successful, they did not avail of the opportunity. Instead, Fegan called to the Institution and asked for money. When his request was refused, none of the trio appeared again. On another occasion, the superintendent prevented two sailors from changing their tickets for cash. In June 1928, a man called Burke applied to be sent to Clitheroe where he wanted to work. He produced a letter purporting to be from an official at the local Water Board where the Institution had sent many other applicants over the years. In this case the letter turned out to be a forgery, and the police were notified.[61] In November 1931, a woman whose application for transmission to London had been successful was arrested before she could leave for larceny of a gold ring and some clothing, the property of her late mistress. Following the transmission to Colne Valley of a man named Calvert who had represented himself to the managing committee as single, his wife complained that he had deserted her and asked for assistance. Unable to help, the managing committee advised her to write to the British Legion, who had recommended her husband for transmission.[62] When Rev E L B Barker proposed the transmission of Mrs Lloyd and her three children to Cleethorpes, the managing committee asked him to ascertain the extent of the help friends in England were prepared to give them and if they would support them until they got employment. This case was a particularly worrying one as Mrs Lloyd was very delicate and the children practically illiterate.[63]

Occasionally, exorbitant demands were made on the service. In 1927 the Council of the St Vincent de Paul Society asked the Institution to pay the fare to Trinidad of £35 for Dr Forrester of Rathgar. When the managing committee agreed to pay a small sum towards the fare, they were immediately asked how much.

The answer came with equal speed: 'To Southampton, and no further'.[64]

Financial problems caused the suspension of the service in October 1939 except for young girls and very urgent cases. The managing committee debated giving up the service completely, and a week later all applicants were informed there were no funds available for transmission. Despite this decision, the managing committee continued to consider applications and an occasional one was granted, particularly if the applicant had a promise of work.[65] An example was the transmission to Belfast in December 1939 of a man who was enlisting in the RAF.[66] Some transmissions were more difficult than others. Patrick and Bernadette Rogers applied in February 1940 to be returned to their native Tory Island in Co Donegal, from whence they had come to Dublin in search of work. However, as there was a political charge against Patrick in Northern Ireland, he could not be sent home through Belfast.[67] The managing committee did not always have to bear the full cost of these later transmissions. Occasionally, the Public Assistance Board, the Dublin Union Outdoor Relief Office, or the St Vincent de Paul Society paid part of the fares. The first permanent chairman of the managing committee, William Boydell, whose family had been connected with the Association since the end of the nineteenth century, personally took responsibility for paying the fares of many people once their transmission was approved by the managing committee.[68]

The Institution could afford to transmit only twelve people between 1941 and 1953. Between 1954 and 1968 there were no transmissions. The final entry in the transmission book, made on 16 October 1969, noted that Paddy Power, aged 23, unemployed and living in the Iveagh Hostel, applied for the fare to Navan Hospital, where he had a letter of admission for an operation. However, a note beside this last entry reads: 'Cancelled; did not turn up at the bus', thus bringing to an end another unique and valuable service of the Mendicity Institution.[69]

CHAPTER NINE

The Institution in the Twentieth Century

TWO FACTORS WERE INSTRUMENTAL in changing the profile of the Mendicity Institution in the twentieth century. Political unrest abroad and at home and increasing state intervention in the lives of the poor affected the operation at Usher's Island considerably. The number of male applicants to the Institution fell in 1900, as men enlisted in the army to fight in the Boer War.[1] For the first time in nearly forty years the proportion of women in the Institution increased, rising from 1:3 to more than 1:2 men. Table 15 describes the average daily attendance of 122 people in September 1900.

Male applications increased by 6,000 during the following year when soldiers invalided home from South Africa were unable to work and sought the Institution's help. At the end of the war reservists returned home and created extra demands on the overstretched employment situation in Dublin. Again many who could not find work came to the Institution with their families.[2] The size of these families, often nine or ten, strained the Institution's finances, and it was soon in debt. The interest on the Institution's investments, mainly held in government funds, had seriously decreased. In 1904 the bank was owed £217, and the committee were forced to make several decisions:

Table 15: Average Daily Attendance in September 1900

	Male	Female
Yard department	3	3
Casual cases	72	42
Children	1	1
Total	76	46

Source: Minutes, 11 September 1900

1. To confine the number admitted daily to 150;
2. To reduce the expenditure on the Christmas dinner by £10;
3. To supervise transmissions more closely.[3]

When these decisions were made public, the *Irish Times* newspaper established a fund-raising campaign, a 'shilling account', which raised £180 for the Institution in six weeks. This sum enabled an increase in the number of daily admissions for a short period, but less than three months later it was again necessary to restrict admissions to 150.[4]

Oat bruising was carried on in the Institution until 1909. The managing committee were approached on several occasions by a committee interested in setting up a labour yard to provide the poor of the city with employment. As the operation of the Institution needed all the space available on the premises, the managing committee did not co-operate in this project.[5] A profile of 148 people attending daily in January 1906, shown in Table 16, highlights the return to the higher proportion of men in the Institution.

In the early years of the twentieth century the Association publicly acknowledged the change that had taken place in the Institution's role, stating that it no longer contemplated 'maintaining the helpless and hopeless mendicant who can find a shelter in the poor house'.[6] Acceptance of this change was facilitated by increasing state intervention in the lives of the poor. 'Systematised help and assistance for the necessitous poor', such as the introduction of old age pensions in 1908 for those aged 70 years of age who were in poor circumstances, relieved the Institution of being the sole support for many of Dublin's elderly poor.[7] The old age pension was the first assistance scheme, outside the poor

Table 16: Average Daily Attendance in January 1906

	Male	Female
Yard department	3	3
Casual cases	108	29
Children	3	2
Total	114	34

Source: Minutes, 2 January 1906

law, where benefit was payable without proof of utter destitution.[8] The Association believed the Institution's role of providing emergency relief to people in temporary distress was a positive and valuable one. Many Irish people had a strong antipathy to the workhouse, and the relief given by the Institution saved many from entering that dreaded place.[9] Not everyone agreed. Williams, a contemporary writer, suggested that it would be better to send people abroad where they would be more likely to prove useful members of society than to spend the same amount in giving them free breakfasts and dinners for a few weeks, 'leaving them a rung or two lower down on the social ladder at the end of that time, and more unfitted to make a fresh start'.[10]

During the lock-out in 1913, it was believed the number of men applying to the Institution fell because the Transport Union supplied their members with food. The fall in numbers was not as great as it might have been. Many men and women, although not sympathising with the strike, were thrown out of work and thankfully availed of the Institution's help.[11] During World War I, 1914-18, the Institution's work was again considerably lightened as men enlisted in the army, more employment became available in the city, good wages were

Table 17: Annual Attendance 1912–18

Year	Men	Women	Children	Total	Daily Average
1912	31,081	10,473	1127	42,681	117
1913	29,094	10,507	1008	40,609	112
1914	23,790	9,450	873	34,153*	94
1915	20,075	10,255	730	31,060	85
1916	13,231	8,743	735	22,709	63
1917	12,012	8,736	736	21,084*	58
1918	10,314	7,740	645	18,699	52

* Note: *Sic,* however, the correct totals for 1914 is 34,113, and 1917 should be 21,484

Source: Annual Reports of the Mendicity Association, 1912–18

paid, and there was more money in circulation. Allowances made to soldiers' wives and families saved many from applying for regular help, but in times of temporary poverty, due to illness or some other emergency, the Institution was still called upon for relief. As Table 17 shows, the proportion of women to men increased again during these years. The fall in the number of children attending was due to the provision of breakfast or dinner in the parochial schools.[12]

On 25 April 1916 the Institution's minute book records:

> Owing to the disturbances in the City during Easter Week there was no meeting of the Committee and no business was transacted. On Easter Monday April 24th, the Sinn Feiners, 25 in charge of one of their officers [Sean Heuston], entered the Institution by the side entrance, the principal entrance being closed on account of its being a holiday. The poor people had been admitted and were at their dinner in the dining-hall. They immediately proceeded to drive them out. They next turned their attention to the occupants and servants of the Institution; the superintendent with his family live on the premises and they were driven out at the point of a bayonet, not being allowed to carry anything with them.[13]

A fierce battle was fought between the group who had taken over the Institution and a battalion from the Royal [later Collins] barracks on the opposite side of the River Liffey. The defence of the Mendicity Institution has been described as 'one of the most glorious episodes of the Rising'.[14] The insurgents held out for three days against 'the onslaught of well-trained, fully equipped and experienced English soldiery' before Captain Heuston surrendered in order to save the lives of his men.[15] 'The House was considerably injured' as a result of this incursion.[16] For three weeks meals were not served and the committee did not meet, although transmissions continued. The bank pass book was mislaid in the confusion but was found several weeks later. The government awarded the Institution a sum of £286 15s 9d in compensation for the damage, although the full cost of repairs was £391 9s 10d. Superintendent Holohan received £6 from the managing committee to compensate him for having to take lodgings elsewhere with his family.[17]

Links with the old days of the Institution were frequently broken during these years as staff and managing committee members grew old. Robert Purcell, the first secretary-manager of the Institution, retired in 1916 after forty years service because of illness. In his letter of resignation, Purcell remarked that no one now remained in the Institution from the time when he began his employment in 1875. The managing committee considered his departure a serious loss to the Institution: his efficiency and integrity had ensured the operation was in safe hands. When his job was advertised, a resolution was passed: 'Lady candidates are ineligible for appointment to the secretaryship of the Mendicity.'[18] Before applicants could be interviewed, Purcell asked the managing committee to withdraw his resignation as he had recovered from his illness. The managing committee were only too delighted to agree, but less than five months later the minutes recorded the death of Robert Maxwell Purcell.[19] Following tradition, Purcell's son stood in for his father during his illness and for some time after his death, until the appointment of his successor, H F Campbell.[20]

In 1917 programmes of modernisation and economy were initiated by the managing committee. The kitchen fittings were declared hopelessly out of date, and the secretary was asked to make arrangements for the renovation and refitting of the dining hall with a gas stove and boiler. June 1917 saw the inauguration of gas cooking in the dining hall.[21] The diet provided in the Institution in the early years of the twentieth century was stirabout and milk for breakfast and bread and soup made from ox heads for dinner. During an inspection of the kitchen in 1917, the stirabout was found to be improperly cooked. An order was given that the rice should be steeped separately and for a longer time than the Indian meal, and water should be added, as the sample tasted was stodgy and insufficiently cooked. The bread order was reduced by five loaves a day, and each loaf divided into six portions instead of four. The milk order was not to exceed five gallons a day, and was reduced to four gallons later in the year.[22]

The last link with the bath and wash-house service was broken with the sale of the lead and brass fittings of the old baths. An offer of £75 for removing twenty-two reclining baths, one Jewish bath, the pipes, fittings, and wash tubs in the laundry was accepted on condition that the buyer put back the flooring once the baths were removed. Henry Harden, a committee member, purchased four dressing room cubicle doors.[23] In a further move towards economy, an advertisement offering bones for sale was placed in the newspapers. The initial tenders were considered too low, but the managing committee finally accepted a tender of eight shillings per hundredweight, noting with satisfaction that the successful firm had raised its original offer by one shilling per hundredweight.[24] An estimate of twenty-five shillings for the repair of the Institution's barometer was regarded as too high, and the secretary was asked to have the instrument valued with a view to selling it. An offer of twenty shillings from the optician who had given the estimate for repairing the barometer was refused, and the matter was dropped.[25] The decision, discussed in Chapter Eight, to pay only half-fare for the transmission of munition workers to England and Scotland, was implemented at this time.[26]

The first National Insurance scheme in Ireland, providing for sickness and unemployment benefit for insured workers, was introduced in 1911. In 1917 it became necessary for the Institution to contribute towards insurance stamps for its employees. A sub-committee was appointed to report on the staff of the Institution. This committee suggested that the superintendent should act as caretaker to the Institution. There was no need to have a separate official for this duty, especially as the present incumbent was a woman. If the post could not be abolished immediately, the sub-committee recommended that it should be allowed to lapse when a vacancy occurred. It was suggested that the hall porter be kept on until he qualified for the old age pension. He had worked for the Institution for thirty-five years, having been in charge of the baths until that service ceased, and was now too old to get another job. The sub-committee found no reason to retain the furnace man as he had no duties since the gas supply had been connected to the Institution. The cook and the yardman were necessary officials, but the sub-committee recommended that the gardener should apply for the old age pension. Any duties 'real or imaginary he is supposed to perform could be done by the yardman or one of the casuals'.[27] The sub-committee disapproved of the system by which the staff received part of their wages in rations, and recommended that rations be withdrawn and wages increased to make up for the withdrawal. They recommended that clients should be given the same quality of food as staff, who appeared to keep all the meat for themselves, the clients receiving the water in which the meat was boiled. 'The oxheads should in future be cooked until the meat on them falls off in rags and becomes part of the soup, and not merely until the meat is boiled to a turn for the officials to eat as at present.'[28] When the staff objected to this curtailment of their rations, the cook's wages were increased from £4 6s to £6 weekly and those of the yardman from £2 9s to £4 weekly. The remainder of the staff was refused an increase, and the managing committee insisted that the ruling on rations was to stand.[29]

There was some disagreement among committee members when a resolution was passed to discontinue the annual subscription to St Audoen's Parochial schools paid in respect of children whose parents attended the Institution. Notice was given of a motion to rescind the resolution. When a vote was taken, this motion failed. Two of the members abstained, and Rev Thomas Byrne entered a protest and another motion to rescind the resolution. Finally, the subscription was discontinued.[30]

The managing committee had continued the long-standing policy of investing legacies or bequests received by the Association. During the early years of the century they also invested money whenever the balance in the bank was more than the amount needed for immediate use.[31] In March 1919, an investment fund was created to provide for much-needed repairs to the premises, to be done when the price of labour and materials fell to pre-war figures. By the end of 1919 there was £750 in the fund.[32] The price of labour and materials did not fall as had been hoped, and investment for future repairs continued during the next two years, as the managing committee continued to economise in the day-to-day business of the Institution.[33] The minutes of 15 December 1920 record: 'In as much as the present cost of management is 30/- for every 20/- spent on the poor, the committee could not consider giving the secretary a rise.'[34] He was granted a temporary bonus in monthly instalments for the next year. After the establishment of the Irish Free State in 1922, many investments made on behalf of the Institution were placed in the new Irish National Loans.

With the closure of the baths and wash-houses in 1909, the transmission service and the provision of meals twice daily were the only services given by the Institution during the next three decades. The managing committee decided it was time to upgrade the quality of the meals service. Various schemes were tried on a temporary basis: Bovril was introduced into the diet on 16 January 1918 and remained on the menu for many years.[35] Meat and potatoes were added to the dinner menu in March 1922. Mrs Campbell, the secretary's wife, apportioned the following quantities to be served to each person: ˘ pound of meat, 3 potatoes and a large piece of bread. The superintendent was given an extra five shillings each week to compensate him for the additional work incurred by the change in the menu. Following a satisfactory month's trial, the system was adopted permanently.[36] Another experiment, which did not last, replaced oatmeal with cocoa and bread for breakfast for two months in 1924.[37]

The minute books continued to reflect events in the world outside the Institution. On 14 April 1920 when the city was disrupted by demonstrations in support of political prisoners on hunger strike in Mountjoy prison, a brief note remarks: 'In consequence of the hunger strike there was no meeting of the committee.'[38] On 28 June 1922, the minute book records: 'There was no meeting of the Committee owing to the disturbed state of the city due to *bombardment* of *Four Courts*.'[39] The Civil War had begun. During the celebrations for the centenary of Catholic Emancipation in 1929 and again in 1932 during the Eucharistic Congress, the St John's Ambulance Brigade manned a first aid station at the Institution.[40] On the first occasion, the superintendent was reprimanded for spending £1 on decorations without permission and warned that no unauthorised expenditure would be reimbursed in future.[41] The International Eucharistic Committee was also given permission to erect a 'temporary attachment' to the Institution free of charge for the duration of the Congress in 1932.[42]

The unsettled and difficult economic situation in the struggling new state brought many newly unemployed people to the Institution for help during the 1920s. The increase in the number of applications and in the number of meals provided continued throughout the decade as unemployment and the price of most commodities continued to rise. In 1923 it was agreed that the upstairs dining room could be made available with light for any charitable purpose. However, when the Kingsbridge branch of the National Union of Railwaymen offered to pay £10 per annum for the use of a room with light and a fire in which to hold twice-weekly meetings, the offer was refused on the advice of the Institution's solicitor that the Institution would be rated for the room rented to the Union.[43]

In January 1924, solicitors for P Hamilton Reid offered to sell the leasehold of the property at Usher's Island to the Association for a sum of £1600, equivalent to twelve years of the net annual rent he received. Before making a decision, quotations for valuing the site were sought from three auctioneering companies.[44] Battersby and Co's quotation of five guineas was accepted, and on the basis of their valuation, the Association made an offer of £1500, which was refused. The Association would not increase the offer, and the leasehold was sold the following year to Timothy Woods of 11 Parliament Street.[45]

The Association did not focus its attention solely on the Institution, but considered the wider issue of social conditions in the city. At the Annual General Meeting in 1925, it reported that the number seeking help in the Institution had doubled during the past year, applications having risen by 26,000 due to unemployment and labour troubles. The Association warned that the effects of the government's industrial policy would not be seen for years, and there was very little prospect of employment for all the people presently out of work. Canon McGill, a committee member, observed that unemployment in the city was aggravated by the number of children who left school untrained, without any prospect of work before they were sixteen years of age. He recommended that children should not be allowed to leave school before that age unless they had a job, and suggested that the government could easily spare a few thousand pounds to help those growing up.[46]

The clientele continued to be predominantly male. Of the daily average of 242 meals provided by the Institution in 1925, 216 were served to men.[47] That year the cost of supplying breakfast and dinner for one week to 1,500 clients was:

	£.	s.	d
Bread	1	15	0
Meat	4	0	0
Potatoes	1	1	0
Bovril		2	7
Oatmeal	1	5	4
Milk	3	10	0
Total	11	3	11

The secretary calculated that this was equivalent to a fraction less than 2 pence per client per week.[48]

In 1927, following complaints from the superintendent about the quality of the meat served for dinner, Mrs Campbell, the secretary's wife, was asked to inspect the kitchen. She reported that she had visited the kitchen without notice being given to the staff or the contractor, and found the meat to be of excellent quality and the cooking extremely good. She had only one recommendation to make: that less water could be used to produce a thicker soup. The apportionment she had made in 1922 was still in force and, in her opinion, could not be improved. She also noted that the utmost cleanliness was observed and each meal was served steaming hot.[49] When the Mother Superior of a nearby convent inspected the dining arrangements in the Institution at the request of the managing committee, she found the dining-hall in reasonable condition but recommended that the floor should be covered in oilcloth, which could be easily cleaned. She also considered that the cook needed more instruction in her duties, the clients should be given tea at breakfast-time, and bacon and onions should be added to the dinner menu.[50]

Occasionally there was trouble in the dining-hall during meals. In November 1929 the superintendent prosecuted two men, who were bound over to keep the peace. As a result of this episode, the managing committee consulted the Garda authorities, and two gardai were placed on duty during meals for some time afterwards.[51]

When superintendent Holohan died, he was succeeded by his nephew, Sergeant James Tiernan, on condition he provided a home on the premises for his aunt, the late superintendent's widow.[52] This generous gesture caused a problem as Mrs Holohan's family lived with her and they occupied four rooms in the Institution. After some years, the managing committee decided that at least one of these rooms should be given to superintendent Tiernan, and that the Holohans' coal allowance should cease. When the family objected to this arrangement, the committee suggested that they become proper tenants at a rent of twenty shillings per week.[53] Mrs Holohan fell behind in paying the rent in 1930 and received notice to quit her accommodation. However, the committee relented and granted her accommodation on the premises for her lifetime, provided that her sons did not live with her.[54]

In the continuing programme of modernisation, it was decided to update the original rules of the Association. A new scheme was drawn up by the Commissioners of Charitable Donations and Bequests and approved by the High Court in 1930. William C Boydell, Henry Harden, Rev William Plunkett Webb, and Rev Ernest Maunsell Bateman became the first trustees for the Institution under the new scheme. The number of members of the board of management was fixed at no fewer than seven and no more than twelve: nine ex-officio members—the trustees, and clergy representing local parishes—and one nominee from each of three charities, the Society of St Vincent de Paul, the Association for the Relief of Distressed Protestants, and the Dublin Presbytery in connection with the Presbyterian Church in Ireland.[55] The Church of Ireland and Roman Catholic Archbishops of Dublin and the Dean of St Patrick's Cathedral agreed to become vice-presidents of the Association.[56]

Two families had a long association with the managing committee during the twentieth century, one of them maintaining a link with the nineteenth-century Institution. James Boydell joined the managing committee in 1898, became a trustee and and remained an active member until his death in 1920, when the minutes record that he had taken 'a great interest in the patient work of this Institution. His long experience of the city made him a wise counsellor, and his kindness of heart endeared him to those associated with him in the work.'[57] He was succeeded by his son, William C Boydell, MA, who became the first annual chairman of the managing committee in 1926.[58] Up to that time, the chairmanship of each committee meeting rotated among the members. William Boydell rendered great service to the Association, and his remarkable generosity to candidates for transmission has been described.[59] He drafted the new constitution and bye-laws for the Association, and in his customary generous fashion, contributed £50 towards the legal expenses for drawing up the new scheme.[60] After many years as chairman, he was elected Honorary Secretary, in which position he remained until his death in 1963. His son, Major Derek Boydell, OBE, was elected to the committee on his father's death, and became chairman three years later. He remained a committee member until his death in 1995. Two members of the Tennant family also gave long service to the Institution. William Tennant was elected to the committee in 1951 and was chairman between 1953-66. He was a hard-working member and a trustee of the Association until his death in 1979. His son, Richard, joined the committee in 1985, became president in 1991, and remained in that position until his death in 1996.

The new bye-laws drafted by William Boydell came into effect in December 1930:

1. Weekly meetings shall be held on Wednesday.
2. The Annual General Meeting shall be held no later than 15 February.
3. Subscribers of £1 per annum shall be entitled to vote in elections.
4. Audited accounts shall be presented annually.
5. A chairman and a vice-chairman shall be elected at the first meeting of the managing committee after the Annual General Meeting.
6. The chairman shall have a vote, and a casting vote, if necessary, at the Annual General Meeting and meetings of the trustees.
7. The quorum for committee meetings shall be three members and for meetings of the trustees, two members.
8. At the first committee meeting each month two members of the committee shall be appointed as visitors to inspect the Institution and the work of the staff during the month.
9. The committee shall have the power to co-opt members to the committee when a vacancy occurs.[61]

From the establishment of the Institution in 1818, the managing committee met on Tuesday afternoon at 3pm. The first alteration in this arrangement came in 1902 when the meeting time was changed to Tuesday morning at 10.30am. In 1916, the time reverted to 3pm and the day was changed to Wednesday. For a period of four years during the 1920s, meetings were held on Fridays at 2.30pm to suit some members of the managing committee. Wednesday became the meeting day again in May 1927. In December 1943, a decision was taken to hold monthly meetings in future on the first Wednesday of each month. The meetings of the present committee of management are held in the Institution on the second Wednesday of the month.[62]

One of the Institution's oldest traditions was broken in 1931 when the annual festive Christmas dinner was discontinued. In the grim economic conditions of the great depression, the financial position of the Institution was precarious, and several other organisations were now providing similar entertainment for the poor of Dublin. For some years, the Institution continued to open and serve meals on Christmas Day, but finally ceased in 1952 due to the poor attendance.[63]

Rather than attempt the long-delayed repairs, the managing committee decided to sell the buildings at Usher's Island in March 1931 and purchase another premises for the Institution. They placed the Institution on the books of several auctioneers, each of whom warned it would be difficult to find a purchaser because the premises needed modernisation. Although Battersby's valued the premises at £1510, the committee decided not to accept less than £3000.[64] The Vocational Education Committee inspected the premises and offered £2500 which the managing committee refused, describing the offer as 'utterly inadequate'.[65] Battersby's suggested two buildings, one in Dominick Street and another in Benburb Street, as possible new premises for the Institution, but these were also rejected as unsuitable. The premises at Usher's Island was taken off Battersby's books, and the matter was dropped for the time being.[66]

Despite the introduction of the dole, unemployment assistance for men in 1933, the number of meals served to men in the Institution increased in the second half of the decade. The provision of non-contributory pensions for widows and orphans in 1935 may have contributed to the fall in the number of meals served to women and children after that date, as shown in Table 18.

The years of World War II, known in Ireland as 'the Emergency', were not as beneficial for the Institution as those of World War I. In 1940 the Institution supplied over 3,000 meals weekly, but the high cost of ingredients and a fall in subscriptions meant that expenditure always exceeded income, and there was an ever-growing bank overdraft. During the Emergency years, the Institution shared the difficulties of the rest of the population as prices rose and goods became scarce. The gas supply was intermittent. Often there was no light in the kitchen by which to prepare breakfast. An electricity supply was installed to overcome this problem. Coal was another scarce commodity, and the Institution had to apply for a license to purchase a monthly ton of coal.[67] Donations of food from parishes and church councils were gratefully received, and a gift from the Commissioners of Public Works of a half carcass of deer from the Phoenix Park provided dinner for three days in August 1941.[68] Due to the bad state of repair of the premises, the managing committee were unable to accommodate refugees from England on their way to the country, when asked to do so by the Red Cross. For the same reason, the air raid warden was refused permission to use the building for meetings or the storing of equipment, and the Institution could not help a man who requested permission to store furniture following the bombing of his house.[69] The committee's opinion of the premises was confirmed in March 1941 when the Board of Assistance of the Dublin Union inspected the Institution and rejected it as unsuitable for accommodating and feeding large numbers of people if the need arose.[70]

A radio appeal on behalf of the Institution was made for the first time in 1940.[71] The appeal became an annual event and was a satisfactory way of fundraising for many years. Following each appeal, requests came from all over the country for the Institution's collection boxes, one in 1943 from a nine-year old girl.[72] A committee member, Rev R J Kerr, made the appeal in the early years. Later appeals were made by Lord Mayors Alfie Byrne and

Robert Briscoe, TD, who also collected money for the Institution in the US.[73] Noel Purcell, Senator Owen Sheehy Skeffington, Mrs Rita Childers, Very Rev Dean Griffin, Milo O'Shea, Maureen Potter, and Gay Byrne were among those who spoke on behalf of the Institution.

The publication in 1942 in Britain of the revolutionary Beveridge report, proposing a comprehensive social policy to attack want, disease, ignorance, squalor and idleness, caused a sensation in Britain and did not go unnoticed in Ireland. William Boydell commented at the Mendicity Institution's Annual General Meeting in 1943 that 'the Beveridge plan was good in its way', but he forecast, rather inaccurately, that it would cause a great deal of disappointment because it would take a long time to come into force, and would be required only for a small number of people.[74] He argued that there would be plenty of work available after the war 'for the re-building of the world'.[75]

In 1949 the Institution's financial problems had grown to such an extent that auditors, Craig Gardner, suggested the premises should be sold and the Institution moved to a smaller building elsewhere.[76] In 1951 the trustees agreed to the sale but were required to ask the court's permission to spend any money received from the sale on the purchase or building of new premises.[77] The Dublin Board of Assistance offered £9000 for the buildings and part of the rear yard.[78] The offer was accepted when the Board of Assistance agreed to pay the Institution £120 ground rent per annum, and to provide a lean-to store on the part of the yard

Table 18: Number of Meals Served Annually 1931-38

Year	Men	Women	Children	Total
1931	82,304	15,213	4,402	101,919
1932	87,900	15,816	10,253	113,969
1933	89,617	14,140	5,328	109,085
1934				99,351
1935	85,668	12,147	2,080	99,895
1936	93,564	8,180	4,868	106,612
1937	102,910	6,180	3,515	112,605
1938	100,247	7,280	1,297	108,824

Source: Annual Reports of the Mendicity Association 1931–38

retained by the Institution.[79] Having viewed other buildings in the neighbourhood, the managing committee decided to build on this site. Their new premises would front on to Island Street. An estimate of £8852 6s 4d for the new building was accepted, and the Bank of Ireland granted an overdraft of £7000 to fund the project. The Board of Assistance agreed to wait until the building was ready before moving into Usher's Island.[80] The erection of the new building proved more difficult than anticipated. It was found necessary to put in a re-inforced concrete 'raft' to avoid extensive excavations.[81] Mrs Phyllis O'Kelly, wife of President Sean T O'Kelly, opened the new premises at Island Street on 3 June 1954.[82]

The Institution's financial situation improved in 1954. The Corporation issued a compulsory purchase order for three yards in Island Street owned by the Institution, offering £1414 and the redemption of the ground rent from £147 to £90 per annum.[83] A new source of income was found when the Institution was asked to supply daily breakfast to people now housed at Usher's Island by the Board of Assistance. Porridge and ∫ pint of milk was provided for each person at a charge of sixpence for each meal. This charge was raised to seven pence two years later. The number of breakfasts supplied by the Institution monthly varied between 304 in September 1954 and 1355 in December 1962 by which time tea had been added to the menu and the price charged for each meal was eight pence. The Institution raised the charge to one shilling plus turnover tax in November 1963. The service continued until 1966 when it was no longer required.[84] Proximity to the Board of Assistance's hostel was not always a plus for the Institution. In 1958 confusion over the roles of each organisation resulted in some 'misleading press reports' about the treatment received by the Institution's clientele, which generated unwelcome publicity.[85] The managing committee succeeded in getting compensation and an apology from Irish Times Newspapers for erroneous reports about the Institution in the *Sunday Review* and the *Irish Pictorial*.[86] In 1972 an apology was sought from the management of the *Irish Press* for a report of the impending closure of the Mendicity Institution, when the closure in question was that of the Eastern Health Board's night shelter for men.[87] The managing committee always worried that such publicity would affect the subscriptions on which the Institution's service depended.

Local traders were generous to the Institution: Miss Egan, of Usher's Quay, donated loaves of bread regularly; while Mr Hickey, of Island Street, supplied 56 pounds of meat every month for nearly 20 years.[88] In October 1962, a gift of bracks was received from Bewley's. The bracks were distributed at breakfast-time and were very popular. Bewley's continued this generous gesture throughout the 1960s and 1970s.[89] Donations of potatoes were always gratefully received; the Institution often had to stop serving potatoes when the price was too high.[90] During the 1960s the Institution extended its service by providing almost one hundred old age pensioners with a bag of coal during the winter months from November to March. In May 1969, the pensioners were each given one pound of tea and two pounds of sugar monthly until November when the delivery of coal was resumed.[91] The committee were occasionally asked to help poor families in distress. In January 1969, on the recommendation of a clergyman, the Institution provided a woman with seven children who had been abandoned by her husband, with tea, sugar, bread, and margarine for one month.[92] In October 1970 the Institution's bank overdraft reached £1993 12s 9d, and the provision of tea and sugar to pensioners was suspended.[93] The Institution applied to the Dublin Health Authority for a grant to meet this deficit on the grounds that the number of meals served had increased, and it was no longer able to provide its service for pensioners. Through the intercession of the Minister for Health, Erskine Childers, a grant of £500 was received early in 1971.[94] As the financial situation had slightly improved by the following year, the committee decided not to pursue an application for a further grant.[95] However, as the cost of food, gas and electricity continued to rise in the inflationary 1970s, and the wages of the staff were raised to keep up with the cost of living, the expenditure of the Institution often exceeded its income.

The appointment of new trustees was an expensive and time-consuming business for the Institution. In 1977 the Institution applied to the Commissioners of Charitable Donations and Bequests to frame a scheme establishing the trustees of the Institution as a body corporate and vesting the property of the Institution in that body corporate in accordance with the *Charities Act 1973*. On 18 April 1978, the charity was established as a body corporate with the name of 'The Mendicity Institution Trust'.[96]

The annual number of meals provided by the Institution continued to rise until 1977 when the number fell by almost 1,500 due to the provision of a similar service in the neighbourhood by another charity. In 1978 the number decreased by almost 7,000 and continued to drop each year. In 1982 the committee asked the recently appointed secretary, Charles Smith, to improve the quality and variety of the meals, and to upgrade the surroundings in order 'to attract more people to the dining-room'.[97] At a cost of £976, a waiting room was provided where the clientele could remain until meals were served. Up to that time, people had to wait outside on the street, whatever the weather. New toilet facilities were also provided at a cost of £1,085.[98] Cooking equipment was urgently needed: one antique cast-iron cauldron was used to cook the morning's porridge and had to be thoroughly cleaned before being used to cook the dinner.[99] Through the help of the National Catering Organisation, a modern gas range and a stainless steel gas boiler were presented and installed free of charge by the RTE catering department. The Institution purchased a new fridge and a chest freezer at a cost of £406.60.[100] A very important purchase was an automatic potato-peeler costing £789.75. The need for this machine was clear. As Charles Smith remarked:

> Can you imagine two ladies in their 70s, one with painful wrist and finger joints from arthritis, peeling three stone of potatoes every waking day with ordinary cooking knives? Our cooks have been doing just that for as many years as they can remember.[101]

Repairs and improvements to the Institution continued throughout the 1980s. For ten years from 1983 to 1993 the Royal British Legion rented office space in the premises at Island Street for three days a week, providing another source of income for the Institution.[102] Dissatisfied with the continuing drop in attendance, the committee decided to provide an additional daily meal for their clientele. The significant increase in the number of meals served in 1987, shown in Table 19, was due to the introduction of 'sandwich teas' from 1 December 1986.[103]

At the end of the twentieth century there are eleven members on the committee of management of the Mendicity Institution which meets at Island Street on the second Wednesday of each month at 2.30pm. They include representatives of the local clergy from the parishes of St James', St Audoen's, and St Paul's, and a representative of the St Vincent de Paul Society. Richard White succeeded the late Richard Tennant as president in 1996. The Institution suffered a second loss within a year when its valued secretary, Charles Smith, died in 1997. He was succeeded by the honorary treasurer, George Sheppard. Three women now sit on the committee. Mrs Dorothy Browne, the current vice-president, made history in October 1986 when she became the first female member of the managing committee. She was joined by Mrs Nell Carley in December 1987 and Mrs Ann Coffey in 1995. The longest serving member is John H Smiley who was elected to the committee in 1978. Patrick E de B Bewley, who joined the committee in 1980, represents a link with the early days of the Association, being a descendant of a founder, Samuel Bewley. The Institution is under the patronage of the Church of Ireland and Roman Catholic Archbishops of Dublin, and of the Deans of St Patrick's and Christ Church Cathedrals.

A visitor to the Mendicity Institution at the end of the 1990s finds a rather unprepossessing exterior to the building on Island Street. For security, all the windows are barred. Inside, there is a bright comfortable dining-room capable of accommodating over seventy people, where the Victorian-style benches and long ta-

Table 19: Number of Meals Served Annually 1984–88

Year	Men	Women	Children	Total
1984	28,637	802	99	29,538
1985	27,013	360	11	27,384
1986	28,237	402	29	28,668
1987	42,052	756	40	42,848
1988	42,558	2,496	6	45,060

Source: Annual Reports of the Mendicity Institution, 1984–88

bles of former years have been replaced by small tables, each seating six people, and individual chairs. Meals are prepared in a modern kitchen by three permanent members of staff and five or six part-time workers. There are always two people on duty. Despite the provision of meals elsewhere in the city by other organisations, nearly 8000 more meals were served by the Mendicity Institution in 1996 compared with the 1990 figure of 44,569. A list of provisions used in 1996 is given in Appendix F. Breakfast, consisting of unlimited porridge, bread and butter and tea, is served at 9am; and dinner between 11am and 12 noon, when soup and bread, meat, potatoes, and vegetables are served. Beef and pork are provided frequently, while bacon and cabbage, Irish stew and fish fingers often appear on the menu. As Table 20 indicates, dinner is the most popular meal. For many of the clientele who do not attend at breakfast-time, it is the first meal of the day. Tea and sandwiches are served at 3.15pm. There is no charge for any meal and no limit to the number of people served. Every one who comes is welcome. No questions are asked and names are not recorded. Members of the committee of management take it in turn to visit the kitchen and dining-room once a month at dinner-time, when the clientele are encouraged to comment on the menu, the quality of the food provided or any aspect of the service they wish. The times of the meals are arranged to suit the clientele, most of whom are regular attenders. The average number of meals served daily is 130.

Table 20: Annual Consumption of Meals by Time of Day 1990–96

Year	Breakfasts	Dinners	Teas	Total
1990	12,749	19,466	12,354	44,569
1991	12,176	20,742	12,094	45,012
1992	14,034	21,069	14,319	49,422
1993	14,826	22,312	16,048	53,186
1994	14,129	22,532	13,120	49,781
1995	12,740	22,407	10,727	45,874
1996	13,752	23,384	15,201	52,337

Source: Annual Reports of the Mendicity Institution, 1990–96

Although there are panic buttons in the kitchen and the food store-room, the management seldom have reason to worry about problems with the clientele. Any potential trouble-maker is quickly made aware that such behaviour is not acceptable by the other diners, who thus operate their own control system.

At dinner-time, some of the clientele come early and wait for the door to open at 11am, most of the remainder arriving within a few minutes. The kitchen supervisor knows the clientele well and has a friendly welcome for everyone as they collect their meals at the counter dividing the kitchen from the dining-room. Although several clients come for company, meals are not social occasions. Perhaps due to the ban on smoking in the dining room, people do not delay once they have eaten their meal. When the committee installed a television set in the dining-room the clientele asked for its removal. The door remains open at dinner-time until 12 noon to allow for late-comers. About half the clientele return for tea when the door is opened again between 2.30pm and 3.15pm. Others go to dining rooms run by other organisations, walk around the city, or return home. As Table 21 shows, the clientele is predominantly male. The majority are over 50 years of age. Several of them live in hostels, but many have a room or small flat where they live alone. Whereas some walk quite a distance to the Institution, the majority live close by. Several living in the suburbs avail of the free bus pass for people over 66 years of age. All seem to enjoy the meals, the porridge at breakfast-time coming in for special praise.

Table 21: Annual Consumption of Meals, by Gender 1990–96

Year	Men	Women	Children	Total
1990	40,793	3,525	251	44,569
1991	44,504	486	22	45,012
1992	48,986	423	13	49,422
1993	52,723	433	30	53,186
1994	49,401	350	30	49.781
1995	45,409	444	21	45,874
1996	51,595	694	48	52,337

Source: Annual Reports of the Mendicity Institution 1990-96

The Institution remains completely dependent on voluntary contributions and does not receive any regular state funding. Subscriptions, donations, dividends and rent from lettings provide its income. Only two collection boxes continue to make a return. Expenditure in 1996 was almost £60,000. Occasionally, grants have been received for specific purposes from the Mercer Foundation, War on Want, the Cork Street Fund, the Department of Social Welfare, and from the People in Need Trust. Some donations are anonymous, but, in 1997, the secretary was invited to visit a house in suburban Dublin. There he was handed a cheque for £1,000—a gift from a son of the house now making a successful career in Australia, who had used the services of the Institution during an unsettled period in his youth.

The Institution has played many roles and met various needs during its lifetime of 180 years. At first it attempted to train the poor for employment and provide those who could not work with food and money for shelter. Alone in Dublin, it catered for destitute people excluded by other voluntary organisations. Its unique transmission service gave many people from Ireland and elsewhere the opportunity to make a fresh start in life. During the Great Famine, it assisted the poor law authorities to provide outdoor relief by feeding many people who were starving. It focused on the sanitary improvement of the population of Dublin by introducing the first public baths in the city. As state intervention in the lives of the poor increased and social services developed, the Institution's role became one of meeting the emergency needs of poor people in times of sickness or other crisis. The temporary relief given by the Institution saved many from entering the workhouse. The committee of management recognise that the present clientele is not destitute but has other needs which the Institution can meet. The task now is to provide three nourishing meals a day for anyone who calls to Island Street. The Institution is joined in this work by other organisations who provide meals in dining-rooms around the city. The Institution's service is no longer unique, but is widely used and appreciated.

This story began in the golden age of the eighteenth century when extreme wealth co-existed with dire poverty in Dublin, and the streets were thronged with beggars. Two centuries later, this dichotomy still exists. The building cranes that mar the city's skyline signify another era of economic boom and great prosperity for many people. Much of this prosperity is attributed to the 'Celtic Tiger', who prowls the streets in the company of many less fortunate members of society, while the number of people begging is still a constant source of complaint by the general public. The Institution's founders and the early managing committees hoped for the day when their objective of preventing and suppressing mendicity would be achieved, and they could voluntarily close the doors because they would have no clients. Their successors, the present-day committee of management, cannot envisage a time when the 'patient work' of the Institution will not be required. Despite the improvement in the economy and in the state provision of social services, they believe that, as long as there are lonely, marginalised people whose needs are not met by the system, the Mendicity Institution should be there to fill the gap. Sadly, they consider that the epithet printed on the cover of the Institution's annual report every year since 1818 will continue to be relevant:

> 'For the poor always ye have with you'—John xii, 8

APPENDIX A

Original Resolutions of the Association for the Prevention and Suppression of Mendicity in Dublin

At a General Meeting of the Inhabitants of Dublin held at the Rotunda on Thursday, January 22 1818
The Right Hon. the Lord Mayor in the Chair.

The following resolutions were unanimously agreed to:

1st. Resolved—That Mendicity has long prevailed in Ireland to a most disgraceful and pernicious extent, and has from various causes increased of late to a degree calculated to shock the Philanthropist and alarm every reflecting member of the community.

2nd. Resolved—That though an immense annual sum is voluntarily paid for the support of mendicants, it is now but too manifest that the profuse and spontaneous liberality of the Irish Public in the indiscriminate distribution of Alms has acted, and ever must act, as a powerful and irresistible stimulus in encouraging and fostering the most idle and worthless Vagrants, and has operated, like the Poor-rates in England, or indeed as any legalized system must ever operate, in increasing the evil it was designed to relieve.

3rd. Resolved—That the cities of Munich, Hamburgh, Edinburgh and Belfast have furnished memorable instances of successful efforts made by their inhabitants to repress Mendicity, and frequently to convert the idle and dissolute into industrious and moral members of society.

4th. Resolved—That Dublin, though from its greater population it presents difficulties more arduous, may yet be relieved by the disgusting and baleful influence of Mendicity, provided the present contributions of the charitable, now but too generally devoted to the support of idleness, imposture and vice, be diverted through other channels, to the encouragement of industry and the promotion of moral habits.

5th. Resolved—That as the prevalence of Mendicity is not only an evil of monstrous magnitude in itself, but has also greatly contributed to the present fatal diffusion of contagious Fever throughout the Country, it is now therefore not merely expedient, but indispensable to adopt such immediate and decisive measures in Dublin, as may, through the influence of its example, eventually lead to the general suppression of Mendicity in Ireland.

6th. Resolved therefore—That an Association be forthwith formed for the purpose of suppressing Mendicity in the City of Dublin, and its Precincts; and that the Association be governed by a President, twelve vice-presidents, and a General committee composed of the Ex-officio members hereafter named, and of forty two members annually chosen by the subscribers of £3, one third at least of the said 42 members to retire each year.

7th. Resolved—That every annual Subscriber of one pound and upwards shall be deemed a Member of the Association.

8th. Resolved—That the Lord Mayor, for the time being, be President and the following Noblemen and gentlemen be Vice-Presidents for the ensuing year:-

Duke of Leinster,	Bishop of Elphin,
Earl of Meath,	The Most Rev. Dr Troy,
Earl of Fingall,	The Right Hon. George Knox,
Earl of Charlemont,	Sir Edward Bellew,
Lord Viscount Southwell,	Richard Power, Esq.,
Lord Viscount de Vesci,	Mr Thomas Pleasants

9th. Resolved—That the following Noblemen, Prelates, Magistates and Gentlemen be Ex-Officio Members of the said Committee of Directors, and be requested to act as such, viz.—the Lord Mayor, the Archbishop of Dublin, the Lord Chancellor, the twelve Judges, the Master of the Rolls, the Most Reverend Doctors Troy and Murray, and their successors, the Chief Secretary and Under Secretary in the Civil Department to the Lord Lieutenant, the Representatives in Parliament of the County and the City of Dublin, His Majesty's Attorney and Solicitor General, the Provost of Trinity College, the Deans of Christ Church and Saint Patrick's, the Archdeacon of Dublin, the Aldermen, Recorder, and Sheriffs, the Police Magistrates, the Governors of the House of Industry, the Commissioners of Revenue, the Commissioners for Paving and Lighting, and the several Members of the Corporation for the Improvement of the Port of Dublin, the Commissioners for Dunleary Harbour, the Governor, deputy Governor and secretary of the Bank of Ireland, the Vice-Presidents and Secretaries of the Dublin Society, the Secretary of the Linen Board, the Serjeants at Law and King's Counsel, the Seneschals of the Manor Courts, the Committee of the Cork-street Fever Hospital, the Treasurers and Secretaries of the Societies for Promoting the Comforts and Educating the Poor, and of the Charitable and Strangers' Friends Societies, and the Treasurer and Secretaries of this Association.

10th. Resolved—That the following Gentlemen, together with the President, Vice-Presidents, and the Ex-Officio Members, constitute the General Committee of Directors for the ensuing year:

1 Thomas Abbott
2 Samuel Bewley
3 Peter Brophy
4 Doctor Barker
5 George F Brooke
6 Richard Cane
7 James Connolly
8 Roderick Connor
9 Richard Corballis
10 Leland Crosthwaite, Jun.
11 John Crampton
12 Richard Darling
13 George Drevar
14 John Doherty
15 George French
16 Arthur Guinness
17 Rev. Thomas Goff
18 John George
19 William Guinness
20 Doctor Gamble
21 Joseph Huband
22 Robert Harty
23 Francis Lear
24 D Kinahan
25 John D La Touche
26 Randall McDonnell
27 Doctor Harty
28 W Shaw Mason
29 Mark Montsarrat
30 George Ness
31 Thomas Nowlan
32 Doctor Orpen
33 Paul Patrick
34 Matthew James Plunkett
35 Richard Palmer
36 Doctor Robinson
37 Edward Scott
38 Sir E Stanley
39 Paulus Singer
40 William Sankey
41 Chas. Williams
42 Rob. White

11th. Resolved—That a Deputation from the Committee do wait on his Excellency the Lord Lieutenant to request that he will be graciously pleased to honour and encourage the Association by becoming its Patron.

12th. Resolved—That the said General Committee, so constituted, be empowered to fill up such vacancies as may occur in their Body by death, resignation or removal, and have the full power to make such Bye Laws and Regulations for the good government of the Association and the promotion of its objects as they shall deem most expedient, and to alter and amend the following outline of a plan in such as experience may hereafter direct:

Outline of a Plan

I. That the City be divided into—Districts, and each District into—Walks.

II. That District Committees of 42 members each be elected by subscribers of £1, and upwards, and the Clergy of every religious persuasion and the Church Wardens be Ex-officio Members of the Committees of the District in which their respective Parishes are included.

III. That the General Committee and each District Committee be divided into the six Sub-committees following:
1st. of Finance and Accounts
2nd. of Employment
3rd. of Investigation
4th. of Supply
5th. of Education and Superintendence
6th. of Health

IV. That the District Committees do act in unison and conformably with the Plan laid down by the General Committee.

V. That the General Committees and the District Committees do meet once a Week, the General Committee on —, and the District Committees on the day preceding, and that the latter make regular weekly reports to the former.

VI. One Member and the Secretary of each District Committee to attend the weekly meetings of the General Committee, and be empowered to vote upon all Questions then and there discussed.

13th. Resolved—that the General Committee be instructed to ascertain as soon as possible the probable amount of donations and Annual Subscriptions that will be contributed by the inhabitants of Dublin for the employment of the Poor, and for Suppression of Mendicity, and also to ascertain the probable number of unemployed Poor and of Mendicants, classing the same under distinct and appropriate Heads, and that the sub-committees of Employment do also report on the best modes of employing the Poor without interfering with the ordinary channels of labour.

14th. Resolved—that the General Committee do also confer with the Governors of the House of Industry as to the accommodation which can be furnished by that Establishment to the Aged, to the Infirm, and to Children; and also with the Lord Mayor, Aldermen, and the Police Magistrates, as to the best mode of removing sturdy Vagrants from the Streets, and of disposing of them afterwards.

15th. Resolved—That the General Committee do also adopt speedy and effectual measures for the general establishment and encouragement of savings' banks, as it is most expedient by every possible means to impress upon the lower orders the necessity of providing for the future by the practice of industry, frugality, and sobriety; and as the promotion of those virtues, the best and surest preventives of Mendicity, would be especially aided by the establishment of such banks.

16th. Resolved—That due public notice be issued by the General Committee, so soon as they have made adequate arrangements for carrying into effect their measures for the suppression of Mendicity; and that to guard, as far as possible, against any misconception of the views of this Association, they be further instructed to adopt the most effectual measures for making it generally known among the labouring poor, that it is not the intention of the Association to afford relief to any, except through the medium of employment, or to consider any individual an object for such relief, who cannot prove a residence within this city or its precincts, for six months, at least, previously to the 1st of January, 1818.

17th. Resolved—That the Secretaries be directed to communicate to the Dublin Society the request of this Association, that the Society will be pleased to grant to the General Committee of Directors the temporary use of the Board-room and Committee-room, in Hawkins-street, until the General Committee shall be prepared to make arrangements for their permanent accommodation.

18th. Resolved—That the cordial thanks of the Association are pre-eminently due to Alderman Bloxham, late Lord Mayor, for the support and encouragement given by him during his Mayoralty, to the early efforts of the Committee, appointed to devise measures for the Suppression of Mendicity in this City.

19th. Resolved—that the Bank of Ireland be requested to act as Treasurer to this Association.

20th. Resolved—That the Rev Edward Groves and Walter Thom, Esq, be appointed secretaries to this Association.

21st. Resolved—That this Meeting, confidently relying on the active and energetic exertions of the Committee this day appointed, do at its rising adjourn until the 1st day of January next, or until such intermediate time as the General Committee shall deem it expedient that the Subscribers should re-assemble.

22nd. Resolved—That the thanks of this meeting be given to the Gentlemen of the late Committee for their laborious and humane attention to the object of the Association.

The Lord Mayor having left the Chair and the Right Hon the Earl of Charlemont being called thereto:

Resolved—that the cordial thanks of this Meeting are due to the Right Hon the Lord Mayor for his dignified conduct in the Chair, and for the countenance and support which his Lordship has individually and officially given to promote the great and important objects of this Association.

Source: 3rd *Annual Report,* App I, pp 29–33

APPENDIX B

The Case of a Mendicant Illustrated According to the Method Laid Down by the Dublin Association

A MENDICANT APPEARED BEFORE THE General Committee on Tues day the 9th of June at the Repository, Hawkins-street. The following questions were asked—What is your name?—Sarah Smith. Where do you live?—In Bow Lane James' Street. A ticket was then given her of the following form:

No. 1

Sarah Smith, Bow-lane James' Street-
Apply to the Office, District No. 6.
in—street on Wednesday the 10th of
June, between the hours of seven and
twelve in the morning
Signed

When she appeared the next day before the District committee, as directed by the ticket, she was questioned according to the annexed form. The paper, with her own answers inserted, was sent to the Visitor of Bow Lane, and she was desired to return to the same office on Saturday the 13th, at eight o'clock in the morning. The visitor returned the paper before that day (as desired by a foot note) with the result of his own enquiries opposite her answers.

This form is nearly the same as that of the Edinburgh Association, from whom it is borrowed.

Question	As stated by herself	As ascertained by the Visitor
1. Married or single?	Married	Believed to be so
2. Age?	Forty	Apparently
3. How long resident in Dublin?	Four years Born in Belfast	Believed to have been so
4. Employment?	Can procure none therefore begs	Said by A.B. and C.D to be unwilling to work as they offered her light work which she refused
5. Capabilities of work	Can spin and use her needle a little; could not do out-door work	Believed, in point of strength to be fit for any work.
6. With what implements provided?	None	Has a wheel at the pawn-broker, pledged for 2s. 8d. Has some needles and thread
7. Earnings per week?	Uncertain Never more than 6d per day	Is known to have collected half-a crown by begging; is reported to spend more than 6d per day at the whiskey shop
8. Rent per week?	Sixpence	True; lodges in a cellar. seldom in during the day
9. Husband/wife how employed? —and where?	Soldier in the 61st regt. West Indies	Believed to be true

10. Earnings of above?	His pay, never remits any	No means of ascertaining this
11. Number, age and sex of children?	Three, the eldest eight years old, a boy—two girls, one four the other three	The eldest girl borrowed from a fellow lodger to assist in begging
12. Employment of above?	None	Brought up to begging
13. Appearance of above?	Ill-clad and sickly	Purposely ill-clad stout in appearance.
14. Relatives? Any Assistance from them?	Has some in country/county of Galway; give no assistance	Recommend enquiry by letter, as it is supposed they are ignorant of her way of life
15. Probable cause of poverty?	Want of work.	Never endeavoured to find it
16. Lodging, when white-washed?	Does not know.	Lodges in a cellar, hardly any appearance of ever being white washed.
17. Clean or otherwise?	Not very	Very dirty and damp
18. Number of family residing at home?	Two families beside her own, in all ten people	True.
19. References for character?	To A.G and A.C. in Bow-lane	*Saw* them; they know nothing of her, except that she has often presented petitions; believe her to be undeserving

20. What aid from charitable sources?	None except from street-begging	Believed to be true

Signed

} Committee of
A.B } Investigation C.D. Visitor

The applicant returned, as directed on Saturday morning at eight o'clock. The committee having the evening before examined the visitor's report, and referred her to the sub-committee of Employment, they settled that she should be employed in spinning. The Member who attended in the morning took the necessary measures for redeeming her wheel, supplying her with one till her own could be stamped with the mark of the Linen board. She had a ticket given her of the following form to the Clerk-

District 6
No 1. Deliver to Sarah Smith
1lb of flax and a wheel,
17th day of June 1818
Signed,
}Committee of
}Employment

The clerk delivered the flax and wheel, entered the number, name, the quantity of flax and date of delivery, and filed the ticket, desiring her to return a sample of her work as expeditiously as possible, holding out prompt payment as an encouragement to do so. The sub-committee of supply had, the evening before, been informed, that Sarah Smith would be entitled to one ration and two ounces of provisions, namely, half a ration for her girl of three years old, and two-thirds for her boy of eight. They found the quantity correct; and the member of that sub-committee, who attended in the morning, gave her a written order to obtain provision from the Clerk with merely Sarah Smith, No 1. Saturday 13th of June, 1818 upon it. To the Clerk he had handed before a printed ticket of the following form

District 6
No. 1 Deliver to Sarah Smith,
Rations of potatoes, two-thirds,
Rations of meal, one half,
Rations of fuel, eight sods
of turf
13th day of June, 1818
Signed,
} Committee of
} Supply

He compared the number, name, and date of this ticket with the written form which the applicant produced, and finding them correspond, issued provisions accordingly, giving her a leaden ticket with No. 1, District 6 upon it in place of the written form. The member of the Sub-committee of Finance who attended at the same hour, paid her sixpence, to be continued, according to the regulations for new workers, till she returned a sample of her work. She brought in her work on the second morning at eight o'clock, when the Clerk having weighed it, counted the threads and examined the quality, under the inspection of a member of the committee of Employment, gave her a printed ticket of the following form:

District 6
No 1.— Sarah Smith returned 1lb of
two hank yarn properly spun, is
entitled to

19th day of June 1818
Signed,
} Committee of
} Employment

This was handed to the member of the finance committee, who immediately paid it, deducting so much from the daily allowance of sixpence. At the expiration of one week she had produced two samples of her work, the committee of employment were thus enabled to ascertain that she was capable of earning 3d per day by her own labour; the first ticket for provision was on this representation, cancelled by the committee of supply, and another filled up, directing that one ration eight ounces should be delivered to her, making the addition of sixpence, This was to continue for one month only when her case would undergo further examination, in order that the allowance of food might be regulated as strictly as possible according to he capability of earning money by work. The case having been thus disposed of, it was registered in its alphabetical order, by the sub-committee of investigation, in a book kept for that purpose

Source: 1st Annual Report, App 3, pp 30–5

Appendix C: Previous Occupations of Clients received between 1 January 1826 and 1 January 1827

Number	Occupation
188	Silk-weavers, throwsters
182	Cotton weavers, spinners
53	Worsted weavers, stuff makers
99	Dressmakers, lace and bonnet makers, plain workers
7	Hosiers
6	Printers and book binders
13	Tailors
4	Stay makers
46	Shoemakers
23	Flax dressers and linen weavers
24	Bakers, confectioners, pastry cooks
3	Pin makers
1	Whip maker
14	Glovers
6	Carpenters
6	Dyers
30	Distillers, brewers, maltsters
13	Skinners, tanners, curriers
3	Button makers
3	Teachers
9	Clerks
21	Shopkeepers, pedlars, huxters
63	Washerwomen
33	Fruit and cake sellers (in street)
6	Dairy keepers
8	Boot sellers
13	Gardeners
12	Painters and glaziers
13	Sailors
3	Cart makers and carters
8	Egg sellers
30	Soldiers' widows
3	Paviours
5	Fish dealers
1	Livery lace maker
1	Game-keeper
3	Tin workers

Number	Occupation
2	Comb makers
15	Cabinet makers and upholsterers
12	Paper makers
6	Tobacco workers
2	Plumbers
12	Bleachers
3	Mat and palliasse makers
2	Chair makers
7	Newspaper and pamphlet sellers
2	Feather dressers
3	Hairdressers
2	Coach-trimming makers
7	Glass cutters and blowers
2	Harness makers
2	Quilt makers
2	Toy sellers
3	Brush makers
2	Farriers
2	Broom makers
9	Chandlers
13	Masons, slaters, bricklayers
27	Smiths, brassfounders etc.
4	Sawyers
3	Butchers
6	Carpet makers
17	Knitters and spinners
33	Hatters
8	Marble polishers
4	Cutlers
5	Coal porters
74	Day labourers
13	Waiters
476	Servants
377	Scourers, charwomen etc

Source: 9th *Annual Report,* p 19

APPENDIX D

Re-Classification of Mendicants in the Institution in 1829

On applying to the Institution every mendicant fit to work was put to stonepounding and received free rations for three days.

First class: Stonepounders
Male stonepounders: one penny a bushel.
Female stonepounders: one and one half pence a bushel.
It was expected that men would pound 12 bushels a week and women 8, although some men could pound up to 20 bushels and some women 15.

Second class: Spinners
Spinners: three and one half pence per hank of yarn spun (four and one half pence per hank from 1 November to 1 February because of the shortness of the days) and a ticket for every working day they attended. When a spinner had accumulated 120 tickets she received enough strong coarse linen to make herself a shift. Unless a woman could spin three hanks per week she was not allowed to remain in this class. Most women spun less than four hanks a week.
Learners: an introductory allowance during the training period of 8 weeks; nine pence for first two-week period, seven pence for the second; three and one half pence for the third and two pence for the final two weeks; they also received what they earned from spinning during the training period.
The overseer and teacher of the spinners: five pence a day;
Reelers (selected for good behaviour): three pence a day;
Young spinners who attended school for two hours a day received an allowance of one half penny a day to compensate for the time taken from spinning.

Third Class: Knitters
Knitters: one penny a day for attending each week-day at the Institution and four pence per pair of socks knitted, or six pence per pair of stockings knitted.
The overseer of the knitters: four pence per day with free rations.
Knitters with infant children: one penny a day to buy milk for their children and to compensate for time spent looking after the children.

Fourth Class: Oakum pickers.
This class received one penny a day for attendance on weekdays and one penny for a half lb of oakum picked each day they were present.
The overseer of this class; two pence a day and free rations.

Fifth Class: Infirm
This class received two pence for each weekday attended.

Sixth Class: Employed in various way
Label holders, Oat-bruisers, Labourers: two pence per day and their rations.
Overseers for this class: five pence per day and rations.
Carters collecting meat in the streets and cleaning and scraping potatoes: three pence per day, free rations and eight pence per hundredweight of meat and bones collected and two pence for the same amount of bread and refuse collected.
Assistants cleaning potatoes: one and one half pence per day and free rations; they were only required in summer when there was more of this work to be done.
Those employed in kitchen: three pence per day and free rations.
Attendants in dining hall: four pence per day and free rations.
Assistants, the gatekeeper, the carpenter: three pence per day and free rations.
Door-keepers: two pence per day and free rations
Scourers: two and one half pence per day and free rations.
Sweepers: one and one half pence per day and free rations.

Seventh Class: Extern Sick
Those unable to attend were visited by the apothecary and received one shilling and two pence weekly.

Those discharged from fever hospital: one shilling and two pence for one week.
Those discharged from other hospitals: six pence and free rations.
The sick with a certificate from the dispensary were exempted from work for 3 days and received one penny per day on handing in this certificate.

Eighth Class: Children
Women got five pence per week to look after orphans in their homes.
Children were given a school dress each day; after three months attendance they received a complete outfit of clothes for themselves out of the school clothes store; this outfit was renewed every eight months.
Every adult who attended on Sunday got an allowance of two pence. Those who did not attend lost this allowance and paid a small fine.

Source: 12th *Annual Report*, App 4, pp 26–30

APPENDIX E

Recipes Recommended by the Institution

Receipt for making Stirabout of Indian meal and Rice at a total cost per day for 192 persons of £1 7s 3d.

Take of Indian meal 4 and one half stone and of rice 1 and one half stone and 64 gallons of water; measure out the water (viz.: 64 gallons) and heat the same in the boiler. Steep the rice in a portion of the above water, taken from the boiler, for at least one hour; mix then the Indian meal and Rice with a sufficient quantity of water, taken from the boiler; then let the water in the boiler come to a strong boil, then put in the mixed Indian meal and Rice and add 2 lbs of salt, and let it come to a boil, keeping same well stirred; then let it simmer for an hour and a half until it thickens, keeping it continually stirred, and thus an excellent stirabout will be prepared. An experiment showed that 6 stone of Indian meal and Rice mixed in above proportions of 3 to 1 produced 192 quarts of food weighing 2 and one half lbs each. With milk and soup 192 persons could be fed for £1 7s 3d per day. Potatoes would have to be 3d per stone to match this.

Soup Receipt

Take one Ox-head, wash it well and put it into the boiler with 12 gallons of water, let it boil for 3 hours, then take it out and cut the meat into small pieces; put all back again into the boiler, then add 7 pounds of good Oatmeal and 1 pound of Salt; let it simmer for 2 hours and you will have 8 gallons of good Soup, at the cost of 2 shillings and 8 pence.

Source: 38th *Annual Report*, pp 9–11

APPENDIX F

Quantity of Provisions Used in 1996

	Tons	Cwts	Qtrs	Lbs
Meat	2	10	3	9
Potatoes	3	5	-	16
Butter	-	3	-	8
Tea	-	1	2	9
Sugar	-	4	3	3
Porridge Meal	-	8	1	14
Cheese	-	3	1	8
Sandwich Meat	-	4	-	14
Soup	-	-	-	24
Canned Vegetables	-	5	2	9
Loose Peas	-	-	3	1
Turnips	-	8	1	2
Carrots	-	8	1	-
Onions	-	2	2	-
Salt -	-	4	9	

Bread	3089	family pans
Milk	436	gallons
Cabbage	1120	heads
Soup Powder	144	25 ltr tins
Fish Fingers	200	dozen

Source: 179th *Annual Report*, p 7

BIBLIOGRAPHY

Books and Pamphlets

Anon, *Arguments in Proof of the Necessity and Practicability of Suppresing Street Begging in the City of Dublin,* Dublin: 1817

Anon, 'First Battalion', in *Dublin Brigade Review*, Dublin: 1939

Bruce, Maurice, *The Coming of the Welfare State*, London: 1965

Burke, Helen, *The People and the Poor Law in 19th Century Ireland,* Dublin: 1987

——, *The Royal Hospital Donnybrook, Two Hundred and Fifty Years of Caring*, Dublin: 1993

Curry, John, *The Irish Social Services*, Dublin: 1980

Craig, Maurice, *Dublin 1660–1860*, Dublin: 1980

Daly, Mary E, *Dublin-The Deposed Capital: A Social and Economic History 1860–1914*, Cork: 1984

——, *Social and Economic History of Ireland since 1800*, Dublin: 1986

Dobbs, Arthur, *An Essay on the Trade and Improvement of Ireland,* Dublin: 1729

Fagan, Patrick, *The Second City: Portrait of Dublin 1700–1760*, Dublin: 1986

Farrell, Patrick, 'Writing the History of Irish-Australia' in *Ireland and Irish-Australia: Studies in Cultural and Political History,* O McDonagh and W F Mandle (eds), London: 1986

Fitzpatrick, Samuel A O, *Dublin: A Historical and Topographical Account of the City*, Cork: 1977

Fownes, William F, *Methods Proposed for Regulating the Poor, Supporting of Some and Employing Others, According to their several Capacities*, Dublin: 1725

Frazer, Derek, *The Evolution of the British Welfare State*, London: 1973

James, Francis G, *Ireland in the Empire 1668–1770*, Cambridge Massachusetts: 1973

Kinahan, Daniel, *System of Relief for the Poor as Used in the Dublin Mendicity Institution, Adapted to General Use*, Dublin: 1847

Liddy, Pat, *Dublin: Stolen from Time: Perspectives of Dublin 1790s–1990s*, Dublin: 1990

McDonagh, Oliver, 'The Irish in Australia: A General View', in *Ireland and Irish-Australia: Studies in Cultural and Political History*, O McDonagh and W F Mandle (eds), London: 1986

McBride, Sean, (ed), *Crime and Punishment*, Dublin: 1982

McDowell, R B, *Ireland in the Age of Imperialism and Revolution 1760–1801*, Oxford: 1979

Malton, James, *A Picturesque and Descriptive View of the City of Dublin*, Dublin: 1794

Maxwell, Constantia, *Dublin under the Georges: 1714–1830*, London: 1936

Nicholls, George, *The History of the Irish Poor Law in Connection with the Condition of the People*, London: 1856

O'Connell, Maurice R. *Daniel O'Connell, The Man and his Politics*, Dublin: 1990

—, *The Correspondence of Daniel O'Connell*, Vols 1–7, Dublin: 1973, 1974, 1977

O'Connor, John, *The Workhouses of Ireland: The Fate of Ireland's Poor*, Dublin: 1995

Ó'Grádá, Cormac, Ireland, *A New Economic History*, 1780–1939, Oxford: 1995

Perceval, Robert, *An Attempt towards a Plan for Rendering the Charitable Institutions of Dublin more Efffective by Co-operation*, Dublin: 1818

Phelan, Denis, *A Statistical Inquiry into the Present State of the Medical Charities in Ireland with Suggestions for a Medical Poor Law*, Dublin: 1835

Powell, Frederick W, *The Politics of Irish Social Policy 1600–1990*, New York: 1992

Robins, Joseph A, *The Lost Children: A Study of Charity Children in Ireland 1700–1900, Dublin:* 1980

Rumford, Bernard, *Essays, Practical, Economic and Philosophical: Vol I*, Dublin: 1796, *Vol II*, London: 1800

Stewart, John W, *The Gentleman's and Citizen's Almanack*, Dublin: 1820

Thom's Directory, Dublin: 1861

von Voght, Baron Caspar, *An Account of the Management of the Poor in Hamburgh between the years 1788 and 1794 in a Letter to Some Friends of the Poor in Great Britain*, London: 1817

Warburton, J, Whitelaw, J, and Walsh, R, *History of the City of Dublin*, London: 1818

Wilderspin, Samuel, *Infant Education or Remarks on the Importance of Educating the Infant Poor*, London: 1825

Williams, George D W, *Dublin Charities*, Dublin; 1902

Woods, Audrey, 'The Evolution of Dispensary Policy in Ireland 1766–1872', unpublished MSocSc Thesis, University College Dublin: 1988

Woodward, Richard, *An Address to the Public on the Expediency of a Regular Plan for the Maintenance and Government of the Poor*, Dublin: 1775

——, *An Argument in Support of the Right of the Poor in this Kingdom to a National Provision*, Dublin: 1772

Parliamentary Papers and Official Reports

Chadwick, E, *Report on the Sanitary Condition of the Labouring Population of Great Britain*, London: 1842

First Report of George Nicholls Esq. on Poor Laws, Ireland, London: 1837

Report of a Select Committee of the House of Commons on Legislative Provisions for the Poor of Ireland, London: 1803–4

Report of the Commissioners appointed to Inspect the House of Industry, London: 1820

Report of a Select Committee of the House of Commons on the Employment of the Poor in Ireland, London: 1823

The Royal Commission into the Conditions of the Poorer Classes in Ireland and into the Various Institutions Established by Law for Their Relief, *Third Report*, London: 1835

Bibliography

Documents in the Archive of the Mendicity Institution Trust

Annual Reports of the Association, 1818–1996

Managing Committee Minute Books, 1819–1996 Sept 1825–July 1830, Mar 1832–Feb 1836, Mar 1839–July 1847, Jan 1975–Aug 1978

Admission Books, 1859–1866, 1884, 1913–16, 1920–29

Bathhouse Memorandum Book 1852–1894

Book of Sales 1857–1866

Cash Books, 1818–1833, 1883–89, 1907–1963

Finance Book 1847–1854

Journals, 1862, 1907, 1925

Ledgers 1824–1841, 1860–64, 1872–1906

Miscellaneous Correspondence Books

Payment Books 1848–1853, 1863–1872

Receipts Books 1841–48, 1861–1870

Rents Received Book 1841–1869

Rules and Regulations Book

Subscription Books 1839–1872, 1908–1963

Transmission Books 1884–1969

Wages Book 1864–1884

Miscellaneous Papers and Reports

The Bath Society for the Suppression of Mendicity, *Eighth Report,* Bath: 1813

The Society Established in London for the Suppression of Mendicity, *First Report,* London: 1819; *Fourth Report,* London: 1822

The Society for the Suppression of Beggars in Edinburgh, *First Report,* Edinburgh: 1814

Typhus Fever Epidemic Papers, Dublin: 1815

REFERENCES FOR CHAPTER ONE

1 Fagan, P, T*he Second City: Portrait of Dublin 1700–1760*, Dublin:1986, p 1
2 Liddy, P, *Dublin: Stolen from Time: Perspectives of Dublin* 1790s–1990s, Dublin: 1990, p 1
3 *Ibid*, p 34
4 Malton, J, *A Picturesque and Descriptive View of the City of Dublin*, Dublin: 1794, p 14
5 Liddy, p 66
6 Fagan, p 217; Liddy, p 66
7 Maxwell, C, *Dublin under the Georges: 1714–1830,* London: 1936, p 84
8 *Ibid*, p 93
9 *Ibid*, p 59
10 Liddy, pp 11, 34
11 Maxwell, p 48
12 Liddy, p 98
13 McDowell, R B, *Ireland in the Age of Imperialism and Revolution: 1760–1801*, Oxford: 1979, p 20
14 James, F G, *Ireland in the Empire 1668–1770,* Cambridge Massachusetts: 1973, p 223
15 *Ibid*, p 212; Liddy, p 3
16 Liddy, p 1
17 Fagan, p 43
18 James, p 223; Liddy, p 3
19 Liddy, p 30
20 Dobbs, A, *An Essay on the Trade and Improvement of Ireland: Part II*, Dublin: 1729, p 10
21 Maxwell, p 121
22 Malton, p 1
23 Warburton, J, Whitelaw, J, and Walsh, R, *History of the City of Dublin*, London: 1818, p 443
24 James, p 212
25 Woodward, R, (1) *An Address to the Public on the Expediency of a Regular Plan for the Maintenance and Government of the Poor,* Dublin: 1775, p 4
26 Fagan, p 43
27 Maxwell, p 122
28 Woodward (1), p 24
29 Fagan, pp 43–4
30 Fownes, Sir W F, *Methods Proposed for Regulating the Poor, Supporting of Some and Employing Others, According to their Several Capacities*, Dublin: 1725, p 15
31 *Ibid*, pp 9–10, 16
32 Dobbs, pp 45–8
33 Woodward, R, (2) *An Argument in Support of the Right of the Poor in this Kingdom to a National Provision*, Dublin: 1772, p 41; Woodward (1), p 23
34 43 Eliza 1, c 3 (1601)
35 Powell, F W, *The Politics of Irish Social Policy 1600–1900,* New York: 1992, p 28; *An Act for the Erecting of Houses of Correction, and for the Punishing of Rogues, Vagabonds, Sturdy Beggars and Lewd and Idle Persons*, 10 Chas 1, c 4 (1634–5)
36 Powell, p 28
37 *An Act for Erecting a Workhouse in the City of Dublin, for Employing and Maintaining the Poor Thereof*, 2 Anne, c 19 (1704)
38 Nicholls, G, *The History of the Irish Poor Law in Connection with the Condition of the People*, London: 1856, p 36
39 Fagan, p 44
40 Burke, H, *The People and the Poor Law in Nineteenth-Century Ireland*, Dublin: 1987, p 54
41 6 Anne, c 11 (1707); Powell, p 32; 3 Geo 2, c 4 (1729); 9 Geo 2, c 6, (1735)
42 Powell, p 34
43 Fownes, p 9
44 *Idem*
45 *Ibid*, pp 6, 13
46 Dobbs, p 48
47 *Ibid*, p 51
48 *Ibid*, pp 54–6, 60
49 11 & 12 Geo 3, c 11 (1772)
50 11 & 12 Geo 3, c 30 (1772); 13 & 14 Geo 3, c 46 (1774); 21 & 22 Geo 3, c 45, (1782); 23 & 24 Geo 3, c 58 (1784)
51 Woodward (1), p 4
52 *Ibid*, p 23

53 *Ibid*, p 8
54 *Ibid*, p 27
55 Maxwell, p 131
56 Nicholls, p 56
57 *Idem*
58 *Idem*
59 5 Geo 3, c 20 (1765)
60 Phelan, D, *A Statistical Inquiry into the Present State of the Medical Charities in Ireland with Suggestions for a Medical Poor Law*, Dublin: 1835, p 8
61 Rumford, B, *Essays, Political, Economic and Philosophical: Vol I,* Dublin: 1796, p 4
62 von Voght, C, *An Account of the Management of the Poor in Hamburgh between the Years 1788 and 1794 in a Letter to Some Friends of the Poor in Great Britain*, London: 1817, pp 8–9, 21
63 *Ibid*, pp 9, 28
64 *Ibid*, p 39
65 Rumford, p 136
66 *Ibid*, p 14
67 *Ibid*, p 15, App 1, p 418
68 *Ibid*, pp 15, 17
69 *Ibid*, App 1, pp 411–21
70 *Ibid*, p 34, 37
71 *Ibid*, pp 41–3
72 *Ibid*, App 8, pp 453–7, App 9, pp 458–64
73 Rumford, B, *Essays, Political, Economic and Philosophical: Vol II,* London: 1800, pp 159–61
74 Rumford, *Vol I,* p 93
75 *Ibid*, pp 106–8
76 *Ibid*, pp 115–188
77 The Bath Society for the Suppression of Mendicity, *Eighth Report,* Bath: 1813; The Society for the Suppression of Beggars in Edinburgh, *First Report,* Edinburgh: 1814
78 Daly, M, *Dublin – The Deposed Capital: A Social and Economic History 1860–1914*, Cork: 1984, pp 1, 4
79 Maxwell, p 76
80 *Ibid*, pp 92–3
81 Daly, M, *Social and Economic History of Ireland since 1800,* Dublin: 1981, p 66; Maxwell, p 93
82 McDowell, p 704
83 Liddy, p 67; Fagan, p 219
84 *Typhus Fever Epidemic Papers,* Dublin: 1815, O P 428/10
85 The Association for the Suppression of Mendicity in Dublin, *First Annual Report,* Dublin: 1819, pp 2–3.
86 *Ibid*, p 1
87 *Arguments in proof of the Necessity and Practicability of Suppressing Street Begging in the City of Dublin,* Dublin; 1817, p 8
88 *Ibid*, pp 8–9
89 *Ibid*, p 8

REFERENCES FOR CHAPTER TWO

1 3rd *Annual Report*, App 1, p 29
2 1st *Annual Report*, App 2, p 26
3 Stewart, J W, *The Gentleman's and Citizen's Almanack*, Dublin: 1820, pp 190, 193, 209
4 Rumford, B, *Essays, Political, Economic and Philosophical: Vol I,* Dublin: 1796, p 118
5 1st *Annual Report,* Committee list
6 *Ibid*, p 3
7 3rd *Annual Report,* p 10
8 1st *Annual Report,* pp 4, 15
9 *Ibid*, p 5
10 3rd *Annual Report*, p 12
11 2nd *Annual Report*, p 19
12 1st *Annual Report*, p 3
13 *Ibid*, p 7
14 *Ibid*, p 4
15 Rumford, *Vol I*, pp 125–6; 1st *Annual Report*, App 2, p 23
16 1st *Annual Report*, App 1, p 20, App 3, p 30
17 *Ibid*, App 2, p 25, App 3, pp 27–30; 3rd *Annual Report*, App 1, p 32
18 1st *Annual Report*, App 3, p 28
19 3rd *Annual Report*, App 3, p 44
20 1st *Annual Report*, p 6, App 2, p 22
21 1st *Annual Report*, p 5
22 *Idem*

23 Minutes, 22 February 1818, cited in 12th *Annual Report*, App 6, p 45
24 1st *Annual Report*, p 9
25 *Ibid*, pp 7, 9
26 *Ibid*, p 9
27 2nd *Annual Report*, p 19
28 Minutes, 6 May 1818, cited in 3rd *Annual Report*, p 16; 2nd *Annual Report*, p 6
29 1st *Annual Report*, p 10, App 2, p 26
30 *Ibid*, App 2, p 25; Fitzpatrick, S A O, *Dublin A Historical and Topographical Account of the City*, Cork: 1977, p 260
31 1st *Annual Report*, App 3, pp 30–5
32 *Ibid*, App 2, p 25
33 *Ibid*, pp 23–25
34 *Ibid*, p 11; App 2, p 23
35 *Ibid*, pp 11, 15
36 *Ibid*, p 12; 2nd *Annual Report*, p 10
37 1st *Annual Report*, pp 12–13
38 *Idem*
39 2nd *Annual Report*, p 9
40 *Ibid*, p 13
41 1st *Annual Report*, p 14
42 2nd *Annual Report*, p 19
43 1st *Annual Report*, pp 10–11
44 *Ibid*, p 11
45 *Ibid*, pp 13–14
46 Minutes, 9 December 1820
47 11th *Annual Report*, pp 14–15
48 1st *Annual Report*, p 11
49 *Idem*
50 *Ibid*, pp 15, 18
51 *Ibid*, pp 10, 14, 16
52 *Ibid*, p 18
53 *Ibid*, pp 7–8
54 *Ibid*, pp 17–18
55 *Statement to the Poor Law Commission*, 15th *Annual Report*, App p 4
56 1st *Annual Report*, p 15; 3rd *Annual Report*, App 2, p 37
57 2nd *Annual Report*, p 13
58 3rd *Annual Report*, App 2, p 36
59 Minutes, 14 February 1820
60 2nd *Annual Report*, p 3
61 *Idem*; 3rd *Annual Report*, App 2, p 37
62 2nd *Annual Report*, p 13; 3rd *Annual Report*, pp 3–4
63 2nd *Annual Report*, p 4
64 3rd *Annual Report*, App 2, p 37
65 *Ibid*, p 36
66 2nd *Annual Report*, pp 1–2
67 *Ibid*, p 5
68 *Idem*
69 *Idem*
70 *Ibid*, p 6
71 *Ibid*, pp 7–9
72 *Ibid*, p 9; Minutes, 21 October 1819
73 2nd *Annual Report*, pp 9–10; Minutes, 9 November 1819
74 2nd *Annual Report*, p 10
75 *Ibid*, p 11
76 *Ibid*, pp 11–12
77 *Ibid*, p 11
78 *Ibid*, p 12
79 *Ibid*, p 4
80 *Idem*
81 *Idem*
82 Minutes, 7 September 1819; 2nd *Annual Report*, p 22
83 3rd *Annual Report*, pp 16–17
84 2nd *Annual Report*, pp 2–3
85 3rd *Annual Report*, App 2, p 38
86 2nd *Annual Report*, p 15
87 3rd *Annual Report*, App 2, p 39
88 2nd *Annual Report*, p 16
89 3rd *Annual Report*, App 2, p 38
90 *Ibid*, p 39
91 *Ibid*, p 41
92 2nd *Annual Report*, p 16
93 *Ibid*, p 17; Minutes, 14 February 1820
94 Minutes, 30 November 1819
95 2nd *Annual Report*, p 19; 3rd *Annual Report*, p 17
96 2nd *Annual Report*, pp 19–20
97 *Ibid*, pp 17, 22
98 1st *Annual Report*, p 17
99 1st *Annual Report*, p 15; 2nd *Annual Report*, pp 17, 20
100 2nd *Annual Report*, p 22

REFERENCES FOR CHAPTER THREE

1 Minutes, 24 August 1819
2 59 Geo 3, c 31 (1819)
3 Minutes, Annual General Meeting 1820
4 *Idem*
5 Minutes, 23 May 1820
6 3rd *Annual Report*, p 8
7 Perceval, R, *An Attempt Towards a Plan for Rendering the Charitable Institutions of Dublin more Effective by Co-operation,* Dublin: 1818, pp 5–10
8 Burke, H, *The Royal Hospital Donnybrook: A Heritage of Caring,* Dublin: 1993, p 38
9 Minutes, 1 February 1820
10 Minutes, 20 May 1820
11 *Idem*
12 3rd *Annual Report*, p 14
13 Minutes, 16 May 1820
14 *Idem*
15 Minutes, 6 June 1820
16 3rd *Annual Report*, p 14
17 Minutes, 22 February 1820
18 Minutes, 17 October 1820
19 Minutes, 22 February 1820
20 3rd *Annual Report*, p 20
21 *Ibid*, p 18
22 Minutes, 9 November 1819
23 5th *Annual Report*, p 12
24 Minutes, 9 November 1819, 21 November 1819
25 2nd *Annual Report*, pp 21, 25, 26
26 *Report of the Commission Appointed, to Inspect the House of Industry and to Report on the Management Thereof;* App 7, p 50, 1820 (84) VIII, 227
27 2nd *Annual Report*, p 24
28 *Idem*
29 3rd *Annual Report*, p 19
30 2nd *Annual Report*, p 26
31 3rd *Annual Report*, App 1, p 32
32 Minutes, 2 December 1819
33 3rd *Annual Report*, p 21
34 *Ibid*, p 22
35 *Idem*
36 *An Act to Amend and Render More Effectual an Act Made in the Parliament of Ireland in the Fifth Year of His Present Majesty, Intitled 'An Act for Erecting and Establishing Publick Infirmaries in Ireland in this Kingdom',* 45 Geo 3, c 111, s 2 (1805); Woods, A, 'The Evolution of Dispensary Policy in Ireland 1766–1872', unpublished MSocSc Thesis, University College Dublin, 1988, p 57
37 3rd *Annual Report*, p 22; Woods, p 57
38 3rd *Annual Report*, p 23
39 *Ibid*, p 22
40 *Idem*
41 Minutes, 23 January 1821
42 2nd *Annual Report*, p 18
43 *Ibid*, p 17
44 Minutes, 27 June 1820, 8 August 1820
45 3rd *Annual Report*, p 8
46 Minutes, 29 August 1820, 2 September 1820
47 Minutes, 29 August 1820
48 Minutes, 22 August 1820
49 Minutes, 4 September 1820
50 *Idem*
51 Minutes, 5 September 1820
52 Minutes, 6 September 1820
53 Minutes, 24 October 1820, 31 October 1820
54 Fitzpatrick, S A O, *Dublin: A Historical and Topographical Account of the City,* Cork: 1977, p 261
55 Minutes, 12 September 1820, 18 September 1820
56 Minutes, 16 September 1820, 18 September 1820, 26 September 1820
57 6th *Annual Report*, p 14
58 Minutes, 11 June 1822
59 3rd *Annual Report*, App 1, pp 29–30
60 Minutes, 13 July 1821
61 Minutes, 5 February 1822
62 Minutes, 28 November 1820
63 Minutes, 14 November 1820, 13 December 1820

64 4th *Annual Report*, App 2, p 38
65 4th *Annual Report*, App 1, p 31; Minutes, 13 July 1821
66 4th *Annual Report*, App 1, p 29
67 Minutes, 16 July 1821
68 O'Connell, M R, *Daniel O'Connell: The Man and His Politics*, Dublin: 1990, p 137
69 Minutes, 24 April 1820, 19 May 1820
70 Minutes, 6 June 1820
71 Minutes, 7 January 1823, 3 June 1823
72 Minutes, 18 November 1823, 30 December 1823
73 Fitzpatrick, p 313
74 Minutes, 4 June 1822
75 Minutes, 18 June 1822
76 *Idem*
77 Minutes, 12 November 1822
78 Minutes, 18 February 1823, 4 March 1823
79 Minutes, 20 May 1823
80 Minutes, 10 June 1820
81 Minutes, 2 September 1823, 30 September 1823
82 Minutes, 21 October 1823
83 Minutes, 4 November 1823, 11 November 1823
84 Minutes, 25 November 1823, 29 November 1823, 2 December 1823
85 Minutes, 25 November 1823
86 Minutes, 9 December 1823
87 6th *Annual Report*, p 13; Minutes, 23 December 1823
88 Minutes, 23 December 1823
89 Minutes, 30 December 1823
90 *Idem*

REFERENCES FOR CHAPTER FOUR

1 2nd *Annual Report*, pp 8–9, 36; 3rd *Annual Report*, App 4, pp 42–4
2 3rd *Annual Report*, App 4, p 43
3 Minutes, 23 December 1823
4 Minutes, 21 November 1820
5 Minutes, 11 March 1823
6 2nd *Annual Report*, p 7
7 Minutes, 12 March 1822, 23 March 1822
8 Minutes, 11 March 1823
9 Minutes 15 July 1823
10 *The Employment of the Poor in Ireland*, Sel Ctte Rep, App p 200, 1823 (561) VI, 331
11 9th *Annual Report*, p 11
12 10th *Annual Report*, p 14
13 Minutes, 15 April 1823
14 7th *Annual Report*, p 16
15 Burke, H, *The People and the Poor Law in 19th Century Ireland*, Dublin: 1987, p 54
16 15 & 16 Geo 3, c 25, s 4 (1775–6)
17 10th *Annual Report*, p 18
18 16th *Annual Report*, p 16–17
19 10th *Annual Report*, p 19
20 16th *Annual Report*, p 16
21 Burke, p 60
22 Minutes, 26 March 1822
23 Minutes, 31 August 1830
24 Minutes, 7 December 1830
25 Minutes, 18 May 1830
26 Minutes, 31 August 1830
27 Minutes, 25 May 1830
28 Minutes, 11 May 1830, 1 July 1832, 29 March 1836
29 Minutes, 27 July 1830
30 Minutes, 22 March 1836
31 Minutes, 3rd August 1830
32 Minutes, 22 March 1836
33 Minutes, 18 May 1830
34 Minutes, 4 May 1830
35 Minutes, 17 August 1830
36 Minutes, 29 March 1836
37 Minutes, 21 September 1830, 28 September 1830
38 Minutes, 26 October 1830

39 Minutes, 29 March 1836
40 Minutes, 11 January 1831, 1 March 1831
41 Minutes, 15 December 1820
42 Minutes, 3 July 1821
43 15th *Annual Report*, App, p 4
44 Minutes, 11 April 1820
45 Minutes, 18 June 1822
46 Minutes, 13 March 1821
47 Minutes, 10 March 1821
48 Minutes, 18 December 1821
49 Minutes, 6 March 1821
50 Minutes, 25 March 1823
51 Minutes, 12 October 1819, 19 October 1819
52 Minutes, 21 October 1819, 2 November 1819
53 Minutes, 11 February 1820
54 Minutes, 15 February 1820
55 Minutes, 14 December 1819
56 Minutes, 22 February 1820
57 Minutes, 28 January 1823, 11 March 1823
58 16th *Annual Report*, App 7, p 70; Minutes, 8 October 1822
59 Minutes, 24 April 1821
60 Minutes, 28 December 1819
61 *Idem*
62 Minutes, 7 May 1822
63 Minutes, 14 March 1820
64 8th *Annual Report*, p 13
65 11th *Annual Report*, p 16
66 *Ibid*, App 2, p 22
67 12th *Annual Report*, pp 11–12
68 *Ibid*, p 14
69 Minutes, 21 March 1820
70 Minutes, 11 April 1820
71 Minutes, 21 March 1820
72 Minutes, 9 May 1820
73 Minutes, 27 May 1823
74 Minutes, 8 December 1820
75 Minutes, 25 April 1820
76 Minutes, 4 January 1823
77 Minutes, 8 December 1820
78 Minutes, 23 November 1830
79 Minutes, 23 November 1819
80 Minutes, 18 July 1820
81 Minutes, 22 August 1820
82 Minutes, 29 August 1820, 2 September 1820
83 Minutes, 22 March 1836
84 Minutes, 25 September 1821
85 *Idem;* Minutes, 15 October 1821
86 Minutes, 27 May 1823
87 Minutes, 5 June 1821
88 Minutes, 17 July 1821
89 Minutes, 22 July 1823, 14 October 1823
90 Minutes, 7 October 1823
91 Minutes, 30 December 1823
92 Minutes, 6 July 1830, 4 May 1830
93 Minutes, 29 February 1820
94 Minutes, 6 August 1822
95 Minutes, 15 October 1822
96 Minutes, 28 December 1819
97 Minutes, 17 November 1820
98 Minutes, 3 September 1822
99 Minutes, 15 April 1823
100 Minutes, 25 May 1830
101 15th *Annual Report*, App, p 3
102 Minutes, 23 March 1823
103 7th *Annual Report*, pp 14–16
104 9th *Annual Report*, p 11
105 Minutes, 19 October 1819, 14 December 1819
106 Minutes, 21 December 1819, 22 February 1820
107 Minutes, 27 June 1820
108 10th *Annual Report*, pp 37–8; 16th *Annual Report*, App 7, p 68; Minutes, 6 February 1821
109 16th *Annual Report*, App 7, p 68
110 Minutes, 1 May 1821
111 3rd *Annual Report*, p 25
112 *Idem*
113 Minutes, 14 April 1820, 31 October 1820, 9 January 1821
114 Minutes, 17 July 1821
115 Minutes, 15 August 1821
116 Minutes, 4 September 1821
117 Minutes, 26 December 1821
118 Minutes, 8 February 1822
119 Minutes, 2 July 1822
120 Minutes, 11 March 1823, 27 March 1823; 15th *Annual Report*, App, p 2
121 Minutes, 1 April 1823
122 6th *Annual Report*, App 3, p 32
123 16th *Annual Report*, p 34, App 7, p 72

124 *Ibid*, pp 69–70
125 Minutes, 3 November 1819, 15 February 1820
126 Minutes, 6 November 1821
127 Minutes, 25 September 1821
128 Minutes, 6 November 1821
129 Minutes, 13 November 1821
130 Minutes, 5 March 1822
131 Minutes, 2 July 1822
132 Minutes, 26 March 1822, 8 October 1822, 5 November 1822
133 Minutes, 28 October 1823
134 Minutes, 11 March 1823, 15 April 1823
135 Minutes, 12 December 1820, 19 December 1820
136 Minutes, 28 September 1830, 5 October 1830
137 Minutes, 5 August 1823, 19 August 1823, 24 September 1823, 30 September 1823
138 8th *Annual Report*, App 2, pp 24–7
139 *Idem*
140 Minutes, 23 October 1821, 30 October 1821
141 Minutes, 24 July 1821
142 Minutes, 11 April 1820
143 Minutes, 25 April 1820, 2 May 1820
144 Minutes, 11 February 1823
145 Minutes, 19 October 1830, 26 October 1830
146 Minutes, 22 November 1821
147 Minutes, 6 February 1821
148 Minutes, 31 January 1821, 13 February 1821
149 Minutes, 2 May 1820
150 Minutes, 16 May 1820, 15 January 1822, 5 March 1822
151 Minutes, 6 February 1821
152 Minutes, 21 February 1820, 21 March 1820, 13 November 1821

REFERENCES FOR CHAPTER FIVE

1 6th *Annual Report*, p 14
2 8th *Annual Report*, p 10
3 Minutes, 30 March, 1824
4 8th *Annual Report*, pp 10–11
5 6th *Annual Report*, p 15
6 8th *Annual Report*, p 11
7 20th *Annual Report*, p 12
8 Minutes, 19 December 1820, 1 January 1821
9 6th *Annual Report*, p 21
10 Minutes, 10 February 1824; 7th *Annual Report*, p 19
11 3rd *Annual Report*, App 2, p 38
12 6th *Annual Report*, p 22
13 Minutes, 18 April 1820, 20 March 1821
14 7th *Annual Report*, p 11
15 *Ibid*, p 12
16 *Ibid*, pp 14, 24
17 *Ibid*, p 19
18 Minutes, 30 November 1824
19 7th *Annual Report*, p 24, App 2, p 32
20 *Ibid*, p 12
21 *Ibid*, p 26
22 Minutes, 7 December 1824
23 7th *Annual Report*, pp 26, 114
24 *Ibid*, p 27
25 Minutes, 21 December 1824
26 8th *Annual Report*, p 3
27 16th *Annual Report*, p 39
28 8th *Annual Report*, p 20
29 *Ibid*, pp 12–13
30 Minutes, 18 January 1825; 8th *Annual Report*, p 19
31 Minutes, 12 July 1825; 8th *Annual Report*, p 19
32 Minutes, 26 April 1825
33 *Idem*
34 8th *Annual Report*, p 13; Wilderspin, S, *Infant Education or Remarks on the Importance of Educating the Infant Poor*, London: 1825
35 8th *Annual Report*, p 14

36 *Ibid*, App 1, p 23
37 9th *Annual Report*, p 9
38 *Ibid, p 9*
39 *Ibid*, p 10
40 *Ibid*, p 16
41 10th *Annual Report*, App 4, pp 50–62
42 *Ibid*, p 10, App 2, pp 44–5; 16th *Annual Report*, p 37
43 10th *Annual Report*, p 11, App 3, p 46
44 *Ibid*, p 50
45 *Ibid*, p 12
46 *Ibid*, p 24
47 *Ibid*, pp 22–3
48 *Ibid*, p 24
49 *Ibid*, pp 23, 25
50 *Ibid*, App 7, pp 74–5
51 11th *Annual Report*, p 11
52 *Ibid*, pp 2–3
53 *Ibid*, App 3, pp 26–7
54 *Ibid*, pp *27–31*
55 *Ibid*, pp 29
56 *Ibid*, p 31
57 *Ibid*, p 4
58 *Ibid*, p 5
59 *Ibid*, pp 1, 6
60 15th *Annual Report*, App pp 6–7; 11th *Annual Report*, App 2, p 22
61 Minutes, 11 May 1830
62 12th *Annual Report*, p 13; Minutes, 11 May 1830
63 12th *Annual Report*, p 7
64 *Ibid*, p 8
65 *Ibid*, p 10
66 *Idem*
67 11th *Annual Report*, p 11
68 12th *Annual Report*, p 11
69 *Ibid*, App 4, p 26
70 *Ibid*, p 9
71 *Ibid*, p 11
72 13th *Annual Report*, p 9
73 *Ibid*, p 10
74 *Ibid*, p 11
75 Minutes, 26 April 1830
76 Minutes, 1 June 1830; 13th *Annual Report*, p 9
77 Minutes, 8 June 1830
78 *Idem*
79 Minutes, Extra meeting 11 June 1830
80 Minutes, Extra meeting 18 June 1830
81 Minutes, 1 June 1830
82 Minutes,, 22 June 1830
83 Minutes, 15 June 1830
84 Minutes, 22 June 1830
85 *Idem*
86 Minutes, 29 June 1830
87 Minutes, Extra meeting 2 July 1830
88 Minutes, 6 July 1830, 13 July 1830
89 13th *Annual Report*, p 16
90 *Ibid*, p 17
91 Minutes, 20 July 1830
92 Minutes, 31 August 1830
93 Minutes, Extra meeting 3 September 1830
94 13th *Annual Report*, p 12
95 Minutes, 7 September 1830
96 Minutes, 14 September 1830, 21 September 1830
97 Minutes, 21 January 1830, 28 September 1830
98 Minutes, 28 September 1830, 12 October 1830
99 Minutes, 28 September 1830, 5 October 1830, 2 November 1830
100 Minutes, 12 October 1830
101 *Idem*
102 *Idem*
103 13th *Annual Report*, p 13
104 Minutes, 23 November 1830
105 *Idem;* Minutes, 7 December 1830
106 Minutes, 14 December 1830
107 14th *Annual Report*, p 9
108 Minutes, 23 November 1830
109 Minutes, 14 December 1830
110 13th *Annual Report*, p 4
111 *Ibid*, p 12
112 Minutes, 11 January 1831, 29 March 1831
113 Minutes, 7 December 1830
114 Minutes, 4 January 1831
115 Minutes, Annual General Meeting 22 January 1831
116 14th *Annual Report*, p 11
117 *Ibid*, p 23
118 Minutes, Extra meeting 15 April 1831, Managing committee meeting 19 April 1831

119 16th *Annual Report*, p 37
120 Minutes, Public meeting 20 April 1831; 14th *Annual Report*, p 11
121 14th *Annual Report*, p 12
122 Minutes, 24 May 1831
123 Minutes, 7 June 1831, 14 June 1831
124 Minutes, 7 June 1831
125 14th *Annual Report*, p 12
126 Minutes, Extra meeting 10 June 1831
127 14th *Annual Report*, p 13
128 Minutes, 21 June 1831
129 *Idem*
130 Minutes, 21 June 1831; 14th *Annual Report*, p 14
131 Minutes, 21 June 1831; 14th *Annual Report*, p 15
132 14th *Annual Report*, p 15; Minutes 5 July 1831
133 14th *Annual Report*, p 15
134 Minutes, 5 July 1831
135 Minutes, Extra meeting 8 July 1831; Managing committee meetings 12 July 1831, 19 July 1831
136 14th *Annual Report*, p 16
137 *Idem*
138 *Idem*
139 Minutes, 26 July 1831
140 Minutes, 2 August 1831
141 Minutes, 9 August 1831
142 Minutes, 16 August 1831
143 *Idem*
144 *Idem*
145 Minutes, 6 September 1831
146 Minutes, 15 September 1831
147 Minutes, 28 June 1831, 20 September 1831, 22 November 1831
148 Minutes, 4 October 1831
149 Minutes, 15 November 1831
150 Minutes, 29 November 1831
151 Minutes, 20 December 1831
152 Minutes, 27 December 1831
153 14th *Annual Report*, p 17
154 *Ibid*, p 19
155 *Ibid*, p 18
156 *Ibid*, pp 19–20
157 *Ibid*, p 18
158 Minutes, 24 January 1832; 14th *Annual Report*, p 21
159 Minutes, 7 February 1832
160 *Ibid*; 15th *Annual Report*, pp 12–13
161 Minutes, 10 January 1832; 15th *Annual Report*, p 8
162 15th *Annual Report*, p 9
163 *Ibid*, pp 9–10
164 *Ibid*, p 10
165 *Ibid*, p 12
166 *Ibid*, p 14
167 *Ibid*, pp 14–15
168 16th *Annual Report*, p 33; 17th *Annual Report*, p 34
169 16th *Annual Report*, App 5, pp 61-2
170 18th *Annual Report*, pp 3, 9
171 *Ibid*, p 8
172 *Ibid*, p 18
173 *Ibid*, pp 14–15
174 *Ibid*, p 15
175 *Ibid*, App 5, p 28
176 *Ibid*, p 16
177 Minutes, 29 March 1836
178 Minutes, Extra meeting 26 April 1836
179 Minutes, 10 May 1836, Extra meeting 24 May 1836
180 Minutes, Public meeting 1 June 1836
181 19th *Annual Report*, p 8; Minutes, Public meeting 8 June 1836
182 19th *Annual Report*, p 8
183 *Ibid*, p 9
184 Minutes, Extra meeting 14 July 1836
185 19th *Annual Report*, p 11
186 Minutes, 20 September 1836, 4 October 1836
187 Minutes, 29 November 1836
188 Minutes, 6 December 1836
189 Minutes, 13 December 1836, 31 January 1837
190 Minutes, 26 July 1836, 13 December 1836; 19th *Annual Report*, pp 12–13
191 Minutes, 1 August 1837
192 19th *Annual Report*, p 6; Minutes, Annual General Meeting 9 January 1837

193 Minutes, Annual General Meeting 9 January 1837
194 Minutes, 14 March 1837
195 Minutes, 23 May, 13 June 1837
196 Minutes, 30 May, 6 June 1837
197 Minutes, 20 June 1837, 27 June 1837; 20th *Annual Report*, App 3, pp 23–4
198 20th *Annual Report*, App 3, p 25
199 Minutes, Extra meetings 30 June 1837, 12 July 1837
200 Minutes, Extra meeting 30 June 1837
201 20th *Annual Report*, p 9
202 Minutes, 8 August 1837; 20th *Annual Report*, p 8
203 20th *Annual Report*, pp 10–11; Minutes, 4 July 1837
204 Minutes, 11 July 1837, 21 November 1837
205 Minutes, 2 January 1838
206 Minutes, 30 January 1838
207 Minutes, 3 April 1838, 10 April 1838
208 Minutes, Extra meeting 4 May 1838
209 Minutes, 15 February 1838, 20 February 1838, 22 February 1838
210 Minutes, 1 May 1838
211 Minutes, Extra meeting 4 May 1838
212 Minutes, Public meeting 7 May 1838; Managing committee meetings 8 May 1838, 8 June 1838
213 Minutes, 8 May 1838
214 Minutes, 1 January 1839
215 Minutes, 15 June 1838
216 *Idem*
217 *Idem*
218 *Idem*
219 Minutes, 12 June 1838, 26 June 1838
220 21st *Annual Report*, p 10
221 *Idem*
222 Minutes, 22 June 1838
223 Minutes, 26 June 1838
224 1 & 2 Vict c 56, s 46–47 (1837–8); Burke, H *The People and the Poor Law in 19th Century Ireland*, Dublin: 1987, p 47

REFERENCES FOR CHAPTER SIX

1 1803–4 (109) V, 771
2 O'Connor, J, *The Workhouses of Ireland. The Fate of Ireland's Poor*, Dublin: 1995, p 48
3 Burke, H, *The People and the Poor Law in 19th Century Ireland*, Dublin: 1987, p 1
4 *Ibid*, p 30
5 *Ibid*, p 48
6 1st *Annual Report*, pp 7, 9; 10th *Annual Report*, App 3, p 46; 18th *Annual Report*, p 12
7 12th *Annual Report*, p 15
8 *Ibid*, p 14; 18th *Annual Report*, p 12
9 11th *Annual Report*, pp 7, 9
10 14th *Annual Report*, pp 12–13
11 Minutes, 21 June 1831
12 19th *Annual Report*, p 28
13 *Ibid*, pp 14–15
14 *Ibid*, pp 18–32
15 *Ibid*, p 23
16 *First Report by G. Nicholls on Poor Laws, Ireland*, 1837 [69] LI 201, pp 7–8
17 *Ibid*, p 8
18 *Idem*
19 Minutes, 21 February 1837, 2 March 1837, 23 May 1837
20 Minutes, 21 February 1837, 2 March 1837
21 21st *Annual Report*, p 14
22 *Ibid*, p 12
23 *Ibid*, p 11
24 Minutes, 17 August 1838
25 Minutes, 21 August 1838
26 Minutes, 28 August 1838
27 Minutes, 31 August 1838; 21st *Annual Report*, App 1, p 16
28 21st *Annual Report*, App 3, p 20
29 *Ibid*, App 14, p 38
30 21st *Annual Report*, p 8
31 Minutes, 21 December 1838; 21st *Annual Report*, App 2, p 19
32 Minutes, 1 January 1839
33 21st *Annual Report*, p 8; Minutes, 24 December 1838

34 22nd *Annual Report*, p 7
35 *Ibid*, p 8
36 23rd *Annual Report*, p 7
37 *Ibid*, p 8
38 Burke, p 73; O'Connor, p 261
39 23rd *Annual Report*, p 8
40 50th *Annual Report*, p 8
41 22nd *Annual Report*, App 1, p 15
42 23rd *Annual Report*, p 8
43 *Ibid*, p 9
44 27th *Annual Report*, p 10
45 23rd *Annual Report*, App 2, p 17
46 23rd *Annual Report*, p 7
47 22nd *Annual Report*, App 1, p 16
48 23rd *Annual Report*, p 10; 22nd *Annual Report*, App 1, p 15
49 23rd *Annual Report*,, p 9
50 22nd *Annual Report*, App 1, p 15
51 23rd *Annual Report*, p 11
52 *Idem*
53 24th *Annual Report*, p 7
54 22nd *Annual Report*, App 1, p 16; 24th *Annual Report*, p 3
55 25th *Annual Report*, p 10
56 24th *Annual Report*, p 4
57 *Ibid*, pp 5–6
58 *Ibid*, p 6
59 23rd *Annual Report*, p 12
60 25th *Annual Report*, p 18; 28th *Annual Report*, pp 11–12
61 29th *Annual Report*, p 14
62 23rd *Annual Report*, pp 12–13
63 48th *Annual Report*, p 14
64 24th *Annual Report*, p 7
65 Robins, J A, *The Lost Children: A Study of Charity Children in Ireland 1700–1900*, Dublin: 1980, p 129; 24th *Annual Report*, p 6
66 24th *Annual Report*, p 7
67 25th *Annual Report*, p 16
68 27th *Annual Report*, p 12
69 26th *Annual Report*, p 8
70 *Ibid*, p 9
71 28th *Annual Report*, p 8
72 27th *Annual Report*, p 13; *Thom's Directory*, Dublin: 1861, p 1197
73 29th *Annual Report*, pp 9–11
74 *Ibid*, p 10
75 *Idem*
76 30th *Annual Report*, App 3, p 22
77 Minutes, 28 March 1848
78 30th *Annual Report*, p 15
79 O'Connor, p 134
80 *Ibid*, p 136
81 30th *Annual Report*, p 10
82 Kinahan, D, *System of Relief for the Poor as Used in the Dublin Mendicity Institution, Adapted to General Use*, Dublin: 1847, p. 8.
83 30th *Annual Report*, pp 13–14
84 34th *Annual Report*, p 15
85 Minutes, 31 August 1847
86 31st *Annual Report*, p 7
87 30th *Annual Report*, p 24
88 Minutes, Special meeting 16 December 1848
89 32nd *Annual Report*, pp 8–9
90 Minutes, Special meeting 16 December 1848
91 32nd *Annual Report*, pp 9–11
92 30th *Annual Report*, p 6

REFERENCES FOR CHAPTER SEVEN

1 Chadwick, E, *Report on the Sanitary Condition of the Labouring Population of Great Britain*, London: 1842
2 30th *Annual Report*, App 3, p 23
3 See pp 32–3 above
4 30th *Annual Report*, pp 22–3
5 Minutes, 24 August 1847, 7 March 1848
6 31st *Annual Report*, p 8; Minutes, 18 July 1848
7 Minutes, 13 June 1848
8 Minutes, 8 August 1848, 15 August 1848, 7 November 1848
9 Minutes, 21 November 1848
10 31st *Annual Report*, p 3
11 *Ibid*, p 7
12 Minutes, 6 November 1849
13 32nd *Annual Report*, p 9; Minutes, 7 August 1849, 6 November 1849
14 Minutes, 22 January 1850
15 Minutes, 5 February 1850
16 Minutes, 7 May 1850

17 Idem
18 Minutes, 18 June 1850, 9 July 1850, 30 July 1850
19 Minutes, 27 August 1850
20 Minutes, 10 September 1850
21 Minutes, 17 September 1850
22 Minutes, 1 October 1850, 22 October 1850
23 Minutes, 15 October 1850, 22 October 1850
24 Minutes, 22 October 1850
25 Minutes, 26 November 1850
26 Minutes, 3 December 1850
27 Minutes, 28 January 1851, 1 February 1851
28 Minutes, 22 April 1851, 29 April 1851
29 Minutes, 23 September 1851
30 Minutes, 11 November 1851, 18 November 1851, 25 November 1851
31 Minutes, 30 December 1851
32 39th *Annual Report*, p 10
33 Idem
34 33rd *Annual Report*, p 8
35 Idem
36 34th *Annual Report*, p 8
37 36th *Annual Report*, p 10; 84th *Annual Report*, p 8
38 Minutes, 23 March 1852
39 Minutes, 11 May 1852, 25 May 1852
40 Minutes, 19 April 1853
41 Minutes, 21 December 1852
42 Idem; 35th *Annual Report*, p 8
43 35th *Annual Report*, pp 7–8
44 Minutes, 19 April 1853
45 Minutes, 12 May 1853
46 Minutes, 2 August 1853, 16 August 1853
47 Minutes, 18 May 1852
48 Idem
49 Minutes, 15 March 1853
50 Minutes, 4 October 1853, 25 April 1854, 27 June 1854
51 Minutes, 10 October 1854
52 Minutes, 12 September 1854
53 Minutes, 17 April 1855
54 39th *Annual Report*, p 12
55 Bathhouse Memorandum Book, 15 July 1852
56 Ibid, 2 August 1852
57 Idem
58 Ibid, 19 August 1852
59 Ibid, 10 June 1853
60 Ibid, 9 July 1853
61 Ibid, 30 July 1853
62 Ibid, 9 August 1853
63 Minutes, 8 June 1852, 7 November 1854, 21 November 1854, 13 January 1857
64 37th *Annual Report*, p 10
65 38th *Annual Report*, p 11
66 Minutes, 5 September 1854
67 38th *Annual Report*, pp 12–13
68 48th *Annual Report*, p 11
69 36th *Annual Report*, p 11; Minutes, 8 May 1855
70 Minutes, 27 November 1855
71 Minutes, 14 March 1854, 19 April 1853
72 Minutes, 28 November 1849
73 *An Act to Provide for the Better Distribution, Support, and Management of Medical Charities in Ireland*; 14 & 15 Vict c 68; Minutes, 6 May 1851, 19 April 1853
74 Minutes, 26 September 1854, 37th *Annual Report*, p 7
75 Minutes, 27 December 1853
76 Minutes, 28 December 1858
77 Minutes, 11 May 1861
78 Minutes, 17 April 1855, 11 March 1856, 20 October 1857, 19 June 1860, 11 May 1861
79 Minutes, 22 March 1864
80 Minutes, 18 July 1871, 3 December 1873
81 39th *Annual Report*, p 10
82 Ibid, p 11
83 Minutes, 2 December 1856, 5 May 1857, 3 November 1857, 14 November 1858, 8 November 1859, 11 September 1860
84 Minutes, 16 July 1850
85 Idem; Minutes, 3 May 1853, 7 October 1856, 2 August 1859, 7 July 1863
86 37th *Annual Report*, p 10
87 38th *Annual Report*, p 8

88 Minutes, 11 May 1857
89 Minutes, 5 July 1859, 12 July 1859, 10 April 1860
90 Minutes, 1 May 1860, 19 June 1860, 31 July 1860, 9 February 1864
91 Minutes, 12 July 1864
92 Minutes, 8 September 1868, 27 April 1869
93 Minutes, 30 July 1861
94 Ó'Grádá, C. Ireland, *A New Economic History 1780–1939*, Oxford: 1995, pp 248–50, 50th *Annual Report*, p 10; 57th and 58th *Annual Report*, p 11
95 Minutes, 2 May 1865
96 Minutes, 18 February 1851, 28 October 1860
97 Minutes, 1 July 1873
98 Minutes, 18 April 1876
99 Minutes, 14 July 1887; 69th *Annual Report*, p 9
100 20th *Annual Report*, p 17
101 38th *Annual Report*, p 8; Minutes, 12 June 1855, 6 July 1852, 14 August 1855
102 Minutes, 26 April 1859
103 Minutes, 14 June 1859
104 Minutes, 12 December 1872
105 Minutes, 1 April 1873
106 Minutes, 18 January 1876; 57th and 58th *Annual Report*, p 8
107 Minutes, 22 February 1876, 29 February 1876
108 Minutes, 7 March 1876
109 Minutes, 14 December 1875
110 Minutes, 13 June 1876
111 Minutes, 17 December 1878; 83rd *Annual Report*, p 7
112 Minutes, 6 October 1874, 18 May 1875, 8 December 1874
113 Minutes, 21January 1873, 22 July 1873, 3 February 1874, 9 November 1875, 21 March 1876
114 57th and 58th *Annual Report*, pp 7–8
115 Minutes, 30 January 1877
116 61st *Annual Report*, p 7
117 59th *Annual Report*, p 8; 60th *Annual Report*, pp 7–8
118 62nd *Annual Report*, pp 8–9
119 Ibid, p 7
120 63rd *Annual Report*, p 12; Minutes, 27 January 1880, 4 May 1880
121 55th *Annual Report*, p 9; Minutes, 11 November 1873
122 Minutes, 9 December 1873, 17 February 1874
123 Minutes, 24 February 1874
124 59th *Annual Report*, p 7
125 62nd *Annual Report*, pp 8–9
126 63rd *Annual Report*, p 13
127 74th *Annual Report*, p 8
128 Minutes, 16 November 1897
129 92nd *Annual Report*, p 8
130 Minutes, 27 June 1899, 21 March 1905
131 Minutes, 4 February 1908
132 Minutes, 12 January 1909, 19 January 1909
133 Minutes, 21 December 1909

REFERENCES FOR CHAPTER EIGHT

1 15th *Annual Report*, App, p 2
2 *Report of the Commissioners Appointed to Inspect the House of Industry and to Report on the Management Thereof*, App 7, pp 47-48 1820 (84) VIII, 227
3 16th *Annual Report*, p 14
4 10th *Annual Report*, p 20
5 1st *Annual Report*, p 10
6 O'Connor, J. *The Workhouses of Ireland. The Fate of Ireland's Poor*, Dublin: 1995, pp 26-7
7 Frazer, D. *The Evolution of the British Welfare State*, London: 1973, pp 31–2, 43
8 10th *Annual Report*, p 20
9 Minutes, 28 October 1902
10 61st *Annual Report*, p 7; 62nd *Annual Report*, p 9
11 10th *Annual Report*, pp 20-21
12 *Idem*
13 16th *Annual Report*, p 18
14 *Ibid*, p 15

15 10th *Annual Report*, p 21
16 *Idem*
17 Minutes, 26 July 1825
18 15th *Annual Report*, App p 8
19 *Idem*
20 *Ibid*, App, pp 7-8; 17th *Annual Report*, p 10
21 17th *Annual Report*, p 11
22 15th *Annual Report*, App, p 8
23 17th *Annual Report*, pp 10-11; 15th *Annual Report*, App, p 8
24 Minutes, 19 August 1836
25 Minutes, 30 August 1836
26 Minutes, 13 December 1836
27 Minutes, 4 September 1838
28 23rd *Annual Report*, p 12
29 *Ibid*, p 11, App 1, p 15
30 Robins, J, *The Lost Children: A Study of Charity Children in Ireland 1700-1900*, Dublin: 1980, pp 201-212; Minutes, 28 March 1848, 22 August 1848
31 McDonagh, O, "The Irish in Australia: A General View", in *Ireland and Irish-Australia: Studies in Cultural and Political History*, Oliver McDonagh and W F Mandle (eds), London: 1986, p 162
32 Robins, pp 209-11
33 McDonagh, p 161; Robins, p 220
34 25th *Annual Report*, pp 17-18
35 *Idem*
36 *Idem; Ibid*, p iv
37 *Ibid*, pp 3-4
38 24th *Annual Report*, pp 3-4
39 28th *Annual Report*, pp 8-9
40 71st *Annual Report*, p 7
41 59th *Annual Report*, p 9
42 62nd *Annual Report*, p 9
43 61st *Annual Report*, p 7
44 *Idem*
45 62nd *Annual Report*, p 7
46 *Ibid*, p 8
47 68th *Annual Report*, p 8
48 63rd *Annual Report*, p 11
49 Burke, H, *The People and the Poor Law in 19th Century Ireland*, Dublin: 1987, p 10
50 Transmission Book, July 1884–August 1886
51 82nd *Annual Report*, p 6
52 Minutes, 1 May 1906
53 83rd *Annual Report*, p 6
54 Minutes, 3 October 1917
55 Minutes, Annual General Meeting, 25 July 1921, Managing committee meetings, 7 September 1921, 29 March 1922, 31 January 1923
56 109th *Annual Report*, p 4
57 Transmission Book, May 1935-June 1969
58 Minutes, 15 January 1926, 12 March 1926, 8 October 1926, 28 March 1928
59 Minutes, 5 November 1926, 12 November 1926
60 Minutes, 19 November 1926, 26 November 1926, 16 May 1934
61 Minutes, 14 January 1927, 3 July 1929, 6 June 1938
62 Minutes, 11 November 1931, 16 March 1932
63 Minutes, 8 May 1838
64 Minutes, 11 February 1927; 25 February 1927
65 Minutes, 25 October 1939, 1 November 1939, 20 December 1939
66 Minutes, 9 December 1939
67 Transmission Book, May 1935-June 1969
68 *Idem*; Minutes, 31 October 1936
69 *Idem*

REFERENCES FOR CHAPTER NINE

1 83rd *Annual Report*, p 6
2 84th *Annual Report*, p 6; 85th *Annual Report*, p 6
3 86th *Annual Report*, p 6; Minutes, 3 May 1904
4 Minutes, 3 January 1905, 10 January 1905, 17 January 1905, 24 January 1905, 31 January 1905, 7 February 1905, 14 February 1905, 21 February 1905, 21 March 1905
5 Minutes, 11 April 1898, 1 May 1906, 26 June 1906
6 86th *Annual Report*, p 6; 103rd *Annual Report*, p 3
7 98th *Annual Report*, p 6
8 Curry, John, *The Irish Social Services*, Dublin: 1980, p 31
9 96th *Annual Report*, p 6
10 Williams, G D, *Dublin Charities*, Dublin: 1902, p 17
11 95th *Annual Report*, pp 6-7
12 97th *Annual Report*, p 8; 100th *Annual Report*, pp 6-7
13 Minutes, 26 April 1916
14 "First Battalion", in *Dublin Brigade Review*, Dublin: 1939, p 16
15 *Idem*
16 99th *Annual Report*, p 6
17 Minutes, 23 May 1916, 31 May 1916, 6 September 1916
18 Minutes, 4 October 1916
19 Minutes, 21 September 1916, 11 October 1916, 7 February 1917
20 Minutes, 21 March 1917
21 Minutes, 21 March, 1917, 27 June 1917
22 Minutes, 21 March 1917, 31 October 1917
23 Minutes, 21 March 1917, 28 March 1917, 18 May 1921
24 Minutes, 9 May 1917, 16 May 1917, 23 May 1917
25 Minutes, 16 May 1917, 23 May 1917
26 Minutes, 3 October 1917
27 Minutes, 17 October 1917, 14 November 1917
28 Minutes, 14 November 1917
29 Minutes, 28 November 1917, 5 December 1917
30 Minutes, 14 November 1917, 5 December 1917, 12 December 1917
31 Minutes, 25 January 1916
32 Minutes, 5 March 1919, 5 November 1919
33 Minutes, 29 June 1921
34 Minutes, 15 December 1920
35 Minutes, 16 January 1918
36 Minutes, 29 March 1922, 23 May 1922
37 Minutes, 14 March 1924, 30 May 1924
38 Minutes, 4 April 1920
39 Minutes, 28 June 1922
40 Minutes, 10 April 1929, 18 November 1931
41 Minutes, 26 June 1929
42 Minutes, 6 May 1931
43 Minutes, 8 June 1923, 6 February 1925, 20 February 1925
44 Minutes, 18 January 1924, 25 January 1924
45 Minutes, 28 January 1924, 30 May 1924, 13 June 1924
46 Minutes, Annual General Meeting 27 July 1925
47 Minutes, 17 April 1925
48 Minutes, 16 October 1925
49 Minutes, 29 June 1927
50 Minutes, 24 August 1927
51 Minutes, 20 November 1929, 4 December 1929
52 Minutes, 31 January 1923, 14 February 1923
53 Minutes, 28 September 1927, 16 November 1927, 25 January 1928
54 Minutes, 23 July 1930, 10 December 1930
55 *The Mendicity Institution Scheme*, Dublin: 1941
56 Minutes, 5 December 1928, 12 December 1928, 19 December 1928, 4 October 1933
57 Minutes, 7 January 1920
58 Minutes, 30 April 1926

59 See p 169 above
60 Minutes, 11 July 1928, 25 July 1928, 10 December 1930
61 Minutes, 3 October 1930, 10 December 1930
62 Minutes, 16 September 1902, 23 May 1916, 14 March 1923, 20 May 1927, 15 December 1943, 18 September 1996
63 Minutes, 7 January 1931, 3 December 1952
64 Minutes, 11 March 1931, 1 April 1931, 22 April 1931
65 Minutes, 10 June 1931, 23 March 1932
66 Minutes, 31 January 1934
67 Minutes, 18 March 1942, 25 November 1942
68 Minutes, 23 August 1941, 24 September 1941
69 Minutes, 25 September 1940, 30 October 1940, 8 January 1941, 15 January 1941
70 Minutes, 12 March 1941
71 Minutes, 13 March 1940
72 Minutes, 10 March 1943
73 Minutes, 1 May 1957
74 Minutes, Annual General Meeting 1943
75 *Idem*
76 Minutes, 18 June 1949
77 Minutes, 3 October 1951, 5 December 1951
78 Minutes, 7 May 1952, 11 June 1952
79 Minutes, 12 December 1952
80 Minutes, 4 March 1953, 13 May 1953
81 Minutes, 1 July 1953
82 Minutes, 5 May 1954
83 Minutes, 1 September 1954
84 Minutes, 1 September 1954, 6 October 1954, 13 June 1956, 5 December 1962, 6 November 1963, 5 January 1966
85 Minutes, 5 February 1958
86 Minutes, 7 January 1959
87 Minutes, 11 October 1972
88 Minutes, 11 January 1961
89 Minutes, 3 October 1962
90 Minutes, 3 September 1958
91 Minutes, 3 January 1968, 21 May 1969
92 Minutes, 7 January 1969
93 Minutes, 7 October 1970
94 Minutes, 2 September 1971, 6 January 1972, 7 April 1971
95 Minutes, 12 April 1972
96 161st *Annual Report*, p 3; Minutes, 20 September 1978
97 165th *Annual Report*, p 6
98 Minutes, 13 December 1983
99 Address given by the secretary, Charles Smith, to the Bray Committee of War on Want, 17 October 1983
100 Minutes, 25 August 1983, 17 November 1983
101 Address given by the secretary, Charles Smith, to the Bray Committee of War on Want, 17 October 1983
102 Minutes, 18 October 1983, 21 July 1993
103 Minutes, 17 December 1986

Index